# A Time to Keep

# A Time to Keep

*Theology,*

*Mortality,*

*and the Shape of a Human Life*

Ephraim Radner

BAYLOR UNIVERSITY PRESS

©2016 by Baylor University Press
Waco, Texas 76798

*Jacket design* by Will Brown
*Cover image*: *Homage to Goya*, c. 1895 (oil on card mounted on canvas), Redon, Odilon (1840–1916) / On Loan to the Hamburg Kunsthalle, Hamburg, Germany / Bridgeman Images

Library of Congress Cataloging-in-Publication Data

Names: Radner, Ephraim, 1956– author.
Title: A time to keep : theology, mortality, and the shape of a human life /
    Ephraim Radner.
Description: Waco : Baylor University Press, 2016. | Includes
    bibliographical references and index.
Identifiers: LCCN 2015049301| ISBN 9781481305068 (hardback :
    alk. paper) |
    ISBN 9781481305099 (web pdf) | ISBN 9781481305075 (epub)
Subjects:  LCSH: Life—Biblical teaching.
Classification: LCC BS680.L5 R33 2016 | DDC 233—dc23
LC record available at http://lccn.loc.gov/2015049301

Printed in the United States of America on acid-free paper with a minimum of 30 percent post–consumer waste recycled content.

# Contents

# Preface
## *Recovering the Context of Life*

My interest in writing this book arose initially as I was engaged in the current debates over sexuality and its proper meaning.[1] That topic has riven both our larger culture as well as our churches. Part of the frustration of these debates, outside of their purely destructive force within the Christian community, is the strange lack of living context they assume. I am not referring to a lack of *personalized* detail injected into the discussion, of which there has been much. Rather, our debates over sexuality have lacked an interest in the lived context of human existence over time. Rarely do we hear the debaters discuss questions such as these: Where do people come from, what do they do with one another, and how do they do it, for their sixty to eighty years of existence within this larger world? And what do they leave behind? This book seeks to recover some of this existential context.

A similar lack of contextual thinking has been evident in the use of Scripture within these debates. Individual texts of the Bible have been analyzed, historicized, dissected, and rearticulated in multiplied fashion, in hopes that they might clarify some central aspect of human sexual life. But it has been hard to place these texts within a populated scriptural landscape, as it were, as parts of an entire scriptural presentation of human life itself. The historicist vivisection of the Scriptures has rendered such a possibility difficult to grasp for most readers, whatever their views about this or that behavior.

The Bible, however, *does* present a single picture, complex though it is, of at least *one* human life: the "image of God" that is granted in the creation of Adam and then presented as the created divine power itself, the Son of God, Jesus the Christ. There is, in other words, one life that the Bible presents as a whole. And the bits and pieces of biblical narrative, of law and praise, of prophecy and warning or encouragement, are all *aspects* of this one life, rather than atomized indicators of diverse and specific truths, whose job it is for readers to organize, order, categorize, and rationalize. The one life that is the Son of God's is the context for understanding Scripture's own discussion of human life.

This book will attempt to look at this context too. For if there is one life, and everything in the Bible describes that one life as it truly is, the distinction between "whole and parts" is probably not a helpful one. To attempt a depiction of human life, yet to leave out from that picture Genesis 1–3 or even just a few verses from them, is not so much to miss some key or perhaps less-than-key bit of information about what a human being is. It is to refer to something other than the one life of the God-Man Jesus Christ, who happens to have these elements as a part of his own self, just because he fulfills the Law in its totality (Matt 5:17; Luke 16:17; Rom 10:4).

The same would be true for the strange portions of the biblical text: the rules of Leviticus (as I will suggest later); or this or that verse of a heart-rent or angry David, the psalmist; or Philemon and Jude, not to mention the ever-inconvenient letters to Timothy, in their different ways. Perhaps we can know the Lord, Jesus Christ, without knowing, integrating, or understanding this or that text of the Bible, just as we might rightly say we "know" the person next to us in church even though we ignore the fact that she has this or that past and this or that family and work. But her past, her family, and her work are truly "who" she is, though we ignore it or misconstrue it; they are not extraneous details or additions to her life. And so, too, with each and every text of the Scripture—they are truly the life of God in Christ. As John Donne put it: "Our sermons are text and discourse; Christ's sermons were all text: Christ was the word; not only the essential word, which was always with God, but the very written word too; Christ was the Scripture, and therefore, when he refers them to himself, he refers them to the Scriptures."[2]

This makes talking about the Bible and human life very difficult when it comes to seeking "practical" guidance. For that, we want the definitions that are possible for discrete truths. If we keep with the analogy above, is the person next to us director or subdirector of her division at this or that agency? Is she allowed to get six weeks' maternity leave or a full year's? These are matters of fact that can be noted and that properly define this person's life. They will determine when and even on what particular dates we can meet. But these practical details do not really define the person. Likewise, to say that "marriage is between a man and woman" may correctly state some aspect of human life, but the meaning of this aspect is opaque without it being a part of the fullness of human life itself. And that is given in the context of the whole man, Jesus Christ, spoken about in all the Scriptures.

In any case, there is a gap between our rule-oriented needs for guidance and the actual meaning of the life for which such guidance is useful and even necessary. In the past, the church, that great gathering of the saints and their wisdom, stood as the historical receptacle of the "whole" in which the rules were enunciated. The gap between the descriptive order of experience and the life of Christ could be greater or less, but simply *living in* the church, with others, often bridged that gap experientially and unconsciously. Why get married? Why fail to have children? Why struggle with a family or find their joys too much to express? Why lose one's spouse or child? What to do in each case of question and expectation? Most Christians could not quite answer these hard queries, and sometimes this failure proved too much to bear. But mostly Christians were simply carried along by the church's common life and by a faith that this "body of Christ" properly held together the image of the one Lord whom the Scriptures, in their often bewildering colorations, were sensed as presenting, and to which they belonged.[3]

One thing that can be said, from the point of view of historical life today, is that this relation of church and people no longer obtains. The gap I have mentioned has grown wider and wider: the rules and the living breath that animates them no longer hold together. There are many reasons for this: conceptual, social, perhaps even the providence of God. I will present one major cause—the withdrawal of socially experienced mortality—in the opening chapter. This will help us consider something of the existential context of human life that is too often ignored in our contemporary decision making. And I will link this context to the context of the whole Scriptures, mainly by trying to follow through with the breadth of scriptural figures that populate the text from beginning to end.

This is, in fact, how Christians have generally read the Bible (if not always in a very skillful or responsible manner) until the nineteenth century. Hence, to know "what the Bible says about the human being," we follow the figure of "Adam" (who includes the male and female human being) through the chapters of Genesis and the Psalms and so on through to the New Adam, Jesus Christ. That is the "figural breadth" of a "human being." And if we will look at the continuities of this figure—I am only using an example here—we will be led from its formulation from "dust," for instance, and be taken through to Job, and to the figures of death and decay that riddle the Scriptures; we will follow, too, the forms of "multiplication" that Adam assumes, which take us to the patriarchs and wives, to David, and the kings and queens of Israel and into the children of the first Pauline churches, and so on. These are all "figures" of Adam and of our human personhood. And we can call this "figural reading," as, in our reading, we touch the figures, hold and handle them, and pass them along within the indwelling of their description throughout the whole range of the scriptural text. This is what I consider to be the Bible's "contextual" truth and the emerging reality for we who read the Scriptures. It is the only one according to which our decisions about human life bear any lasting value.

More than Scripture is at issue here, however. Context, as I indicated, is a time frame of breadth as well, especially in the church. Context is a gathering, a communion, a historical reach that does not simply develop but grows without ever changing in some sense. It is the flood of peoples, flowing from Adam, gathered at Babel, dispersed around the globe, touched person by person through the movement from Jerusalem to Samaria "unto the uttermost part of the earth" (Acts 1:8). This gathering—"a great multitude, which no man could number, of all nations, and kindreds, and people, and tongues" (Rev 7:9)—is real, not imaginary: it is made up of people who were born, lived, grew, weakened, and died, suddenly, or only quickly, or more gradually, though all in all in short order and finally. Their multitude derives from the ramified outline of their generation and progeny, as well as encounter and interaction. All of this is the "body" that is Christ's and that Scripture presents. And it is given in the breadth of fleshly detail and in the heart's struggles and joys.

This reality of human extension over time, or of genealogy, is also part of the context that has been missing in our debilitating debates over the human body. Here I come to a somewhat more personal motive to this volume, one whose collision with the cultural debate over human sexuality has done nothing but trouble me and disturb my theological reflections in ways that I should simply walk away from, but cannot. After all, if the Bible is, as it were, the life of the One Man (Eph 2:15) unfolded for us, and if this carries along with it the whole train of sisters and brothers on their way to God (cf. Heb 2:11-13), then this horizontal temporal reach must also be reflected somehow in the vertical relations of individuals within their more discrete life spans. That is, my life and your life, as lived in this or that instant and minute, hour and year, must contain some intrinsic connection with the vast gathering of human beings who represent the movement from the First to the Second Adam. I can look at my own life, such as it is, and discover within it the truths of who I am as a human being more broadly and representatively before God, who is the God of and in Jesus Christ.

Here, a different context comes to bear, as we reflect on our relationship with our ancestors and descendants, with our parents and with our own children or those close to us. I was, for instance, a teenager when my mother died, and I am now older than she was at her death. So I remember her as a child remembers, looking up to and being led by someone whose wisdom I might now be supposed to have exceeded. As we consider what it means to be a human being, we are forced to take on these different outlooks toward those we know intimately over time and to make sense of their disparities. In my own case, my mother killed herself at the end of many years of deepening depression and anguish, much of which I could not identify as a child, yet surely sensed, and certainly now in retrospect recognize in all its details. If the question of a human being's life as bound to generation and parentage is to be raised at all, it must be raised also within this contextual setting.

One thing that repeatedly gnaws at me is this: something very sharp indeed cut deeply through the truth of things in my mother's act, for good or ill. It was surely for ill, I imagine mostly. But in any case, I must come to know what this "something" is. Hopes and trust were wiped away here, including the simple confidence that life's bonded purposes are more real than its dissolving center. It is, furthermore, easy for most people to imagine how this would be the case. But there was a residue of good as well. For my mother's suicide also exposed for me a profound truth, even if one under threat: because such a death is "not how it should be," what is truer even than this has come into light. In being constantly haunted by the fact that the mother who gave me life, and in so doing invented for me that nature of love in the flesh, walked away from this, I have also had constantly laid out for me, like a fruit cut open to its pit and ranged before the sun's heat day by day, the very workings of my life. I can watch and examine them, in all their bright if fading and slowly deadening clarity, over and over: mothers and fathers; passion and lust; conflicted loves; long yearnings and disappointments; children embraced, led, and abandoned in the midst of this, struggling for food and purpose, searching out, gathering in—each of us have been made by this, because, in a real way, this is the nature of human life itself.

One of my siblings, too, would one day follow my mother's lead and take her life as well. These things are not so unusual within the patterns of love's strange teaching and its wrenching and twisting struggles. Families have their own "clusters" of instructed demise, as sociologists have clearly demonstrated. This is one reason, perhaps, that our contemporary age seeks to overthrow the power of genealogy. But whatever the mistakes our families breed into our bones, their essential and immovable nature is difficult to dismiss. We are born to a mother and father, and the whole world stretches out to mime this reality. All metaphor runs behind our familial genesis, gesticulating. Brothers and sisters, rivalries and growth—all this forms the branches of some great tree set at the center of human being. Each of us finds ourselves somewhere in the midst of its expansive foliage. The tree grows over time. Some critics of traditional families in our culture have argued that "marriage" is first of all a metaphor—that is, that marriage does not, in the first instance, describe a man and woman joined and having children and so on across the course of a generational expanse of time. Yet, the history of the world and of human beings as they have looked at who they are in time seems to indicate otherwise: everything else in human experience—in its striving, brokenness, and sometimes happy resolution—is but a kind of running after that which *comes* to them first in their genesis. The "vertical" truths of biology, then, are not simply the impersonal structure of an evolving and changing set of ingredients; they open up and provide the experiential categories of the human person's very form.

I would not yet wish to call all of this "natural law." The structuring genesis of our being-in-the-world is, however, a natural context to life. The ground that is procreative coupling and the familial life that proceeds from it are simply the *place* we move and have our being temporally; we come from it, we move through it, and we leave it behind, in some condition of health or disarray. Contemporary culture has mitigated the experience of this natural context, by obscuring the traversal of its edges—that is, of birth, growth, maturation, aging, and death. Genealogy, after all, is the measure of our origins and disappearance, but also our connections within this strange episode of existence. Yet today, Time, with all of its limits and necessitating adjustments, seems to have lost its ability to press itself upon the form of life as life's great questioner, such that each of our lives must give an answer in the form of "this is who I am," given that "Time," of course, stands for nothing else, in Christian terms, but the fact that God has made us, and not we ourselves. Thus, this particular context of temporality is, in some measure and must be, the same as the Scripture's: "Be ye sure that the Lord he is God; it is he that hath made us, and not we ourselves; we are his people, and the sheep of his pasture" (Ps 100:3—rightly known by its first Latin word as "Jubilate": "O be joyful in the Lord, all ye lands").

Hence, the extended temporal shape of our mortality is where the contexts of our experienced lives and the context of Scripture's unveiling of their meaning come together. I want to examine this shape, and, taken as a whole, this book seeks to engage the coincidence of scriptural and temporal reality. Their synonymity is the great single context of our life as human beings. Indeed, the cultural pulling apart of this coincidence and synonymity is a major aspect to our confusions about sexuality. To have a body and deploy it is bound up with the fact that we are born and we die within a short span of years. And this being born and dying is itself—in all of its biology of connection, memory, and hope—a mirror of and vehicle for the truth of God's life as our creator. That will be the central argument of this volume. In what follows, I will look at a range of elements in human existence: the clock that seems to measure the limits of mortality; its divine givenness; the nature of procreative genealogy; the shape of our extended life spans; human particularity and singleness; working and eating; and finally, the moral shape of counting out and down our allotted days. But my purpose in all of this is not only to reassert the reality of all these elements, in the face of forgetfulness and modern obfuscation, but to show how just this life, made up of these elements, unveils to us the mystery of God. In the end, I believe that the truth about our lives as natural beings is itself a source of hope, leading us to, even as it is uncovered by, the truth about who God is in Christ.

# I

# Clocks, Skins, and Mortality

## The Clock

In 1574 Strasbourg Cathedral unveiled a marvelous machine, unlike any that the people of the time had seen. The clock was enormous, with several ingenious features of measurement, built up on many levels, and including an array of artwork and moving statues. The clock's maker, Conrad Dasypodius, wrote a book about his invention and became a celebrity. Visitors came from afar to see this wonder, and, as the years passed, the clock became the exemplar of numerous analogies regarding God and the created universe.[1] The Strasbourg clock can also stand as a historical symbol of the kind of contextual argument about human life this book will be pursuing. Within its fabulous complexity of gathered mechanisms and temporal layers, the clock stands as a testimony to the single, if textured, way that all time, and with it human life, is given and held by God. The visual presentation of this fact in the Strasbourg clock's construction aimed at drawing the human observer into a knowing submission to the truth of this divine creative reality.[2]

The clock itself is one of the few existing examples of the technological genre, others being found in Prague and Lund, for instance. And the current remarkable machine is actually the result of a complete refabrication by Jean-Baptiste Schwilgué in the mid-nineteenth century. Schwilgué was tasked with rebuilding a working mechanism but with

1

keeping to the decorated framework of the sixteenth-century clock that had preceded it but that had ceased working in the late eighteenth century. Schwilgué's work was designed to compute and display intricate aspects of timekeeping for up to ten thousand years, and to this degree it far surpassed earlier mechanisms. But the iconography of the clock, in which the mechanism was placed, remained fairly traditional and represents a steady Christian vision that had persisted over many centuries.

The clock is really a series of several measuring devices, each laid on top of the other in a stone and wooden framework, almost like a gigantic and many-tiered altar. Each level points to one aspect of time lived, and each is part of a larger decorative scheme that, although including some disparate elements, is due most prominently to the skill of the sixteenth-century Swiss painter Tobias Stimmer. The entire machine is eighteen feet high, eight feet wide, and five feet deep.

On the floor level of this great vertical contraption is a globe representing the heavenly sphere. Its rotation presents the movement of the stars, and it stands before the lowest clock face, which demonstrates the "apparent" time of each solar and lunar day. These two divisions are set within the measures of a twenty-four-hour period. In the center of the clock face is the projected map of the northern hemisphere, and around the outer circumference of the face are all the days of the year, each detailed by its link with the church's calendar of dominical feast days and saints' days. Here, Schwilgué's genius can be seen in the way he worked into his mechanism the means of following the movable feasts and leap years. In the quadrants of this large face are Stimmer's depictions of the "Four Great Empires": Assyria, Persia, Greece, and Rome, the last of which Europe still inhabited. Each empire, however, is depicted as but a passing set of rising and falling human efforts. This initial layer of the clock, then, represented human history, set in the shadow of the heavens, impregnated by the church's life, yet all still located in a limited and dwindling round of days.

On a narrow layer immediately above this lowest floor of the clock is a sculptured mechanism presenting each day of the week with the rotating figures of the Roman days associated with it, ending with Saturn devouring his children. To each side Stimmer provided a pair of paintings: *The Creation of Eve, The Triumph and Judgment of Christ, The Resurrection of the Dead,* and the contrasting *Deaths of the Pious and Impious.* scriptural verses accompany each image. Between these are squeezed the reclining allegorical figures of the fall and redemption, the former shown as a woman enveloped by the delights of the world, the latter by the Scriptures and the Eucharist. Each figure reprises the scene of the last quadrant's representation of the good and bad death. These two uphold what we might call the clock face showing "normal" time, the hours of the day as we still perceive them, divided into twenty-four. On this layer, then, the dailiness of life is set before us in its scriptural frame: the minutes are given in the one reality of divine creation and redemption.

Right over the clock face of normal time, there are the mechanized statues of two small and cheerful angels. The first sounds the initial strike of the quarter hour, and the second, at the end of each hour during the day, turns its hourglass upside down to begin another hourly round. These two happy creatures are coordinated, however, with automated sculpted figures on the sixth level: the four ages of man who follow suit with the infant chimer for each quarter hour, as child, youth, adult, and old man. At each hour, as the cherub below turns the hourglass, Death appears above, ringing its bell, something it continues to do through the night, even as the small angels below take their rest.

So we move to the fourth level of the clock. Here we find another clock face that traces the changes of the planets as the year progresses. In each of the quadrant corners in which the face is set, Stimmer painted allegorical male figures representing, respectively, the four seasons, the four ages of man, the elements, and the hours and temperaments, bound up as these were with the movements of the heavenly realm. A "year" in this context is a period of time that both repeats itself in toil and in character and winds itself down into old age and weakness.

On the fifth level is a globe that follows the phases of the moon. And just above it, on each side, are depictions of the Church as Virgin Queen, standing upon the moon, and of Antichrist, facing her. This lunar realm evokes the scene of Revelation 12—struggle, exile, and trembling survival all at once.

The sixth level, as mentioned, has mechanized figures of the four ages of man appearing each quarter hour and submitting finally to the hourly tolling of the bell by Death. Yet just above this, on the seventh level, is the summation of all these elements, set in motion every noon hour. Here stands a figure of Jesus, holding his banner of the cross. After the angels and ages have had their say, and Death too, at twelve o'clock figures of each of the twelve apostles make a turn before their Lord, who greets each one of them with his hand. As they file out before him, a large automated rooster, to one side, crows three times. Betrayal, passion, and the new day are all wrapped together in this intense moment. Lastly, Jesus gives a final blessing to the cathedral crowd watching below. To this day, noon hour is the moment when tourist and worshipper gather together before the clock.

A final pinnacle to the tower contains fixed figures of Isaiah (holding a scroll with Isaiah 9:8 written upon it—the word of judgment and light to Israel), the four evangelists, and several musicians. There are other elements: a stone staircase to one side, with a small angel reminiscing on death; a wistful onlooker, sculpted into an adjoining wall; a pillar of angels gazing out; images of the Fates, of the builders and artists of the clock, emblems of the city. But the marvelous clock itself is held in these layers, wrapped in the net of heaven and earth, death and salvation, seasons and their possibilities and exhausted exclusions, and most especially the relentless insistence of limits whose measurability is but the mark of their utter dependence upon God for their very manifestation.

Christians have long been encouraged to gaze upon clocks like this, at least figuratively speaking. Strasbourg's "astronomical" version is only an early modern form of the book of Ecclesiastes in this respect. Some historians have argued that the invention of mechanized clocks changed Western perceptions of the self. But the Strasbourg clock shows that the advent of modernity and temporal measurement did little to alter the basic premise of human unfolding that was articulated already in scriptural reflections on human life. As in Ecclesiastes, the Strasbourg clock explicates that life in terms of birth and death, embedded in a world woven with change but also incapable of recreating itself. Human life is bound to a world of growing and weakening, of aging among other agers, of years laid out one after another in the course of fragile and ultimately passing human constructions. At the same time, however, the Strasbourg clock points to deeper meanings in this temporal passage. The details of human growth and death, the clock says, are themselves the very points of contact with the God whose creative hand has allowed being to be at all, birth to be the coming-to-be, and death to be the going-forward and out of view. The advent of mechanical clocks did nothing but permit the publicizing of these facts and thus the standard-bearing of such truths that creatureliness must constitute. That Schwilgué, with his admittedly new technological methods, was made to hew to the older sixteenth-century framework of the clock, with Stimmer's historical and allegorical panels nailed to the evangelical announcement of daily life, was but a sign that such creaturely time would be dismissed only with difficulty.

Since Schwilgué's nineteenth-century era, however, a sense of creaturely time has indeed been diminishing. The Strasbourg clock tells us
that we die, not simply because of our mechanical limitations. Human
machines, after all, wear out and break, as every commentator on clocks
since Donne has pointed out.[3] Rather, the time of our life, the clock tells
us, is settled with the moon and with the sun and stars of heaven in all
their passing magnitudes. Our lives, therefore, are best seen not simply
as time spent but as time offered, because they have been offered to us by
God and they come to us *as* our very being. Perhaps that is why, to this
day, crowds of tourists in Strasbourg buy tickets to wait in line to see,
each noon, the rooster crow Peter's face-to-face encounter with the God
of mercy: they are drawn to a deep truth about the character of their
lives. But it is a kind of fleeting memory that draws them—a whispering
spectacle of something long forgotten. In the place of such a spectacle
today is a world without clocks for *time*—but rather with clocks aimed
only at ordering the *now*, coordinating present moments in their multiplied and discrete details. Clocks today tell us what to do in the instant
only, even while the creaturely context for our moments has been culturally obscured.

In a similar way, our problems with reading the Scriptures for clarity
and guidance with respect to the pressing practical problems of our day
are related to the way creaturehood no longer provides us with a context
for our reading. In order to regain this context, our own thinking must
slowly change, as must our habits of reading Scripture and thereby our
sense of who we are. We will regain our true context as creatures if we
can recover a way of thinking that is bound more to Strasbourg's peculiar clock time than to the coordinating of moments by which today we
tend to measure our lives. The Strasbourg clock time is one of filiated
tremors and textures; it is the time of the One Man, Jesus Christ, whose
one life is the life by which we have the privilege of being made. This life
moves from first Adam to second Adam, as Stimmer showed in his quadrants painted around the moving dials. This human life indicated by the
Strasbourg clock engages a wholeness that is set by God and no one else,
and that lies within the tiny realm of time, outside of whose bounds
there is only the disturbing uncertainty of nothingness. "Could ye not
watch with me one hour?" Jesus asks his tired disciples in the Garden of
Gethsemane (Matt 26:40). We, in our turn, are asked to dwell upon this
extended reality of our time set against God's making of it.

## Being a Creature

This book will reflect on what it means to live as a mortal human being—as someone who must die. Human life, in its most basic significance, is bound up with the fact that we are temporal beings. We emerge from an inexplicable nothingness; and at their end, lives disappear into what is perhaps that same nothingness. Mortality may be obvious, but in our era it is no longer a central concern of discussion, even of theological discussion. In popular discourse about life's significance, even many Christians will point to something that lies outside of time. We often hear people describe the "meaning of life" in terms that stand beyond the limits of birth and death. A common religious presupposition is that life is "more than" the stuff that happens in being born and in dying, and certainly more than simply the things that happen in between birth and death. This presupposition is itself not wrong insofar as it assumes the meaning of life in that which gives life—that is, in God. Still, while we can rightly say that human life is both oriented to and grounded in God, we must begin a reflection on our lives elsewhere than in the simple fact of God if we are to be faithful to what is *human* about our lives. It is, after all, God who has fashioned this particular humanness that is given in birth, living, and dying.

Questions regarding "eternal life" must therefore be raised only after we have faced carefully the realities of temporal existence. For the ways by which God becomes known to us are the same ways by which we come to be, persist, and pass away as temporal beings, pressed up against the edges of an existence we cannot explain. We know God only insofar as, yet also precisely because, we come to be and live in a temporally limited fashion. This is what makes us God's *creatures*. But it is also the case that only as creatures do we know God. Every other aspect of our knowing, and every other aspect of our peculiar *religious* knowing, derives from and is shaped by this one fact—that we are creatures. Creaturely knowing means that God stands to us as the one who gives the very possibility of knowing anything, even while we are beings that cannot know how to come into existence or leave it. Whether, as some writers of the Christian tradition have speculated, this being that we are contains a "soul" or "spirit" to be distinguished from the bodies and flesh of our lives is fundamentally irrelevant to our creaturely condition. Whether we are more flesh than spirit or more spirit than flesh or both fused together, we stand before the one who made us as fragile and transitory things, laid across the plane of reality that is God's alone.

To say we are creatures is, therefore, a quintessentially *religious* claim even if it is a claim we can make only because we are mortal beings. We cannot claim to be creatures apart from some fundamentally religious understanding of reality. That is why, although I will be suggesting a far more physically focused understanding of the human being than the spiritually oriented emphases of some strands of the Christian tradition, there is no way in which this focus can be viewed as reducing human life to physicality. It is true that the Latin from which our English word "create" derives can easily refer to biological begetting. But the English term "create" has, from its original fourteenth-century usage, always been attached to God. Only God "creates" in any substantive way; and the work that comes from God's hands is always, by definition, some kind of "creature." Obviously, the Christian faith further specifies this creation as somehow being "in Christ," but the basic relationship of creature to Creator is undisturbed by this christological specification. Human beings are somehow "made" by someone beyond their scope of action and being. Human beings are not self-given; they do not "emerge" from something else in a basic way, even if we adopt evolutionary biological frameworks for explaining the origin of human life. Whether we are talking about atoms or the forces that order them or hold them together, it is not possible to avoid the question of what it means that any of this exists at all. The question of this original existence of all things and of their order is one that goes beyond physics. The Christian affirms that all things, including our very selves, "come to be" *because* of the specific act of the Creator. This relationship to a divine act outside of us and outside of our own times makes our creaturehood something singular, in comparison with other relationships we have with people and things, past and present.

If this is a book about human life and its meaning, then it is one that will focus on the contours that are intrinsic to a life given solely and fundamentally by its Creator. In addition, then, such a focus on creature and Creator must also turn toward the Scriptures as a fundamental point of departure. A central claim of the Christian gospel is that we are "creatures of the one Word" who is the cause and source of our life in every way. "For in him all things were created, in heaven and on earth, visible and invisible, whether thrones or dominions or principalities or authorities—all things were created through him and for him" (Col 1:16 RSV; cf. John 1:3; Heb 1:2). If we are creatures of Christ, then we are creatures of those words of Christ that are his own "spirit and life" (John 6:63). To be, in the traditional Latin phrase *crea-turae Verbi*, creatures of the Word is thus to have our life given in the scriptural description of that great movement from Adam to the New Adam, Christ Jesus.

We must, then, assert a fundamental link between human life and the life of God: the times of our life, insofar as they are scriptural times, are God's time. And these times must include not only a limited set of special times—the Sabbath, say, or only acts of devotion or holiness—but all times, of every kind. Most importantly for our self-understanding as creatures, God's time includes the times that mark our coming to be, our survival, and our passing away: times of birth, growth, eating, learning, sexual engagement, relating, work, birthing, forming, weakening, and dying. These personal existential times are scriptural times, in that the Scriptures are God's word speaking about the times we are living. Traditional Christian reading of the Bible could always find this or that aspect of a given human life in the scriptural text for just this reason: all of our human times are created by the Creator; each of them lies somehow "in Christ," who is the original, the truest, the one human life.

The great mystery and wonder of being a creature is that the very realities that mark our human lives are all gifts of the Word: the limits, the changes, the boundaries of nothingness that hold us in; the densely, if often loosely, populated realm of our habitations; the symbolic clock of Strasbourg. The Word itself creates our time and times and the things that make time something discernable. What this means is that every time of our life is Christ's time and is thus scriptural time. There is no "life" that somehow exists apart from God, and thus apart from the God who is in Christ, and thus finally apart from the God in Christ who is revealed to us singularly and exhaustively in the Scriptures. Such an exhaustive divine comprehension of our temporal life does not mean that non-Christian and non-scriptural realities have nothing to tell us about the truth of who we are. Science, anthropology, and other investigative disciplines all stake their claims on our understanding. But such disciplines cannot do so in an ultimately discrete and independent way, as if these realms of inquiry and discourse were hermetically sealed from the more primary realities of the Christian scriptural life. Creaturely life itself finally shows us that scriptural life is primordial to all other ways of construing life.

## The Scripture as the Context for Our Human Life

The modern difficulty with thinking this way does not derive simply from the sequestering of the physical from the spiritual. This separation is indeed a great problem. But it is only a symptom of something else, a habit of thought that impressed itself upon Christians and then the general population only over time. To be sure, this symptomatic habit of dividing physical from spiritual has profoundly shaped our attitudes. It has driven us (for example, when looking at concrete documents like the Bible that seem to be defined in terms of historical constraints of time, composition, historical context, and change) to search for some method of ridding their meaning of such constraints—of getting "beyond" the history. And this has led us to sift out messages from the Bible that are somehow "timeless" and therefore "spiritual" rather than concrete and physically oriented. Birth and death and the in-between times are left in the discarded heap of the physical and given over to science and history to pore over. Surely the Bible can have little to say about such times because, to the extent that Scripture does speak about such things, it is itself too constrained by their limitations: its bits and pieces are bound to ancient Israel, Canaan, Egypt and Greece and Rome, Palestine, and Jewish and Hellenistic attitudes and accretions and moldings.

Still, all this is a symptom of something else that lies deeper: a failure to acknowledge and face into the mystery of our beings as creatures of God, and of God as our Creator. This failure has grown and spread over the years. I will have something to say below about *why* this failure has spread. But the fact that it has spread must be stated up front. What is at issue is not so much a failure to believe in God. That is obviously not the case, given the breadth of religious life that continues even in the so-called secularized West and its cultural reach around the globe. Rather, this failure consists in a particular kind of belief: one that can no longer look, as unhesitatingly as possible, into the eye of our own nothingness, over and against which we exist from God's hand and exist only through divine grace. The spiritualized entities that we tend to see ourselves as constituting—"consciousness," extended "selves" roaming about the world, bundles of meaning and intentions, desires and wills—these are self-understandings that inform Christian and non-Christian people alike in our day. And these self-understandings, very precisely, have turned away from articulating the basic limits of our lives as creatures. This fundamental limitation on our lives, in conjunction with the God who has let it be, is the great mystery of our identity. But, if even

only vaguely grasped, this limitation so thoroughly relativizes the apprehended character of our physical being—and thus also the Scriptures'
documentary limits—that the priority of a temporal definition of reality
as it is commonly assumed must give way to divine claims on that time
in an absolute way: whatever "time" is, it must be defined first as God's
creative act out of nothing. Within such a vantage, the plausibility of
"scriptural time" as fundamental to our own existence becomes overwhelming to those, at least, who have a sense of the compelling truth
of the God of Israel come to us in Jesus Christ. How that truth itself
becomes compelling to this or that individual is a complex matter and
not the subject of this reflection. But the present reflection itself, I think,
is at least a part of that process of conversion.

### The Scriptural Contours of Life
#### *How to Talk about Human Creaturehood*

Our challenge when we address our creatureliness, then, is how to speak
of the scriptural time that constitutes our life in Christ. And <u>we must
find a way to do so as a creature rather than as a disembodied spirit or
being</u>. The Scriptures speak of things a person does in a variety of circumstances and ways. These styles of discourse tend to come down to
discrete laws, narratives of law keeping and law breaking, and the consequences that unfold. In addition, the Scriptures include exhortations,
descriptions of problems, and warnings about possibilities. The variety
and detail of these elements have given rise to discussions by scriptural
commentators that focus on thematized elements gleaned from the text,
ones out of which one might finally construct a "purpose" or "end" for
life: justice, worship, praise, communion. None of these thematized
scriptural meanings, by which a theology of human purpose has been
construed, are necessarily wrongly articulated. But theologically ordering these themes is a task that is distinct from a scriptural discussion
of creaturehood itself. That kind of discussion must be able to take in
the exhaustive shape that gathers these details together. I use the term
"exhaustive" deliberately because, in the end, the details of any given
creaturely life are limited in their temporal extent and are thus subject
to exhaustion if we seek to find their order through our own imaginative
forces, as it were.

By contrast, if we were to seek a scriptural discussion of this exhaustive aspect of creaturehood, we would turn to the comprehensive figures
the Bible offers for that whole that we call a human person, and one

that moves from birth to death. Job comes to mind immediately as such a comprehensive scriptural figure. Indeed, Job has been the figure of human life most turned to as a kind of "everyman" in Scripture, much as Gregory the Great described him at the opening of his vast series of sermons on the book of Job. Although only a small portion of Job's own life is actually discussed in narrative terms within the book of the Bible that bears his name, that book as a whole is a prolonged reflection on what it means to be born, to struggle in existence, and to die, bound to other human creatures of one's origins and passage—parents, spouse, children, and friends and enemies.

This kind of comprehensive figure is described in the Bible in terms of a "span" of years. The theologian Karl Barth devoted a lengthy part of his great *Dogmatics* to thinking about this "life span"—what he called "allotted time"—that defines the human creature.[4] In its particularity, this life span is the very means by which human beings relate to God. And as a time that is shared by Jesus, such a life span is also, as Barth puts it, a "gateway" that necessarily *is* this place—the one place—through which the life of God is shared with us. The great paradox of creaturehood is that the very limits of our existence, which are ineluctably imposed upon us and are immovable to each of us, are also that which is our bond to God. The temporal walls that hem us in are not existential limits to be transcended; rather, they are our connections to God just in their limitations. Our life span is just "God's taking time for us." Many implications may be drawn from this observation—some contested, some simply speculative. But at the least we must see that our limits also *coincide* with God's relationship to us, and we must consider all that this could mean.

The Psalms are particularly explicit about relationship: the years of our lives are three score and ten years or, if we are lucky, four score, or eighty years (Ps 90:10); we are formed in some kind of direct fashion by God even in the womb, before our consciousness and lively shape are given over to the world (Ps 139:13-16); our lives move from youth to age, and with this passage comes some measure of understanding about what our aging involves (Ps 37:25); but also in each life there are vicissitudes, expectations held onto, and expectations ruined (Ps 55). Finally, growing out of this internal ordering of the life span are the tendrils of other life spans: children, families, companions, the great congregation, and Israel and her future (Pss 127–128; Ps 66). The life span of the creature is the place of God's time with and for the human creature; but it is also the time through which we find "our place in time," in a wider sense.

Birth and death, then, stand as definitive markers of our creatureliness. From a theological perspective this leads to scriptural questions about human origins: Why did God "make us" at all? And we also face, of course, the perennial and gnawing questions concerning the character of our created lives—what has come to be seen in terms of "the fall," as it illuminates both God's original purpose and our "in fact" existences. The Bible never treats these questions systematically, but it is replete with their posing: sin, death, the "sting" of our disordered lives, justice and mercy, and with it what is called "the law" and grace. We shall return to some of these issues when we speak of the character of creaturely life itself in the next section. Here, however, I simply want to lay out the bordered scope of scriptural discussion about human life—its walls as well as its building blocks.

To get our bearings, let us return to one of the Christian tradition's classical scriptural figures of human creaturehood—the figure of Job. If birth and death do indeed stand as definite markers of our creatureliness, the way they comprehensively order our lives can be seen in him. Here we have all the questions posed within a single individual: the question not only of *being* born but of its character and the looming problem of purpose and end. "You made me," Job affirms, "yet it would have been better had I not been born!" Much of this complaint, however, is framed in terms of the specific measure of Job's existence: the days, the years, the beginnings and endings. All these temporal elements constitute what we call the "span" of a life, as the psalmist says in 90:10, though it be filled with "labor and sorrow."

More importantly, however, Job's figure is given in terms of a *range* of other figures. That figural range is part of the very premise of his voice: a wife, riven by grief and anger; children showered upon him and lost senselessly; friends from near and far, with their loving touch and disquieting rebukes. It is important to see this: from a scriptural perspective, Job may be the "everyman," but he is only such because he is *not alone* in his filiated existence. (I shall be using the word "filiated" frequently in what follows. While its full meaning must be given cumulatively, here I mean simply the fact that Job has a family and a set of relationships that includes children.) In Job's filiated relationships, the figure for the human creature widens and elongates. And thus Scripture moves from Job to Job's children and beyond. Gregory the Great was able, indeed pressed, to write his multivolume study of Job in terms of a *moralia*, a vast set of reflections on human life and Christian existence, because Job's "everyman" quality was in fact embodied in a socially networked form. That form "ranges," as it were, over generations: from Adam to Adam, as we said. But that also means, textually, that it ranges from Eden to the New Jerusalem, Genesis to Revelation.

The point here is that any scriptural study of the human creature—and only a scriptural study can suffice for understanding the human creature, if in fact Jesus is the Son of God—must order its focus according to the Bible's generational breadth and scope. We must discern how these are laid out and what constitutes their figural coherence in both commonality and change. One way to approach these questions is pursued in Jacques Ellul's notable, though rarely read, study of the city, known in English as *The Meaning of the City*.[5] Ellul was one of the great social theologians of the twentieth century, and he was very influential in the 1960s for his more radically Protestant critiques of modern society. Written early in his career, in 1951, just after World War II, this book provides one of the first careful critiques of the so-called historical-critical method of reading the Bible—that is, of the approach that demands that an understanding of Scripture depend on a full grasp of the contextual concerns and outlooks of its "original" human authors. Ellul notes both the practical impossibility of this criterion and its incoherence with a full understanding of the Scripture as the word of God. More importantly for my purposes, Ellul chose to reflect upon "urbanism," the particular concern of his book, in a way that turned the social science project upside down and also pressed against the piecemeal regulative approach of his conservative and generally sectarian colleagues. He simply followed the "figure of the city" through the Scripture, and he reflected on its shape and meaning as he read. After all, he reasoned, there *are* cities in the Bible, many of them. And their form is given primordially in Genesis and worked out in varying contexts through to the New Jerusalem or Scripture's final book. It is not simply a chronological ordering that comes up here but the theological skein that ties together the various biblical urbanisms, as it were, in a coherent yet historically experienced existence. The result of Ellul's reflection was admittedly a deeply pessimistic vision of the city and of human history. But his reflection was also easily misread (and dismissed) by equally pessimistic social critics because of its integration into the realm of specifically *scriptural* meaning, wherein human communal existence was necessarily bounded by and ultimately accomplished by God.

I believe something similar should be pursued when it comes to considering the meaning of human life more broadly. In this case, we should trace the life span itself as a figure of Scripture. So, for instance, if we are to reflect upon humanness, it is not enough to look at Genesis 1 and 2 —God's forming of Adam and Eve, which constitutes the key but difficult verses regarding human beings' material and personal relationships. To be sure, Genesis 3 and the various "curses" follow immediately upon these first two protological chapters, and Christians have obviously had to deal with this as well. But the tendency in commentary has been to bracket out Genesis 3–4 as incapable of providing positive illumination on human existence and instead to use them only as contrastive coloring, over and against which the "true" meaning of human life is given in the preceding chapters. This allows for a short bridge to be made to "eschatological" texts in the New Testament, especially Revelation, where "redeemed" existence is coordinated with divine "original intention" and human life is telescoped into the woefully unrealizable form of angelic perfection. This tendency, alas, is still with us today: in debates about human relationships, sexual and otherwise, it is as if the entire Bible between Genesis 2 and Revelation had disappeared as the figure of our lives. The very covenant with Noah—in which still we stand "perpetually" (Gen 8:21–9:17)—is, after all, founded on Genesis 4 and 5 in particular. Ellul, rightly, does not shy away from these texts as he tries to understand urban life in particular; nor should we when we engage the character of human life as a whole. Exodus and Leviticus, 2 Samuel and Ezra, Lamentations and Zechariah, not to mention the grating words of the Letters to Timothy and Titus, cannot be overleapt without imposing a fundamental obscurity over our lives as creatures.

This is not to deny that Christians are right when they point to the grace of God in Christ as deeply and utterly transforming this world, and the human creature in particular. The question is how this happens with respect to the clock of our existence. Even with and in Christ, the facts of our existence are still offered us—and ineluctably so—genealogically: we are still born, each of us, and we still die, every one of us. And we do so bound to one another, and ripped from one another. Given Christ Jesus, there is of course much over which to ponder in this light. We can at least say, and we *must* say, that the temporal contours of the life span, immovable in their experience, are nonetheless informed by divine grace. And if this is so, we can go further and say this: if grace in Christ informs our temporal realm, then, from a scriptural perspective, it is proper to say that whatever is not temporal is figured by that which is temporal; resurrection is figured by the grace of (for example) the Psalms' divine action—protection, sustenance, listening, mercy, renewal, healing, comfort, hope. That is, what we read about our filiated existences of birth to death—and what we know of them in experience—*itself* reveals to us the truths of resurrected life in Christ. This revelatory direction of temporal to nontemporal is a crucial theological point: we cannot pry apart the concrete realities of our life spans from the redemptive claims made about our beings in the gospel. The latter come into profile not *apart* from the former but only within them. This great truth of the Christian faith has been obscured in our day. And hence, the generationally elongated figure of human life—the multiplication of scriptural figures that mark the fullness of human existence in its divine creaturely form—is exactly where we ought to turn our gaze to understand who we are: Adam to Adam, yes, but also Cain, Abel and Enoch, Adah and Zillah, to Abraham and Sarah, and more. Our gaze must also move to Paul, a widower perhaps, with all that this implies. *This* is our life.

Eden to Revelation marks the collection of these figures, and then, in Revelation 21, their fullness is unveiled, as, in other places like Isaiah and Ezekiel, that unveiling is previewed. Something emerges out of the "times"—an unknown time, a new clock, or maybe the end of all clocks, and it is given without our ability or intervention. This will be a "new creation," one in which life and death are not simply reinterpreted but have given way to some new thing. Yet we must note this limit that the "new creation" puts upon our lives: that is, because it is "new," the "old" is, in a manner, left intact in its own form. From this fact a key truth emerges: in the "old," in birth and death, and in the life span that marks their coherence, we are "made ready" for what is new. But the span itself, however marked by grace, is not itself the new. Life and death, therefore, the creaturehood that constitutes our being, have their own integrity. We cannot do away with them. There is no truth beyond this that is more basic to the articulation of Christian anthropology and ethics. The grace of the life span's integrity provides the theological meaning of human creaturehood. There is where we must settle if we are to understand ourselves.

## Tunics of Skin
### *A Scriptural Figure of the Life Span*

The vast stretches of Scripture that lie between creation and new creation, and that therefore trace our created lives, are set off with a simple verse, to which early Christian interpreters gave much thought: "Unto Adam also and to his wife did the Lord God make coats of skins, and clothed them" (Gen 3:21). This detail precedes the human couple's setting forth into the world outside of the garden and follows God's statement of their created reality: "In the sweat of thy face shalt thou eat bread, till thou return to the ground; for out of it wast thou taken: for dust thou art, and unto dust shalt thou return" (Gen 3:19). This reality, we are then told, is to be the form for all human beings: "And Adam called his wife's name Eve [*Chava*, "living"]; because she was the mother of all living" (Gen 3:20). God "speaks" us back to the earth in the same way as he creates us, as part of the same miracle of giving, and hence it comes to us as a vocation: "[Thou] sayest, return ye children of men" (Ps 90:3). The garments of skin, then, signal that which God provides for life outside of Eden, a life of birth and death, toil and generation. They are, as it were, the "form" of temporal creaturehood.

To this extent, the skins are elements of grace. To be sure, early Christians (and Jews, for that matter) were not so sure of this, and here, again, we see the temptation to overleap the figure of the Scriptures themselves. Early commentators wondered whether the "skins" here refer to mortal flesh and hence to mortality itself, the consequence of sin. These *tunicae pelliceae*, "tunics of skin," therefore, must be things that in themselves reek of destruction, that signal our "entropic" nature, as it moves inexorably to annihilation. And thus many early interpreters insisted that, as skins, they are therefore to be let go of as progress in godliness is gradually achieved. In this way these early readers defined godliness in part as a casting *off* the skins given in the departure from Eden. When Adam and Eve were first made, they had no fleshly covering at all, some surmised, but were clothed in a kind of effulgent glory. The ascetic premise was here laid out "from the beginning": animal skins, as Jerome asserted, are inherently less "pure" than linen; they are, for instance, linked with hair and nails and hence with transient growth and decay. In this tradition of interpretation, in fact, the skins came to describe the "passions" of this life that weigh us down in life and must be overcome.

It is worth noting what the flip side is to this anticorporeal thrust that is admittedly visible in certain strands of Christian thinking. If bodies themselves, in their enfleshedness and mortal character, constitute only our fallenness, there is in place a nihilist logic that comes to the fore once bodies thus conceived are simply embraced. In its anti-Christian mode, contemporary corporeal affirmation presents just such a situation. With "only bodies," deprived of any divine significance within their moral limits, the world becomes devoid not only of God but of the ugliest of godless realms. "Just the body" in this life leaves us with the crude emptiness of an Antonin Artaud (1896–1948), the early twentieth-century French dramatist, so influential among contemporary modernists. His final play, *To Have Done with the Judgment of God* (1947), announces God's disappearance, gleefully embraced, but then leaves us with nothing but blood and excrement, the bare bodily fluids that make up life and whose ebbing away colors our deaths. "There where it smells of shit / it smells of being" (*Là ou ça sent la merde / ça sent l'être*), he writes in what has become almost a modern French proverb.[6] Of course, there is more to Artaud than this. But the bottom line of "the body only," understood in the immortality-grasping drive of a certain vagary of Christian thinking, is no more than Abel's blood robbed of that voice that "crieth from the ground" (Gen 4:10). "Just blood" remains—sticky, drying, and fading. This inevitable logic is important to discern because it represents the dregs of a de-Christianized culture, which itself reflects what a certain form of distorted Christianity leaves behind as its trace.

We need, therefore, to listen to another strand of the Christian tradition as it pondered the skins of Adam and Eve. While Augustine did not dispute the sign of sinful mortality that these garments represented, simply in being offered at all, he was, however, one of the first to rethink the intrinsic meaning of their giftedness from God, which Genesis seems to indicate. In so doing, he set up another tradition that moved all the way, at least, to Milton: if nothing else, the skins were signs of God's *compassion* on the now denuded Adam and Eve. In the first place, Augustine argued, bodies themselves preceded the fall and are thus intrinsically "good," as God pronounced all his works to be. But more than this, now that they were thrust into a difficult and dangerous world, God had at least offered Adam and Eve the means both of protecting themselves against the elements and of readjusting their bodies' relation to the world in response to the shame of their debased condition. The offering of the skins was grace, after all. Augustine and others went further still: we cannot consider the tunics of skin laid upon our first parents without also realizing that it was just this covering that Jesus himself took upon his own frame. Though imbued with the scent of mortality, then, here we find also the savor of humility, that by which our lives on earth are mysteriously rendered pure. As Milton wrote:

> [T]hen pittying how they stood
> Before him naked to the aire, that now
> Must suffer change, disdain'd not to begin
> Thenceforth the form of servant to assume,
> As when he wash'd his servants feet so now
> As Father of his Familie he clad
> Thir nakedness with Skins of Beasts, or slain,
> Or as the Snake with youthful Coate repaid;
> And thought not much to cloath his Enemies:
> Nor hee thir outward onely with the Skins
> Of Beasts, but inward nakedness, much more
> Opprobrious, with his Robe of righteousness,
> Araying cover'd from his Fathers sight.[7]

The tunics of skin, therefore, are a gracious means of survival, a "way." This way, furthermore, is Christ's own—indeed, it is Christ's first, before all others. (Hence, for some interpreters the skins derived from the first animal "sacrifice," performed in Eden itself, an act that originally typified the cross.)[8] The "way of the skins" is one that carries the human being, as the order of the Genesis narrative itself lays out, into and through the world. The garden of first and last creation frames the scriptural story, and in it all things find their proper place, from beginning to end, in their dependent glory and miraculous givenness. In the midst of this garden—and we are left unsure if the first and last gardens are the same, but surely the two are at least cognate—the perfect "knowledge" of creation is found, as is creation's perfect "life."[9] The skins accompany the human being from one garden to the other.[10]

And just this wandering—from a beginning to an end, from garden to garden, covered by skins—is the story of a human life. The story of the skins is one of wilderness peregrination—in contrast to Eden. It is also the story of toil within this wilderness, of work, of building, of community, of families and their fates. Ellul's city takes its place here as one element of wilderness wandering, but only one. The figure of the skins, after all, reappears in several key places, always pointing to this peregrinating existence by which humans move through time and by which human life is defined in terms of such extended movement.

So, for instance, there is the tabernacle, built by the Israelites in the desert and carried from place to place. It is not by accident that its outer covering was made of skins, according to the divine directive (Exod 26:7, 14; 36:14-19). Both Jews and Christians noted this and sought to grasp its meaning. Origen, and the medieval tradition following him, tended to read the skins allegorically and to develop, according to the order of the tabernacle's coverings, a hierarchy of ecclesial virtues to which each referred. They reasoned that something as mean as animal skins, taken only literally, could never actually adorn the yearned-after precincts of the holy God. Jewish readers, for their part, extended the figure of the skins to the ordering of the cosmos.[11]

But that animal skins should in fact cover this movable dwelling seems quite consistent with their original donation in Genesis. The skin, after all, becomes the mark of created life itself, in that it "holds" that life within itself, in the form of blood. This is what Leviticus, and its intriguing interest in mysterious dermatological disease, seems to indicate (e.g., chap. 13): life dissipates, literally oozes away, as the skin dissolves, and thus the very character of created existence's mortal dependence upon God is bound up with the visible presence of an integral "skin." This notion is crystalized in the central figure of Job, whose own final testing is given in the suffering of his *owr*, the covering of his life (Job 2:4) "from the sole of his foot unto his crown" (Job 2:7). It is, as Satan says, "skin for skin" that is at issue (2:4). And throughout the book, Job's skin becomes the token of his unjust fate, eaten by worms (7:5, etc.) and embodying the Levitical sign of ebbing life. Yet his skin is also, famously, the ground from which the redemption of his flesh is disclosed (19:26). Taken from the goats and rams, however, the skins of the tabernacle in Exodus are also given and received in life's temporal finality—death, and here explicitly, in the death of other creatures. The skins are always God-referring in the form of their creature-rooted being that acts as life protecting. As the skin-covered tabernacle is carried through the desert, it follows the movement of Israel through time in the wilderness.

This idea of linking "tabernacle" and "skin" is taken up most clearly by Paul in the well-known text of 2 Corinthians 5:1-4. Here, Paul describes his life of mortal flesh as a "tabernacle" with which he is "clothed" but that will "dissolve" and be replaced in the glorious "life" that is to come in the future "building of God." The point, however, is not that this mortal life is somehow *not* the true life of the human creature. After all, it is also the case that the Son of God himself "tabernacled" in the "flesh" when he came to dwell among his people (John 1:14). Rather, the life of the human creature, according to Paul, is like the skin-covered tabernacle of the Israelites: it is a "pilgrimage." This life aims, to be sure, at something new, yet it is integrally ordered as the extended place of passage. This consistent perspective frames Christian conviction about creaturely existence from Hebrews through the nineteenth century, passing through Augustine, Hildegard, the Reformation, and the great spiritual tradition of the Western American evangelical revival. The *tunica pellicea*, in all these Christian expressions, marks human existence as a journey of labored survival within mortal limits through time and generational extension.

I have mentioned Leviticus in passing. But it is worth noting how, in this scriptural book, the figure of "skinfulness"—that is, of life lived and life leaked out and drained away—is bound to all the concrete elements of quotidian order and experience. Leviticus is the most "earthy" of the Bible's volumes. Of course blood itself is central (in the treatments of sacrifice, human conception, and birth), but so are all the other aspects of survival: sexual acts, to be sure, but also planting and tilling, family ties, clothing, hygiene, cooking, money and debts, homesteads and land, and then the poor and their needs. We see, however, that the Levitical text's multiple interests in the everyday are located not in the stable existence of a settled lifestyle but in the ever-changing locale of the wilderness people. Skinfulness is ordered not by city walls but rather by the ongoing movement of the liturgical calendar of the clock, which undergirds the outreaching of mortal life. Hence, Leviticus orders Israelite time through its legal imposition of the weekly, monthly, yearly, and finally sabbatical festivals—even while this ordered time is punctuated by the contingent demands of penance and thanksgiving. Everything, as the book makes clear, is founded on "offering," on the gift that wells up as the basis of the human heart's own intentionality. Sacrifice lays out the skinfulness of life in an immediate way, enacts it, draws us into it, and shows us finally, in the elaborate demands of repentance and forgiveness, the dangling thread by which God allows our lives to be.

Not by coincidence, then, the greatest skin-man of Scripture after Adam—and before Christ—is John the Baptist (e.g., Mark 1:6). He "came," clothed in the skin of animals, preaching just the kind of life his own form announced: "For I say unto you, that God is able of these stones to raise up children unto Abraham!" (Matt 3:10).

If we take seriously this scriptural orientation, by which the "garments of skin" mark the tending of our wilderness between the two gardens, then the clock can properly be understood. The Strasbourg timekeeper is nothing other than the complex visual coordinating of this "movement through." The "life span" that it measures and places within this movement marks the way that survival extends itself through these measured spheres. Perhaps the mixing of metaphors or figures here is confusing. But it is important to hold them together. For as I said earlier, though it is with difficulty that creaturely time can be dismissed—that the clock itself can be turned into a vestige—that difficulty is precisely one that has been confronted, however unhappily, in our own era. And as the clock is relegated to the church's closet (and the church herself becomes such a closet), so too are the *tunicae pelliceae* peeled off, as it were, and strung upon a hanger in the dark, leaving our bodies exposed to something unforeseen. This is the story of just the past 150 years of human history; indeed, for many in the world it is the story of only the past 15.

## Casting Off the Tunics
### *The Great Transition and Modern Nakedness*

Having glanced at the scriptural story of the skins, I now turn to the modern story that has taken its place. The modern story is one of obscuring skinfulness and, in the wake of this obscuring, allowing a range of other realities to emerge as dominant. This story is ultimately a deceptive one. But it is powerful. The modern story is basically this: life span extension, along with birth survival. The two, as it turns out, go together. Beginning in the 1920s and 1930s, with the work of scholars like the Americans Warren S. Thompson and Frank W. Notestein as well as the Frenchman Adolphe Landry, the notion of "demographic transition" began to develop in the young science of population studies. The assertion of such a "transition" constituted a theory that founded the understanding of population changes over the long haul, and especially in the modern age, on the birthrate/mortality-rate ratio. Scholars had begun to engage the European and American correlated statistics of lowered mortality rates (which translates into longer life spans) and lowered fertility rates.[12] As people live longer, it seems that birthrates go down. This was quickly linked to what we now call economic "development," and the theory of the "demographic transition" stated that as countries develop and life spans increase people have fewer and fewer children.

Certainly, the basic statistics bore this theory out and remain mostly uncontested. The question of life span, or mortality rates, was especially striking. Using some particularly good data, Alfred Sauvy laid this out quite clearly:[13] if you were born in Sweden in 1750, you could expect to live for thirty-five years; if you were born in 1800, that life expectancy had risen a bit, to thirty-nine; by 1860, however, it had jumped all the way to forty-eight; and, with a huge leap, if you were born in 1960, life expectancy in Sweden was seventy-five. Today it is around eighty years. In the United States, except for the terrible episode of the 1918 flu epidemic, life expectancy at birth from 1900 to the present has steadily risen from about forty-seven years to almost eighty.

The causes for these changes are also generally accepted, although details for this or that place remain in dispute. Some significant changes occurred in the seventeenth century, in parts of Northern Europe especially, as agricultural technology and transportation resulted in better food production and distribution. This trend continued, and its results were seen in the eighteenth-century rise in life expectancy. A more obvious jump occurred in the later nineteenth century, as a confluence of medical innovations, including vaccines and sanitation, had a key role in reducing deaths at birth and during childhood. And finally, the huge jump in the twentieth century is generally attributed to much better distribution of wealth and to major advances in treating disease and applying health care widely. In non-Western countries, these kinds of stages have been either telescoped into a much shorter period or simply leapt over to the final ones.

All in all, and for all the debate over details, this aspect of the "demographic transition" has been about health, as it relates to nutrition and disease. (I will return to the birthrate aspect shortly.) Indeed, while theorists of demographic transition set the focus on industrialization and today on "development" in a way that rightly includes a whole host of social factors like education and employment, the driving center, experientially, in this very recent phenomenon has been health. Apart from war and natural disaster—which obviously have major and immediate effects on life expectancies—the long-term trends in life span are all about our health. And in any case, the pressing issue is always therefore about mortality—death as the limit to our lives.

So, going further than the economists, more recently some scholars have come to designate the recent past's great existential changes in life span more broadly: we have not only been going through a "demographic" transition; we have been going through a more comprehensive *human* transition as well—one tied specifically to the ordering of our mortal bodies. James Riley, one of the pioneers in collating this material, thus prefers to speak of "*the* Transition," which is basically a "health transition."[14] He pinpoints the late nineteenth century as the experiential center for Britain and other parts of Europe and North America; other parts of the world followed later on. For example, Japan began its "Transition" after World War I; Russia after World War II; Africa only—and very haltingly—after the 1960s.

Not everyone has embraced this notion of a single and great "Transition," though not necessarily because the facts are incorrect. Rather, they prefer to engage the issues I will be noting in a moment from a perspective other than demographic "causality," or indeed any kind of causality. The philosopher and historian Rémi Brague, for instance, has wrestled with a number of the same matters I am talking about in this volume: the contemporary denigration of human life, in particular, that is shown in a range of behaviors from the acceptance of suicide to the dismissal of procreative responsibility. Brague, however, believes that questions of causality—too complex in any case to lay out clearly—should take a back seat to "reasons," in the sense of intellectual structures of thought. From this perspective, the cultural problem of the "Transition," he argues, has to do with rejection of the "metaphysical" framework that can posit human being in its essential relation to the good that is God. For Brague the causes of the past—for example, the historical causes of the loss of Christian faith in the contemporary West—cannot tell us anything about the future; rather, only metaphysical groundings in our behaviors can offer predictive visions. Our metaphysics themselves may not "cause" anything, but they do foretell our destiny. If we believe that we live a life that is but one of "brute existence," unattached to any reality other than material chance and its "necessary" imperatives of force, then we will embrace a future that will, in this case, lead to species disappearance, among other things.[15]

There is a logic to this sense of our metaphysics' predictive power. But the demographic causes of our behaviors are actually clues as to the "true" character of our lives. They tell us more than that $y$ follows $x$; they indicate a larger reality—a complete alphabet—that tells us something about who we are. And I will use the phrase "the Great Transition" because of its history-defining character that therefore implies a curtain drawn on the intrinsic limits of human life itself. This phrase has been used of late by those theorizing a new global moment of economic mutual dependence and equilibrium—but this usage seems not only utopian but somewhat blind to the more basic issues at stake in what we are talking about here. What I will call the Great Transition (or the Transition) refers specifically to the rapid increase in life expectancy of the population on average, from around thirty-three years in 1800 in Europe to almost eighty in the year 2000. Wherever this transition has occurred, an astonishingly rapid shift has taken place in how long most people live. But this shift was not only astonishing—it was simply unknown in human history before this time. As McMichael shows, a life span of thirty years was average in ancient Athens, Jesus' time, the Middle Ages, the Reformation, always and everywhere, until the European eighteenth century slowly pushed this up, followed by the late nineteenth century's sudden spike. Since before the dawn of written records until the actual occurrence of the shift in this or that place since the nineteenth century, always and everywhere one could count on a 25 percent infant mortality rate—a quarter of one's children dying as infants (and the rate was often higher). There were people who lived considerably longer—and the longer one survived, the greater one's chances of surviving longer still. But the ranks of survivors thinned out drastically as the years passed childhood.

If one could get to twenty, there was a good chance of living to forty; and if to fifty, then possibly to seventy. But for those who survived into adulthood, living much past forty was rare enough.[16] The numbers varied dramatically from place to place, of course, but not enough or over long enough time to make much difference. In one otherwise unremarkable British diary from 1625, we read an entry concerning the safe delivery of a certain Nehemiah Wallington's son and his wife's survival. "The Lord's Name be praised for it," Nehemiah writes, adding that "one or two weeks before my wife fell sick, I did hear of three score women with child and in childbed that died in one week in Shoreditch parish, and scarce two of a hundred that was sick with child that escaped death." His own family's survival is due only, as he notes, "to the great mercy of God."[17] That mercy was tangible and constantly lifted up before the eyes of those for whom human life hung by a thread.

As I have mentioned, the study of life expectancy and its causes is in fact very recent and, consequently, still undeveloped.[18] After passing through various stages of theoretical assertion, the commonly accepted view today—based on the study of varying rates of life expectancy change in contemporary societies around the world—is that the causes for high mortality in the past were multiple, not singular. And experts argue precisely over what is "most important" in this large set. Malnutrition ranks high (centered around crop production, general economic systems, climate, violent dislocations, and the cultural misunderstandings about the health effects of breastfeeding), as do, of course, epidemiological factors—disease, plagues, infections. Sanitation, public water, and water distribution are considered crucial as well. One should add war, of course. Accidents, which tended to be more lethal in nature, must be considered a factor, as well as common security (e.g., in the prevention of murder) within communities and in the much more extensive and underpoliced open spaces outside of them. But here, in any case, we need to make a clear statement. In the sixteenth century—when we tend to see "modernity" stretching its limbs—and indeed until the nineteenth century, it made no difference if you were rich or poor on this score: your life expectancy was similarly low (and sometimes lower if you were rich, due again to the strange calculus of nutrition and breastfeeding). And it made no difference if you were Christian or pagan, if you were Protestant or Catholic, or what form your doctrine took. Mortality was fastened into your existence from your birth and through every relationship from then on and at every point in your existence. Death was all around, all the time.

This is a crucial observation in light of the Transition and its relationship to our own concern with creaturely life. The *shape* of skinfulness has been altered only very recently; and given these changes in life span, that alteration has been inevitable. One of our theological tasks is to relate the *tunica pellicea* of mortality to the humility of God in Christ, and to consider its meaning as a gracious reach over time's transitory passage, when the garments of mortality itself have suddenly become lighter, their bristling hairs less grating.

A good deal of political policy—and ideology—is determined by the answers one gives to the question of the Transition's causes, causes that remain debated, as I have noted. Is it nutrition and its economic base? Sanitation and its educational foundation? Epidemiological factors and the systems of health provision that navigate them? These are critically important debates to engage in public policy. But the *consequences* of increased life spans are also of great importance—and not for public policy alone but for theology and the Christian life. And the question of consequences has received little attention—except in terms of mop-up responses, behind the curve, to unexpected challenges on the ground. Mostly, the church has been silently bewitched.

Let us consider fertility: here we come to the other side of the "demographic transition," one that its original theorists were most interested in. The issue of contraception, to be sure, has been much scrutinized. But artificial contraception's widespread use actually *followed* the tendency toward lowered birthrates in transitioning societies—it did not precede it. (And here, the moral question thus needs to be placed in this larger context of the Transition and not extracted from it as if it were a discrete item for evaluation.) It is well known that the average birthrate has fallen dramatically in societies that have gone through the Transition. But the extent of this change is rarely appreciated. In Canada alone, the birthrate per 1000 women has fallen from close to 250 births in 1962 to around 50 in 2004. Similar reductions can be seen all around the world, and generally (if not uniformly) they are linked to the Transition as it has touched a given society. The reasons for this are not self-evident. But there are persuasive arguments to be made that increased chances of survival for one's infants deeply affect the need and ability of mothers (and fathers, to a lesser extent) to conceive more children. This approach to childbearing is not simply a rationalist or utilitarian one but rather shaped by affective bonds and responsibilities. The relationship between life span and birthrates is so strong that many economists, like Sauvy, have long argued that, to the degree that the Transition reaches all peoples, the world's population must necessarily reach an equilibrium "on its own," without the need of state interference.

But we should note that the Great Transition must affect more than population numbers. For whole economies are similarly reordered by increased life span and decreased birthrates in drastic ways that touch upon schooling, work, and retirement. One of the most common areas of change has to do with the participation of women in both higher education and in that part of the labor pool that is informed by educational attainment. Women's overall participation in the workforce has tended, for instance, to explode wherever the major aspects of the Transition take hold. Part of this is clearly linked to questions of fertility, in terms of both the average age of first births and the number of children brought into the world and raised. And all of this shifts as the confidence in child-mother survival rises significantly.

At the same time, of course, longer life spans mean that new challenges to long-held traditions of retirement age and retirement activity—or simply the "third age," as Europeans often called it—have arisen. Sometime after 1945 in America, the average life span began steadily to rise beyond the average age of retirement—to seventy-eight to eighty years. So a person now can expect at least fifteen years of life after professional labor has ceased. We are familiar with this, usually in terms of arguments over taxation for social security and the reach of pension and medical insurance support. But, in addition, a range of profound issues have come up around the character of an "elderly" life—its meaning, form, and pursuit. So different do these issues now appear, compared to those that confronted older persons in the past, that sociologists have begun to speak not only of a "third age" but of a "fourth age"— the life that follows retirement's immediate engagements and that now extends with an uncertain center, in terms of both financial substrate and human significance.

We hardly need remind ourselves of the related question of health care and its costs. But deep moral dilemmas are being pressed upon us by the rapid expansion of these costs, with extended lives that require medical support and for which such support has been made possible through technology. "Aging populations" tend not only to monopolize the health system's resources but, in proportion to lowered fertility rates, to create generational value stresses and economic tensions that have already exacerbated traditional divisions in political priorities between young and old. The fact that many churches, almost by default, have generationally separated services and ministries is, obviously, linked to a range of cultural factors. But these factors themselves are fundamentally driven by the Transition. And, at the same time, these struggles can obscure deeper moral challenges that touch upon social infrastructure and planning.

All these areas of consequence of the Great Health Transition are sweeping but also politically straightforward (though probably not in their resolution). But let us turn to the specifically moral aspects of the Transition that touch upon human relationships in particular. These aspects engage the filiated and interwoven fabric of the *peregrinatio in deserto*, the wilderness wanderings of Israel's tabernacle. It is possible here simply to list some of these outcomes, many of which have their own complex feedback dynamics that continually reshape our cultural and social contexts of expectation and response.

    *Shape of the family and relationships*—The Transition has changed decisions about family size; the average age of parents when their children are born; the number of parents deemed necessary; how children are born; and whether biological parents must be those who raise the children (the development of artificial reproductive technologies is important here).

*Maturation and its meaning*—Lengthening of life span has come with clear changes in both the "stages" of life themselves and their number (something we will look at later) as well as their length and thus their meanings: childhood and adolescence; young adulthood (a relatively new category, which designates those who, after university, are, among other things, now increasingly living in parents' homes); work and parenthood; and old age and its relation to work, family, and our physical bodies.

*Gender roles*—This is a well-plowed area of concern, but it is inescapably reshaped by new health, economic, and maturational arrangements: who works, how to prepare for this, fertility and childbearing and at what points in a "life history" this takes place, marriage, and so on. Not only do these elements obviously represent a set of shifts that pertain to women, but women have been the primary focus of study up to this point. Still, these factors have necessarily changed the way men both function and view themselves—as workers, generative beings, fathers, protectors, and wisdom providers.

*The meaning of work*—With extended life spans, new questions arise as to what work is for and how it is related to our ages and bodies and especially to other people (i.e., spouses, children, larger family, self).

*The meaning of the body*—The question of the body's significance is maybe the most complex outcome to consider. Increasingly, people wonder what bodies are "for." They ask how they are to be "used"; what is the role of pleasure in our own or other people's bodies; what is the place of "healthiness," pain, image/look, and so on when it comes to our bodies.

We can note a few examples here of how the Great Transition has shaken up these categories within the cultural realm of various peoples. And these examples are merely indicators of the vast terrain, and often subterrain, that marks our lives today, wherever we are.

So, for instance, the most stark element of the Great Transition, the extended life span, has dramatically altered cultures like Japan's that were founded on close generational ties and integrated engagement. This can be traced fairly clearly, as a cultural crisis emerged in 1960s Japan in which the care of the now very elderly was quickly relocated outside the children's home to nonfamily domiciles, something that earlier generations simply would not have imagined. The development of a new individualism, over and against an earlier embedded communal understanding of generational bondedness, created tensions that deeply rattled Japanese society.[19] And, obviously, this kind of change has been experienced in numerous societies besides Japan.

In another instance, James Riley himself, one of the deans of this area of research, studied the Transition's apparent effects on the shifting character of physical patience: as life spans have expanded, there have been adjustments in the kinds of pain and suffering we are willing to bear in our bodies. Riley identified how contemporary persons in Britain, despite living longer, seem to have allocated for themselves the same amount of time for healthy-bodied work as did their ancestors before the Transition. That is, we are all still "laboring" the same amount in terms of productive years as did our pre-Transition ancestors. Riley theorized several possible reasons for this. Better health care means that people survive longer while suffering chronic disease, which still, however, prevents them from work. An alternative theory, he suggests, is that we contemporary persons have a lower pain threshold than did our forebears, simply because we are not used to it from an early age. Or perhaps it is simply that, in the culture of the post-Transition, we have developed new notions of what both the body and work are "for." In any case, the question of work and its relation to our bodies has been altered profoundly, and so also has our understanding of what physical suffering is all about and how we make sense of that suffering.

This leads to another instance, one more familiar to religious discussions at least, and that is the sequestering of death in contemporary life and the effects of this on both identity and sexuality.[20] As the experience of other people's deaths becomes more primarily located amongst the elderly, and therefore more frightening at other ages, death itself has been integrated into quotidian self-understanding with greater and greater difficulty. Until later old age, death is a kind of surd, and hence is often faced as such even when finally encountered. Certainly, it is left existentially unexamined. In place of lives that are experienced as filiated elements of generational engagement, our selves within the post-Transition society are apprehended as more fragmented and isolated individual constructions of meaning and embodiedness. We live as selves largely detached from the mortal character of our peers and families.

This detachment in turn renders sexuality something focused upon personally embodied pleasure or satisfaction, something simply divorced from genealogy altogether. The "child-free life" is the statistical endpoint of the demographic transition's model. But that life is also, for reasons intrinsic to the dynamic that model presents, built into the emotional self-understandings of the individuals who are, as it were, living out the Transition itself.

To be sure, the marginalization of mortality as an integral part of our self-definition can be achieved with greater or lesser "success," based on all kinds of factors. Thus, we can consider the "Russian drop" in life expectancy in the 1990s, when by 1995 the life expectancy of the Russian population dropped by almost six years (from around sixty-eight to sixty-two). This reversal was arguably based on alcoholism and other health threats tied to the social disruption and the crumbling of psychic confidence in the wake of the Soviet Union's disintegration. An odd possibility—at least for the demographer—thus arises: it is always possible that we are headed for a vicious circle of increased life expectancy and decreased sense of integrated meaning, which in turn will decrease life spans.[21]

Whether correlated through more indirect causation (e.g., economic liberalism leading both to increased life span and to individualism) or more directly caused, we can see how one of the key effects of increased life span is tied to the dilution or even dissolution of what early German sociologists called *Gemeinschaft*—that is, communally founded life meaning. It is certainly the case that we have not yet learned *how* to live as such communally bonded beings within the changed circumstances of the Transition's new parameters of existence. Robert Putnam's popular book *Bowling Alone: The Collapse and Revival of American Community* spoke to this concretely for many North Americans.[22] But parallel—and in many ways far more socially wrenching—changes in the disintegration of communally defined selves have been observed in the lives of those millions of persons caught up in the vast and absolutely sudden urbanization that has engulfed the societies of Africa, Asia, and South America at the very moment the Transition is being passed through. Human identities are being reevaluated as a result—unexpectedly, unpreparedly, and in the most profound ways imaginable.

What we see here, very precisely, is how the change in "life span," seen more specifically in terms of its theological categorization in Genesis, seems to have effected a deep change in, indeed even a dismantling of, "genealogy." The "bondedness" through time that exists through the named linkage of parent, child, grandchild, and familial descendants has been loosened. The clock has been pushed to the side; it is at best a touristic artifact of fascination. Immediacies of demand and response proliferate, and the burgeoning availability of digital communications has rushed in to facilitate and fulfill these requirements. It is not that human life no longer follows a temporal pattern, that one thing does not arise after another, that aging is not real, or that death does not finally and inescapably meet us rather quickly in the scheme of things. Rather, the basic "withdrawal of death" into very specific and limited quarters of controlled illness and geriatric dissolution has left, as the only alternative to this withdrawal, the surd of its violent and seemingly inexplicable eruptions into an otherwise assumed tranquility—"tragedies," "madness," the "criminal," and the "demonic." <u>Death has increasingly become no longer a part of life, where once it had supplied life its background threads, running into its colors.</u> And the ordering of human life, so long  arranged by this design and stirring up what for so long we called "love" itself, in the form of genetic existence and its struggles, has quickly—astonishingly so, given the frame of human history—melted away.

All of this brings us back to the question of our figural existence in scriptural terms. After all, the "skindom" of human life within the landscape of the world's uncertain forms inevitably reasserts itself. It is one thing we continue to admit, whether or not we count on it. But if this is so, one ought certainly to ask whether the reevaluation of life brought by the Health Transition and its demographic consequences is coherent with our Christian faith, our understanding of Christian truths. And the ineluctably looming reality of life span as fundamental ingredient of humanness must answer that in the negative. That is, the Christian life, in its fundamental character of expressing the body of Christ, is explicitly opposed to, or at least in deep tension with, the individualism generated by increased life spans and their causal matrix. And if that is so, one of the great challenges for Christian life and witness in our day is to articulate and represent—to *live*—some form of human life that stands in contrast to the effects bequeathed us by the *blessings* associated with increased life expectancies. That is a real challenge: living longer, and all that can make this possible, is a *good*; it is itself bound up with the "compassion" that God's provision of the *tunica pellicea* itself embodies. But the cultural dynamics this longer life have set in motion must also be resisted and somehow overcome. Otherwise, a gift becomes the means of rebellion or at least a willing forgetfulness plunging us into despair.

Thus, we should hardly assume that the Great Transition is a "mistake," in either human or divine terms. As C. P. Snow said of his grandfather, when discussing the benefits of Great Britain's industrialization:

> The industrial revolution looked very different according to whether one saw it from above or below. It looks very different today according to whether one sees it from Chelsea or from a village in Asia. To people like my grandfather, there was no question that the industrial revolution was less bad than what had gone before. The only question was, how to make it better.

That is because, as Snow explains, although his grandfather had never risen beyond being a manual worker for the tramway, and in many ways resented the terrible limits that had hemmed him in socially and economically, nonetheless, compared with his grandfather, he felt he had done a lot.

> His grandfather must have been an agricultural labourer. I don't so much as know his Christian name. He was one of the "dark people," as the old Russian liberals used to call them, completely lost in the great anonymous sludge of history. So far as my grandfather knew, he could not read or write. He was a man of ability, my grandfather thought; my grandfather was pretty unforgiving about what society had done, or not done, to his ancestors, and did not romanticise their state. It was no fun being an agricultural labourer in the mid to late eighteenth century, in the time that we, snobs that we are, think of only as the time of the Enlightenment and Jane Austen.[23]

Hardly anyone would wish to "go backwards" to the "nasty, brutish, and short" existence of our ancestors in their valiant efforts to forge decency and embody love against tremendous existential odds. Those of us who have lived in societies that have not yet straddled the Great Transition (I did so, for instance, in 1980s Burundi) have sometimes perversely enjoyed the fruits of a traditional life span culture—its stable connection with the rhythms of the larger world of growth, death, and renewal—without having to pay the physical price. This can render us both naïve and blind. For the price was always great and for most people horrendously wrenching and depleting. By contrast, the Great Transition is a part of the "skins" that God has given us in great compassion. But it is *compassion* that this gift of an increased life span represents—not progress and certainly not a right. There are no guarantees on its perdurance, as every rattling pandemic from AIDS to Ebola makes clear, or as human violence and natural disaster overrun this part or other of the globe, and the huddled masses of camp refugees, among them doctors and teachers, children and old women, make clear.

On this score, we must resolutely push back against the still powerful assumptions of human progress that drive our social imaginations. We are long past, surely, those hopes for inevitable and beneficent human development that were proffered in the eighteenth century by philosophers like Condorcet and then witheringly critiqued in the twentieth century by most sober-minded thinkers, including self-styled thinkers of "the Left" like Christopher Lasch.[24] It is painful to watch medical scientists valiantly struggle to address a disease like HIV infection, desperately holding on to hopes that it will finally be "cured," even as they have settled into an acceptance of long-term "management" of the illness. It is painful because the efforts involved bespeak the deepest form of human solidarity, while the admission of intractable infection seems to relativize so decisively the effectiveness of that solidarity. And yet our cultural attitudes remain lodged in the vise of completely incongruous claims: we insist on human cultural progress (rights, respect, articulated dignity) even as we helplessly bemoan the degradation of human life due to cultural corruption (consumerism, indulgence, environmental violence). Oddly enough, sexuality stands as a key component of each competing perspective.

But if we should hold notions of fundamental human progress at bay, we must also be wary of a sharp turn into what is today called an "eschatological" viewpoint, the place where endings are sublated into something "beyond" endings—beatitude, heaven, eternal life. This was, after all, a standard Christian claim of a sort: the fallenness of bodies and their mortal character are redeemed in another and transcendent world. The Great Transition, in this light, is meaningless. Yet, as the analogy drawn with Snow's discussion of industrialization indicates— and as each of us knows deep down—the Transition *is* a good. While "the hope of heaven" is a central Christian commitment, it should not be one that is based on the theological rejection of the grace that marks our being alive at all, given within the form of mortality. To say that mortality limits our being in a definitive fashion, theologically, is not to deprive our self-understanding of transcendent elements. That could happen only if our mortal existences were not *created*—that is, if they were not utterly dependent upon God. Indeed, the loss of a sense of *creaturehood* is what has determined the desiccated character of modern "immanence," noted by critics like Charles Taylor in his studies of secularism.[25] But fears regarding the immanentization of meaning have too often been taken as a reason for demanding a rejection of the finality of mortal existence itself and a rejection of both its inherent responsibilities and its transcendent joys.

The ordering of the traversal of the world, clothed in skins, is itself a divine gift. Its embrace and pursuit is itself a transcendent occupation. This is in part what I will be arguing when it comes to the areas of maturation, family, and work: their character as aspects of survival is, for the creature, precisely what makes them transcendent, and not purely immanent, goods.

Thus, it is appropriate to say, as Christians, that the Great Transition must be acknowledged and given thanks over. But Christians must also recognize that the Transition is only "skin deep," as it were; it is only a contingent and limited blessing from God. That is all any gift of the sort could amount to. It cannot mask the fundamental character of our lives, which has remained steady and uniform. Amortality is certainly a myth, Promethean of sorts, but also simply silly. The best estimates for longevity press toward a life span of one hundred, so that even if we can alter Psalm 90 to "five score" years of life span as a piece of normal luck, the meaning of the figure will hardly have changed. The reason, then, for coming back to the pre-Transition realities of human experience as they are scripturally etched is simply that they are clearer to grasp and less obscured by the fond hopes of a forgetful culture. The clock can still be seen in them, and this is good: for the clock ticks away in all its complicated and coordinated movements, whatever our life span.

The pre-Transition life span unveils a *creature*: a being with limits, whose life belongs to God. The hard part of this reality is mortality—and inevitable dying is as hard today as ever. This is what the stark limitations on survival made clear but what today's death-marginalizing life expectancy has obscured: we are fundamentally limited creatures who depend on God, and that will never change. The converse of knowing this, however, is the inescapable quality of "miracle" that attaches to life: the miracle is love, which is about giving the self over in the face of limits and mortality. It is impossible to understand the cross of Christ apart from grasping this fact about ourselves. For only to creatures, existing as a divine gift, can the cross be given as the font of fruitfulness.

Only mortal creatures can understand how birth and death constitute the place of generation.

So John the Baptist, wearing openly the skins of Adam, must precede the Messiah. He is, as forerunner, another "Elijah," we are told (Matt 17:12-13). He is among the servants of God clothed in the *tunica* of Eden's gate (cf. 2 Kgs 1:8). His message, like the movable tabernacle itself, is a "voice crying in the wilderness" (Luke 3:4) and is calling for repentance in the face of the inevitable reordering of creation's material form, a form that, as Paul says, is "passing away" (1 Cor 7:31). It is in the shadow of this passing form that John speaks: God can raise up children to Abraham from the stones themselves; he "calls into existence the things that do not exist" (Rom 4:17 RSV). To the one who gives life, all that the creature can offer is some measure of that life: "fruit" (Luke 3:9). Such fruit, furthermore, must betoken the creature's own intrinsic character *as* creature: repentance and other acts that befit a life lived in common with other creatures (3:11-14). It is a "life" that is bound to this kind of service, bound and bowed, "decreasing" that the life giver in his mercy might "increase" (John 3:30).

Let us now consider what this mercy might mean. The skins of the wilderness represent the way we traverse a landscape whose shape is outside our control, even while the manner of our passage remains subject to our ordering. If we dwell in the land, we do so as "sojourners," in the consistent language of both Scripture and the entire Christian tradition. Thus we order life in a way that can maintain it, nourish it, carry it forward—and yet by which we can also move on in the face of its fragility and passing. Such a creaturely existence marks the character of a life that is clothed by God. Life, in fact, is shown here to *be* in itself that which is clothed by God. The skins of Adam become, in this movement, "garments of salvation," as the early Fathers of the church described them.[26]

# II

# How Life Is Measured

The journey of traversal, Adam's journey, covered by skins, begins with the fact that we are alive at all. Being alive is a mysterious fact, as it turns out. For its reality is given, as we have said, as an intrinsically unstable claim. On the one hand, we know we are alive because we discover it as given to us; on the other, just because it is given and not taken or earned or made, our being alive is something we sense as removable, bound to not-being-alive. It is God who "creates" "peace" and "evil," light and darkness, as Isaiah says (45:7), using words from Genesis 1. It is God who "makes dead" and who "makes alive," according to Moses (Deut 32:29), again echoing the categories of Genesis. Thus, this mysterious condition that is mortal life is both invented and given over to us as our created identities by God himself.

## Life as Mortal

This fact of divine donation itself, further, charges the mystery of our lives with a divine dynamic that has always puzzled, as well as energized and sometimes even misled, Jewish and Christian reflection. Mortal existence is, in itself, a given. Being born and dying is all we know. Presented as such, it is a biological and ultimately physical datum, with as little intrinsic interest as the bits of rock that fly across the spaces of the heavens, like comets or burning dust, only arbitrarily stimulating.

Much scientific discussion of human life follows this line on constricted interest. But once seen as dependent, and utterly so, upon God, mortal existence is, for better or worse, charged with a compelling call to trust (if often a trust some feel to have been betrayed). Hence, when God says, in Jeremiah, "For I will set mine eyes upon them for good, and I will bring them again to this land: and I will build them, and not pull *them* down; and I will plant them, and not pluck *them* up" (Jer 24:6), this direction of promise carries a weight driven by existence's primordial openness to its divine origin. If we are alive at all, and alive in such a way that our lives are ever colored by their ending because, at root, they are not ours, then that which grants us existence is always a *giver* even more than a destroyer.

The sense of this "giver" and "giving" is a great source of hope. But we should note that this hope emerges from the apprehension of an existence—of our own selves, that is—that escapes our hold. Mortality is at least fundamentally about this existing in way that we cannot maintain of our own. And thus, to the degree that we are distracted from this escape of life from our grasp and to the degree that we cannot feel the slippage of our hold upon our lives, then their givenness itself will fade, giver and all. The Christian tradition has, in fact, debated whether our first parents in the garden were created without mortality as part of their constitution. They wondered if, after all, since "death" entered because of "sin," it must be a kind of extraneous imposition upon an otherwise unimpeded vitality, as Paul writes (cf. Rom 5:12; 6:23). On the other hand, Genesis 3:22, which speaks of the *danger* of the first human beings eating of the Tree of Life and so "living for ever," would indicate some more inherent limit to their life spans, which was at risk of being overcome. Athanasius represents the most celebrated discussion of this view, insisting that Adam and all human beings are "by nature mortal" but are kept alive by the grace of God through obedience to his commands. This grace-filled obedience constituted the "likeness" to God that was also given to our first parents in creation (Gen 1:26).[1] But on the whole, the Western catholic tradition, including the Reformation, followed Augustine in shifting its emphasis from the "naturally mortal" aspect of human creation.[2] While Western Christians accepted created mortality in principle, they preferred to focus on the prelapsarian gift of unending life conditional upon their obedience.[3] This went so far as to reject any concrete sense of "mortality" for created Adam (cf. Council of Carthage, Canon 109: "If any man says that Adam, the first man, was created mortal, so that whether he sinned or not he would have died, not as the wages of sin, but through the necessity of nature, let him be anathema").[4] Not everyone, including Jews, accepted this shift away from created mortality: perhaps Adam and Eve would simply have lived a very, very long life—say, one thousand years; but die they would. Still, the insistence on the inevitable death of Adam and Eve remained a minority opinion.

But if Adam and Eve were "intrinsically" mortal, whether they would have actually died or not apart from sin, we might wonder if they *felt* "mortal." After all, if mortality is of the nature of our very creation, the unfallen Adam and Eve must have "known it in their bones," such that their bones did creak and whisper to them, as the days went by. It is probably a pointless reflection to bring to scriptural narrative about human origins, which seems to take no interest in the matter of our first parents' internal affections. Yet our first parents' sense of moral self goes to the issue of creaturehood directly, whether in speculative terms or not. Calvin, commenting on Genesis 3:19, suggested that, while an "unfallen" Adam would maybe have died physically, it would have been a smoothly untroubling transition of the human spirit to God, without the disordered suffering and anxiety attached to corrupted human passing. I can only think, however, that—whatever this might mean (and Calvin hesitates to call this truly "death")—such gliding into death cannot have obliterated Adam's sense of mortal finitude, even if such a sense was without the fear that came from the fall.[5] "The first man is of the earth," writes Paul, and hence was "earthy" (1 Cor 15:47). Or, more familiarly, he was made of the "dust," as Job will reiterate, drawing men and beasts together as a single created set (Job 34:15; cf. Gen 3:19). That there is such a thing as a "second death" (in, e.g., Rev 20:14) seems to indicate some realm of the undoing of life that surrounds even those creatures destined for the New Jerusalem. Those later critics who worried about the justice of a God who consigns creatures to "eternal torment" (e.g., the Seventh-Day Adventists) have preferred to see this "second death" as a pure annihilation of being.[6] However the exegetical question is resolved, "annihilation," as a comparative baseline for *creatio ex nihilo*, at least indicates a certain envelope of mortality that surrounds being from the start. In any case, although immortality—literally, *athanasia* or "deathlessness" in the Greek New Testament—is a gift given in Christ to those bound up with him, it is not intrinsic to the creature. "Only"

God is immortal (1 Tim 6:16), and only the Second Adam, Christ, has immortality as his very being.

The *tunicae pelliceae*, the skins of survival, are therefore not best seen as, in themselves, the mark of mortality, as some in the Christian tradition have thought. They are that, to be sure, now only in the particular aspect of their gracious promise of divine engagement. Mortality is of the stuff of life and always so. But mortality's creaturely aspect is just that: the mark of creaturehood as a living thing itself—no more, no less. Christian concern with original sin or the fall certainly orders that mortal existence in new ways, but it does not alter the fundamental character of creatureliness. This is one of my main arguments, and it is aimed in part at the modern theological drift to merge two questionable emphases: first, looking at "the human" in purely eschatological terms, as if the perfection of a transformed "new creation" is the benchmark of our self-understanding; and second, introjecting that futuristic understanding of human perfection into present political reconceptions of human flourishing. (An example of the mistaken emphases today would be using Mark 12:25 on the analogy of angelic existence after the resurrection to make claims about the shape and meaning of sexuality within the world of mortal life.) By contrast, we should speak of human creaturehood in an integral way only by basing our self-conceptions on our present existence. Whatever transformations we may think are promised to us in some future divine gift cannot be ones that in any way subvert the integrity of this present. The *tunicae pelliceae*, after all, are given in the image of the incarnate Christ just as much as they are laid over the form of the exiled Adam. We live Christ's life "away from the body" by engaging the fulcrum of bodily mortality in him and in his death (cf. 2 Cor 4:11-12). If we say—or sing—that, in the great future that awaits us, "there's no more cryin' there" and that every tear shall be wiped away (Isa 25:8; Rev 21:4), it can only mean that our hearts will be as full as the heart of Christ who himself wept for his friends (John 11:35), which itself is a "perfect love" (1 John 4:18). To repeat, the "garments of skin" are the "way" into the future; they are a creaturely way given and adopted by God and cannot be thrown off without also throwing off our oneness with Christ himself.

This commitment to mortal existence as the way to and way of Christ need not rule out a "teleological" view of what a human being is: we can still rightly say that we are headed toward something fuller than we now are, whatever that might mean. This last view is often associated with the early Christian theologian Irenaeus, who occasionally spoke in terms of Adam's creation as a "not-yet" man, still on his way.[7] This is probably not the best way to put it. But Irenaeus is surely right to stress this "being on the way" and, more importantly, that this way is a way that God himself has taken upon himself to follow at our head. If we are heading *toward* something as human creatures, it is toward the One Man who can walk this "way" and whose perfection is bound to this traversal. Hence, the life of this way that mortal creatures walk is the very life of God. And the death given in its form is one whose contour must also reveal the God whose life has been given over in this creation. The tale of creatureliness is not exhausted by, or even founded upon, the tale of the fall. It is rather the tale of the revelation of God.

In the wake of the Great Transition, it is necessary that we renew our sense of our weak grasp upon our lives, and in a fundamental way. We live in an unusual moment of social consciousness, at least within the history of human experience; and with respect to our knowledge of God, we have been steadily stripped of our created tools for his apprehension. Death, most especially, has been bracketed as the necessary inner clothing of life. If not exactly "unreal," given who we are and where we all end, death is nonetheless seen by many today as at least *potentially rendered* unreal. And this hope has driven a demotion of death's density: death, even our own deaths, has become unimportant for at least much of the time of our living.

To be sure, few people would wish to repeat the almost vulgar-seeming announcements of philosophers like Edgar Morin, who in the 1950s proclaimed a quite unapologetic Promethean vision of human "amortality." Morin argued that we could—indeed, we *ought*—to consider the human being as at least theoretically now able to hold death at bay, more and more. This, he said, is precisely what the press of modern medical technique demands of our thinking. Yes, he admitted, we are *vulnerable* and hence substantively "mortal," but our lives are in fact and properly governed by another direction of development. Subsequently, the movement known as "transhumanism" has taken up this kind of vision, led by scientists and inventors like Raymond Kurzweil.[8] Given the heavy weight of human experience, Morin would recast this vision into what he called "anthropological immortality"—the species-oriented vision into this open future, based on the hope that the human race as a whole would survive indefinitely. And finally, in the face of the unyielding tenor of human sin, Morin leaves aside such projections altogether.

But just posing this vision of indefinitely extended life as a conceptual possibility is disturbing, for it assumes, in the end, an empty universe, bereft of all but humanity and its hollow companions: self-making becomes evolution, and death itself is an epiphenomenon within this solitary effort.

The contemporary experiential withdrawal of death has not, however, been achieved through some compensatory reaction to the elevation of its opposite, as if "life" has been enhanced somehow in the exchange. After all, a truly intensive scrutiny of life would necessarily identify something of the mysterious mortality lodged within it, as part of life's definition. At least conceptually, death's retreat has been won at the expense of life. The philosopher Michel Henry's notion of "distancing" is important in this respect. Henry uses the term to denote the way human beings and their culture today conceptualize themselves *apart* from the experienced realities of their unconstructed subjectivity, their givenness as existent beings who know themselves to be such. That subjective aspect of our lives, Henry insisted, itself arises from nothingness and takes hold of reality comprehensively just because it is bound to an inexplicable gratuity of being. To look at life in a distanced fashion—from the "outside," and hence without grasping life's interior fragility in all its voraciousness (and beauty)—is to set off on the road to "barbarism." (Cf. Ps 139:6: "Such knowledge is too wonderful for me; it is high, I cannot attain unto it.") And a culture that looks at life in this externalized way out of engrained habit is also, then, a "barbaric" culture.

How could anyone presume, Henry asks, to understand the nature of, say, "suicide" (or for that matter, sexuality, he adds), by ordering their enactment according to the statistics of frequency and distribution, as modern sociologists do in their efforts to "understand" the phenomenon of self-murder or sexual being?[9] Life cannot be articulated this way at all—far better to study Kierkegaard's exploration of a human being's (his own) passage through anxiety and hope than to read, presumably, a sociologist like Durkheim, who gathers the data on thousands of human individuals, tabulates and correlates it all, and then pronounces that suicide or family life, or whatever he is studying, is "this" or "that" on this basis.

Life without death, death apprehended and death experienced as the pressing boundary of our subjective beings, then, is inhuman and leads to inhumanity. This judgment may sound like a paradox, but, in this case, it is not. The inhumanity of deathless humanity is the simple working out, in culture and psychology and finally in politics, of a profound distortion. The great challenge and scandal of contemporary Western culture grows out of just such a distortion. Euthanasia and embraced sterility (in, e.g., same-sex partnerships), for instance, are today lifted up as "humane" developments in our societies, as opposed, say, to the normal cultural disintegrations of war. Yet all three phenomena are actually death-embracing in parallel ways. The "humane" shakes hands with the detritus of violence. The Great Transition has contributed elements to this dynamic wherein what is humanly compassionate becomes destructive of what is human: the prolongation of life via medical care and technology as well as life's "rational" ordering by the same (contraception, fertility controls, etc.) together give rise to euthanizing sterility. And to this extent, the cultural obscuring of mortality is a cause of death itself. In response, we need a way to pursue the thread of mortality into the center of our life actions.

## Gauging Mortality at the Center of Our Existence
### The Freudian Example

In fact, we have been taught modern habits of such a pursuit, although the Transition itself intervened to block the fruits of this learning. Still, we are at least familiar with the habit, one given most famously in the Freudian approach to sexuality. Indeed, the history of the psychological and social study of sexuality more narrowly indicates that our sexual character as human beings has an essential connection to mortality itself, and the connection is one worth pressing, in order to see the kind of thread we are after and why creaturehood is rightly concerned with the sexuality of specifically mortal beings.

Most social theorists recognize, for instance, that there are no simple instinctual orderings of our sexuality. There may be instinctive *drives*, but, as I have tried to indicate by the cursory review of change in sexual behavior in the wake of the Great Transition, the physio-emotive character of sexuality is but a tiny part of what we in fact experience as our sexual beings and meanings. It is the ordering of our entire life spans that in fact and properly defines our sexuality in the sense of "setting it up" and providing the constraints and channels for sexuality's enactment. And that ordering is something that both must take place and takes place in multiple ways in time and space.

To admit this is not to turn one into a crass postmodernist, who sees all experience, even the deepest human self-reflection, as but the residue

of some process of human social construction. For there always remains
the question of *why* sexuality is a human construction in the first place. Of
course, biologists and philosophers will have different assumptions that
they bring to answering such a question. From a Christian perspective,
however, the seemingly postmodernist claim that experienced sexuality
is a human construction derives largely from a conviction that sexuality's
purposes and meanings have been primordially deformed—what we call
original sin in the tradition. The *history* of sexual construction—what
we might want to call sociology, psychology, cultural analysis, and so
on—is therefore all, from a theological perspective, "hamartiology," the
theological analysis of our sinful character. This must inevitably mark
Christianity off—even if one does not adopt an extreme Augustinian
notion of original sin's "corrupting" force—from other outlooks when it
comes to understanding sexuality.

But acknowledging original sin as deforming human experience
does not make the study of sexuality easier or clearer; in fact it renders it
intrinsically problematic. For the fact of original sin tells us that we do
not really have any clear standpoint of experiential purity from which
to figure the topic of sexuality out. Thus, a Christian would rarely deny
innate drives and would readily admit that sexual reality is not simply
something we make up. But its "constructed" character, whose form follows the intricacies of our own sinful thinking and feeling, is such that
we cannot really tell what is constructed and what is not. Instead, we
encounter our sexualities as an enormous knotted set of feelings, hopes,
physical urges, pleasures, and fears all mixed up and messed up. We can
only try to make sense of these elements in what will be many different
ways. But why we have this material and where it all comes from is very
difficult to figure out.

The Christian, therefore, studies all this, not to "see" the truth of
sexuality clearly in the present, but, as it were, to identify threads that
can be followed back—back historically, back psychologically, back to
the depth of their meaning. And these must then lead us to the deepest
recesses of human life and purpose before God. Studying sex, in other
words, leads us to the same place that studying our deaths leads us—this
primal reality of who we are *coram Deo*, before God, from God's hands,
for God's loving if often unknown purposes, and in a world that, apart
from God, is utter confusion and Babel. The profound confusion that
marks our sexual beings as divinely created beings is why the veiling of
death after the Transition is so important and probably so unhelpful.

Once we forget how to engage death, we lose also the capacity to engage sexuality and the aspects of our sexual beings that so fundamentally order our human relationships.

For much of the church's life, Christians have taken the deep creaturely connection of sexuality and death for granted, more or less. In more recent times, Freud, most famously, agreed with some of the non-theological aspects of these assumptions. There is indeed, he argued, something deep, primordial, and outside our comprehension that founds our sexual lives and that we *must* and properly do seek in one way or the other to *order*. It is that ordering that is our human "construction" of sexuality. At the same time, however, Freud argued that this ordering is bound to the deeper realities that strain against our best (and certainly our worst) ordering efforts, that color them, and that finally most overcome their purely human forms. One of the most accessible, and also direct, places he discusses this is in his essay "Reflections on War and Death" (1915), which he wrote in the midst of World War I.[10] It is in this difficult context that Freud initially confronts the terrible "disappointment" of German "civilization's" and European civilization's crumbling descent into unimaginable brutality. It is fair to say that Freud articulates, in his careful and correct German educated prose, what anybody who has experienced war (and a number of other social and collective tragedies) has cried out about in perplexity: How can human beings do what they do? And it is important to realize that significant elements of Freud's thinking were shaped by experiences far closer to the pre-Transition than to our own often, though falsely, buffered existences.

What does war tell us? asks Freud. It tells us, first, that human beings are driven by things that are frightening and violent. But war also tells us, by contrast and surprise, that we tend at other times to deny and obscure these realities—these often frightening and violent drives that are generally hidden within us as we go about our lives within more peaceful and secure contexts. Yet, again, war tells us that these "drives," in all their pitiless violence, are nonetheless part of who we are even in the midst of our normal and quieter lives. War unveils the shape of our hearts in their stable form. And finally, Freud says, war tells us that human history—that is, the shape of culture—is about taming these hidden drives, controlling them, and hiding them, so that we can get on with other things, even as we skate upon the surface of our innate and brooding violence.

We recognize here many of the central features of the Freudian vision, which he will discuss at greater length, and with all kinds of elaboration, in works like *Beyond the Pleasure Principle* (1920) and *Civilization and Its Discontents* (1929). For Freud, this hidden world of our lives—often frightening and violent—is our "unconscious." His theories about the unconscious are more complex than popular portrayals often suggest. But in his reflections on war, at least, he presents its reality as a force in a way that is hard to gainsay in any fundamental way. The unconscious is, as it were, the "primitive" aspect of the human race, "repressed" and ordered by society and its historical forms. And from a Christian standpoint we can easily interpret this claim by saying that the unconscious is a major part of that link we have to Adam: here is the place we confront where we have come from and who we are, at least in terms of our historical identity. The *tunicae pelliceae* cover the nakedness of this linkage.

> There is in fact no "eradication" of evil. Rather, psychological—more strictly speaking psychoanalytic—investigation shows that man's deepest essence lies in drive-impulses that are elemental in nature and identical in all people, and are aimed at the satisfaction of certain primal needs. . . . It should be admitted that all those impulses abhorred as evil—let us take selfishness and cruelty as their representatives—are among these primitive ones.[11]

As we know, Freud's way of looking at things was not something he himself invented. His vision is congruent, on this score at least, with a steady set of traditions derivative of Christian thinking, from the theology of original sin in the early Western church especially, to the notion of a "natural state" in which human beings press for survival one against another, as Hobbes presented it in the seventeenth century. Some of Freud's more specific explanations about the shape of these drives and the dynamics and meaning of their social ordering, on the other hand, are clearly open to debate, and few accept their details any longer. But at the same time, few deny the larger shape of his argument, which insists that we all share a deep ambivalence over those we live with—parents, friends, neighbors. And because of this, both Freud and common wisdom understand, love and hate get mixed up in us; we all experience terrible fears and anxieties over our deaths and the deaths of those we love or live with, so that we construct ways of explaining death, justifying it, answering it (often with more death of others).

Freud himself linked specifically *sexual* drives to all these internal conflicts. This is precisely a major part of his theory that many have rejected. But leaving the details aside, the *structure* of this linkage Freud made does indeed make sense more generally: we do not know who we are; and we are in the grip of things within ourselves that we do not understand or of which we are fundamentally unaware; these involve our loves and hates, our pleasures and aversions; and these unknown motives often end in destructive violence when left unchecked, unformed, or unconstructed, even as our "constructions" are shaped by the very forces of which we are ignorant. But "construct" our inner drives we *do*, because construct we *must*. If we pull down the constructions, then, literally, all hell breaks loose.

To take a present case—over a period of several years, at least until 2013, estimates of rape in the Eastern Congo reached over 410,000 per year.[12] This does not include the increasing number of rapes of men and boys that began to be reported during that time—a phenomenon that goes far beyond the Congo.[13] During this period, of course, conflicts of raging violence have gripped the area, with anywhere from three to five million persons dying. The victims of rape and murder have included not only adult women and men but girls and boys, victims of rampaging, and various groups of Congolese, Rwandans, and Ugandans. With Freud, we must conclude that if we claim that what has just happened in the Eastern Congo has nothing to do with *who we are* today, as human beings of whatever society, we are wrong; and if we say that even the specific *acts* of sexual predators in the Congo have nothing to do with our own sexual natures, we are also wrong. To examine the realms of death-dealing and the realms of sexual existence is to explore common paths that all human beings traverse.

Obviously, on a far less terrifying and destructive level, the modern era has brought into light other aspects of sexual life that in the past were rarely discussed—sadomasochism, for example, or pedophilia and fetishism. These aspects of sexual desire and expression, we now know, are a part of the interior life of far more people than we had been wont to acknowledge in the past; and their enacted forms of life have not only become more openly discussed but also more socially accepted and asserted. A book like the journalist Daniel Bergner's *The Other Side of Desire: Four Journeys into the Far Realms of Lust and Longing* follows the "normal" lives of a sadomasochistic woman, a foot fetishist, an amputee devotee, and a pedophile. Each of these persons is, on the face of it, "normal": married, successful job holder, law abiding. (The pedophile in question, to be sure, skirts the legal line.)[14] A reader of Bergner's account wonders where these desires and practices come from or what they mean and represent. The cultural, moral, and legal critic will pose the question of whether these sexual proclivities are to be affirmed. For all the strong, and sometimes intricately complex, views we have about them, we do not really know. Morally and religiously—the Bible, for instance, has little directly to say about any of these matters—they point precisely to a realm of life beyond our common sense of order and meaning.

But surely Christians must join Freud (or he them) in asserting, but far more robustly, the constructed character of "civilized" sexual life as something that properly responds to the more obviously negative realities of this hidden life. Realities of sexual violence and predatory thirst seem to drive outward from our internal depths—as do, as well, the less obviously negative but quite bizarre, on a purely quantitative level, elements of sexual desire someone like Bergner describes. Beyond Freud, Christians would also want to say that these drives, if rightly though only imperfectly ordered, also contribute to a vision of redemption that touches the deepest joy imaginable, because the drives themselves lead us to the place where life is given and sustained solely by God.

The Christian must rightly adopt something akin to Freud's general (if not specifically detailed) understanding of the deep, hidden, and tangled ambivalence regarding our interior being, within which sexual realities find their experienced home, for otherwise we cannot make sense of Christian, and earlier Jewish, thinking on the matter. Indeed, we cannot make sense of much of the world's diverse thinking and practice about how human beings strive to relate to one another, sexually among other things. Without something comparable to a Freudian archaeology of the self, we will, in other words, valorize a tiny cultural moment and divinize a limited subjective claim of our own. And that way lies madness.

To conclude from our example—to explore our sexuality is to explore the factors that form our existence as living beings over and against our disappearance as being of any kind. Death marks the place where the complexities of our ongoing mechanisms of life generation are shown in their miraculous purity and vulnerable givenness. If we look carefully at the way we live our lives—sexuality, work, food, relations—we necessarily come face to face with our deaths. This is not simply because death is the flip side of life but because death is the fleeting vantage from which to see life as it is. We gauge our mortality by attending to the wildly unsteady limits of our living practices. And as we do this, we see how these practices themselves are defined by the mortal nature of our createdness.

## Suicide and the Revelation of Life

The thread of our sexual selves, then, leads us back to our mortal created-ness and the power that our mortality seems to hold over us. This power is itself the revelation of our lives as something that is not our own. We must, with Freud, peer over the primal ledge, in order to be grasped by an unexpected light.

Suicide, as I indicated earlier, is a key place to engage the reality of life as gift. The sexually generated being, in his or her suicide, turns back on the entire history of human selfhood, its origins, its sustenance, its actual being. Everything that is real is unveiled at this point. Suicide wrestles with the very sense we have of what "life" could possibly be, taken, at least, from the subjective standpoint of those who alone can touch its reality, the living person. Studies of suicide—including Durk-heim's own pioneering work in the late nineteenth century—showed divergences in the rates of suicide and its form according to different social contexts. And already in the sixteenth century, the fact of cul-tural difference on this score was noted and pondered over. Today, we are better informed about cultures where suicide is not only accepted but demanded in certain situations, and we tend to nod with a certain knowing sense that this kind of diversity is to be expected. And if moral diversity over suicide's meaning is expected, suicide itself can hardly be the indicator of essential human character.

Nonetheless, for all the diversity recorded and appealed to, in our day suicide is universally viewed negatively.[15] The pioneering 1897 work of the French sociologist Émile Durkheim on suicide, which involved careful study of a limited area in France, explained suicide as something reflective of patterns of social expectation and of an individual's integra-tion into that society—suicide is, as we say today, "socially constructed" just like sexuality. Hence, one would expect to find different patterns of and judgments about suicide in different cultures and at different times. The fact that men generally kill themselves far more frequently than women, and this across cultures, indicates some kind of either role-shaped or biologically determined difference (or both). But suicides seem to be on the rise around the world; certainly that is the perception (how-ever poor the statistics may be) of observers in different areas from Africa to Asia to the Americas, and there is a common sense that this rising rate of self-killing is a "bad" thing. Indeed, cultural diversity pales in comparison to this larger reaction. There is, as it turns out (and contrary to the popular sense just noted), little evidence of *any* "positive" view of suicide cross-culturally.

The exceptions might be those situations Durkheim called "altruistic," ones in which suicides involve fulfilling some kind of duty that is ultimately seen as a communal good. (Counterintuitively for many, suicide bombing by Islamic jihadists would fall into this category. But perhaps the category of "altruistic suicide" simply makes no sense.) In cultures of honor or shame—from Japan to the Hehe of Tanzania—self-killing is sometimes viewed, and by a small group only, as a supreme kind of moral act in the face of a crisis, and in a way that represents something done in continuity not with other acts but as their transcendent answer somehow. It is "another thing" altogether. And this is one reason that such transcendent suicides are rarely consistently embraced as such by other members of the larger society. (Earlier descriptions of Japanese society as being suicide affirming, were, for example, based on the values of a limited and self-enclosed warrior class. And these descriptions have now been vigorously criticized on the basis of this lack of social representativeness.) Suicide is a good example of something that, despite cultural variation in evaluated practice, turns out to be almost universally rejected as a specific individual act. Thus the transition to more modern and universal legal or simply medically ordered restraints upon suicide's enactment has been fairly easy to accomplish (the press by some for euthanasia, however, being the exception to this trend).

Thus, the question of why such "restraints" on suicide are intuitively accepted around the world is the interesting one to ask, not the question of why—here and there—we find variegated and marginal exceptions to the intuition. To be sure, there is a standard historical judgment these days that views "modernity" as in fact overturning this universal intuition (and hence, the notion of a "modern" intuitive sense of restraint may in fact be overstated). The argument goes like this: In the sixteenth century, for the first time, what were only the marginal suicides of classical Rome became the exemplars for a new morality altogether. The ancients of Greece and Rome had diverse practices with respect to suicide, after all. And the famous Stoic suicides of the Roman worthies Cato and Seneca were reexamined in the sixteenth century by influential writers like Montaigne, who seemed to bring to bear a new openness to discussing suicide as at least a potentially virtuous act in certain circumstances. These sixteenth-century discussions have been seen as one sign of the shift toward an embrace of individual freedom, distinct from the old communal values of the church in the West, which had for so long demonized suicide and imposed, through its cultural sway, sanctions against it.

The standard historical argument, then, states that the modern de-demonization of suicide is a kind of assertion of "voluntarism," by which the act of suicide can become an *affirmation* of self, in an otherwise self-constraining social context. Certainly, Montaigne, the sensitive mayor of Bordeaux observing the sorrows and follies of his compatriots during the so-called "wars of religion," lived within a time of civil anarchy and violence. Faith in the old "coherent" ways of the Catholic universe had been deeply shaken. Set adrift from such certainties, and battered by the arbitrary powers of roaming brutality and moral confusion, Montaigne wondered what a person could do to prove his or her self's integrity. One could at least assert the power to end one's life. This has been, as I said, a contemporary claim—and with it a claim that, in the sixteenth century, the gate was opened to explore self-annihilation with a new freedom.

Let us assume for a moment that this common historical claim about the sixteenth century is true. (Others read Montaigne, and later Donne, who wrote on the subject, quite differently.) And let us take the purported argument on its own terms—that is, that a supreme act of self-assertion, of human *freedom*, can be achieved in suicide: it is still one of the strangest of arguments one could make. Indeed, few people believe suicide is an act of freedom any longer, even if euthanasia is argued for in part on the basis of such assertion of free will. Legally, the "free will" approach to suicide was actually assumed in *earlier*, not later, Christian prohibitions: it founded the main idea in the Middle Ages that people could "choose" to kill themselves, and hence they were liable "perpetrators" of "self-murder." It is, by contrast, the "deterministic" interpretation of suicide—that suicide is due, for instance, to mental disease, which some will then think stands as the "cause" of death—that grounds more current legal approaches. British and British-dependent law did not decriminalize suicide until the 1960s, because of the long hold of the free-will assumption, while other European countries did so in the late eighteenth century and the nineteenth century. And just because of this shift to a "deterministic" view of suicide, we see people being held responsible for *preventing* (or failing to prevent) another person's suicide (e.g., therapists, schools, etc.): lawsuits on these matters, upheld by judicial opinion, have multiplied. If a patient or student under my care commits suicide, I may well be liable for the death. The assumption of morally (and now legally) demanded "intervention," aimed at stopping the acts of the unfree by the free, remains almost universal. "Suicide prevention" is now internationally deemed a "necessary" policy for all societies, and the World Health Organization, among others, monitors these matters.

But perhaps the whole issue of freedom and determinism here is a red herring, at least for our purposes. From the perspective of creaturehood, the human "will" is nothing but an unwilled gift. To say that it can be given in its self-negation is incoherent: it is not possible to negate a gift. Gifts can be refused or belittled, or they can be thrown away. But they remain always gifts nonetheless, whatever one does with them. Whether our moods and impulses are freely chosen or run within our mental veins like a subterranean river, unknown and powerful, our being as persons who encounter ourselves as living is neither willed nor determined in human terms. It is given. Hence, the giftedness of the human will cannot be "undone," no matter what one does with it. The vast asymmetry between the Giver and the Receiver here is important to grasp. In the eighteenth century, the great skeptical philosopher David Hume wrote a short essay on suicide (1755, published only posthumously, for obvious reasons, in 1777) in which he dismantles the traditional Christian argument about life being a divine gift that we cannot undo on our own. If this were such a gift, he says, then we should not undo *anything* we are "given" by God in the natural world: we should not, for instance, avoid rocks that are falling on our head or engage the acts of building something that did not already exist. All these "invade upon providence," which, if taken literally, would demand a completely quiescent existence (and hence, a passive death). As in most of his writings about God, Hume here seeks to render God in the form of a human analogue: God is like a person who carries material in a cart, dumps it out, and lays it before us. Hume does this while also insisting that God be viewed as an impersonal and comprehensive set of "universal" laws ("Providence"). But just here, Hume's entire argument slips away, for God, with respect to life itself, cannot possibly stand in any analogous relationship to human beings, to us. God is not a master builder whose access to material and tools is simply greater than ours. Nor can God simply be the sum of the "laws" that we can identify in the universe. The asymmetry lies not in the power of God versus human (in)capacity—that is, that God is like us but infinitely more "powerful" or infinitely more comprehensive than us. In the case of suicide, the divine asymmetry lies in the fact that our lives are not our own, *at all*, in any meaningful sense of grasping their origins and ends and even of understanding their constituents and their context. As the early Jewish commentary (perhaps from the era of Jesus) *The Ethics of the Fathers* (Pirke Avot), later to be included in Mishnah, put it:

> [R. Eleazar ha-Kappar] used to say, "They that are born are doomed to die; and the dead to be brought to life again; and the living to be judged, to know, to make known, and to be made conscious that He is God, He the Maker, He the Creator, He the Discerner (47), He the Judge, He the Witness (48), He the Accuser; He it is that will in future judge, blessed be He, with Whom there is no unrighteousness, nor forgetfulness, nor respect of persons, nor taking of bribes (49); and know also that everything is according to the reckoning (50); and let not thy imagination give thee hope that the grave will be a place of refuge for thee; for perforce thou wast formed, and perforce thou wast born, and thou livest perforce, and perforce thou wilt die, and perforce thou wilt in the future have to give account and reckoning before the Supreme King of kings, the Holy One, blessed be He."[16]

"Perforce" in the translation here refers to the giftedness of every aspect of our life and destiny. The "gift," in this sense, is always fundamental of all being, of all reality. And self-destruction is thus always incomplete, and profoundly so. This is a basic point around which we can only circle because it defies analogical thinking.

## Adeodatus
### *The Gift of God*

The classic Christian arguments against suicide were articulated by Thomas Aquinas, and it is worth citing them because they cover the range of intuitions and theological claims that led the Christian church fairly early on to declare suicide a sin against God. Thomas thus reflects and articulates the views that shaped the Western consciousness regarding suicide in ways that some critics have tried to relativize as both historically discrete and ethically suspect. In the great *Summa Theologiae* (II.II.64.5), Thomas poses this question: "Whether it is lawful to kill oneself?" (He does this within a general discussion of killing—hence suicide falls within the same category as does abortion and murder.) After listing arguments as to why it may be permitted, he offers three arguments as to why suicide is in fact *unlawful*, beginning with a supporting claim from St. Augustine:

> *On the contrary*, Augustine says (*The City of God*, i, 20): "Hence it follows that the words 'Thou shalt not kill' refer to the killing of a man—not another man; therefore, not even thyself. For he who kills himself, kills nothing else than a man."
>
> *I answer that*, It is altogether unlawful to kill oneself, for three reasons. First, because everything naturally loves itself, the result being that everything naturally keeps itself in being, and resists corruptions so far as it can. Wherefore suicide is contrary to the inclination of nature, and to charity whereby every man should love himself. Hence suicide is always a mortal sin, as being contrary to the natural law and to charity. Secondly, because every part, as such, belongs to the whole. Now every man is part of the community, and so, as such, he belongs to the community. Hence by killing himself he injures the community, as the Philosopher [Aristotle] declares (*Nicomachean Ethics* v, 11). Thirdly, because life is God's gift to man, and is subject to His power, Who kills and makes to live. Hence whoever takes his own life, sins against God, even as he who kills another's slave, sins against that slave's master, and as he who usurps to himself judgment of a matter not entrusted to him. For it belongs to God alone to pronounce sentence of death and life, according to Deuteronomy 32:39, "I will kill and I will make to live."[17]

There is much to investigate in this brief text. But for our purposes, I can summarize the three reasons Aquinas offered in a simple fashion: suicide is a sin because it goes against natural charity, community, and God as giver of life. Philosophers and theologians have tended to focus on one or other of these reasons as more or less compelling and have therefore emphasized natural law, or social responsibility, or what is viewed as a kind of "divine proprietary rights" in their arguments for or against suicide's ethical status. The distinctions are useful, but ultimately I think they can distract us from what is, from the Christian viewpoint that Thomas articulates, a much more unified and coherent claim. As is often the case, Thomas leaves the third reason against suicide—in this case, God as the sole giver of life—to the end because it is in fact the most important and fundamental. The first reason, "charity" toward oneself as a mark of "nature," is not some alternative secular or philosophical claim. It is instead an expression of the character of the creature who is made by God—and also of the kind of intrinsic relationship that the self has to its own existence spoken of in terms of responsibility or responsiveness to this fact. What we do "naturally" is not so much an inner drive but rather a fitting expression of "who" we are as structured in terms of creatureliness. The next argument, the communal one, is in fact no different, though it is couched in terms of human relationship. Such relationships are, after all, "built in" to the character of our natural—that is, created—existences. Hence, the third reason is simply the explanation for the shape of the previous two: we are not our own but God's from beginning to end.

The fact that life is God's, in a basic and metaphysically (and thus ethically) inevitable way, hovers over much of the Christian discussion of suicide and cannot ever quite be extinguished from the argument. The sixteenth- and early seventeenth-century poet and Anglican preacher John Donne notoriously wrote a long discussion in which he seems to counter this Christian tradition, and Thomas' exposition in particular. Donne's effort, however, actually proves the Thomistic rule. Donne wrote his book in 1610, before his career had found a foothold, indeed while he was in rather desperate straits financially and professionally—a large family to support, a strong ego, and little means to fulfill either demand. Although he shared the extensive manuscript with a few friends, and seems to have sought its destruction when he was dying, his son published it after Donne's death in 1647.[18] *Biathanatos*, as Donne entitled the book—"the violence of death" or "death by violence"—is a long essay that laboriously works its way through traditional arguments, like Thomas', against suicide and seeks to demolish each, at least until the very end of the book. Although rarely read today, and almost universally dismissed as irremediably tedious, the book has proved an important touchstone in discussions about changing attitudes toward suicide.

Donne tries to show, using only scholastic and biblical texts as his benchmarks, that the arguments against suicide on the basis of both natural self-love and communal responsibility are not airtight and in fact admit of exceptions. (He actually pursues the formal "objections" that Thomas opens his own discussion with, and he seeks to show that they are too quickly dismissed by Aquinas.) When Donne comes to the final question of God's proprietary rights over human life, he stumbles somewhat from his line. Jesus himself is seen as an exception to the rule, since his own death is self-willed and thus should fall into the category of suicide, or self-killing. But, of course, Jesus is also God. The paradox here proves daunting to Donne. Here, he says, is the example we are called to imitate, quite explicitly giving up our lives for our friends, as well as for God, and doing so in "perfect charity." And thus, in such imitation, we are bound to transgress Thomas' categorical strictures, which in any case, as Donne has tried to show previously, admit of exceptions. Yet in following Christ, we also inevitably *fail* to incarnate the "perfection" of his divine-human life of love, and hence in our efforts at faithful discipleship we cannot *but contradict* the fullness of the self-giving way that Jesus offers.

It is a strange manner in which to end his book, one that has puzzled many readers and given rise to much interpretive controversy.[19] Some critics have come to the conclusion that Donne's elaborate exercise is in fact a kind ironic joke on the whole question—it is subtitled a "declaration of that Paradox . . . that Self-Homicide" is not "naturally" a sin, and "paradox" is part of the play. Others have seen the essay as a sort of private prayer to find some way to serve God, even in the midst of what then, in the context of his writing, must have been experienced as confusion and possibly despair. (Donne, in his preface, remarks that he is prone to seeing suicide, almost by habit, as a solution to whatever problem confronts him: "whensoever any affliction assailes me, mee thinks I have the keyes of my prison in mine owne hand, and no remedy presents it selfe so soone to my heart, as mine own sword.") What Donne describes here may well constitute a rather clear example of what some modern psychologists would see as the engrained and automatic thinking that some ultimately suicidal depressives engage in. Whatever the case, we can at least say that the *logic* of Donne's piece moves back, almost despite himself, toward the totalizing assumptions that govern Thomas' work as well: we cannot address the issue of suicide apart from the logic-defying stance of the one who is *not* God in the face of the God who *alone* has "power" over life's appearance. As one critic has persuasively argued, Donne ends in a place where, far from extolling the human will, he senses freedom's opacity and deformity in the face of the unscalable heights of divine life and so settles back into a humility that, however deeply unresolved logically, seeks a moral "therapy" rather than deeds of liberating self-negation.[20]

It *is* true that literary attitudes toward suicide in the West begin to stretch in the early modern period. The historian and poet Jennifer Michael Hecht, in a compelling volume entitled *Stay: A History of Suicide and the Philosophies against It*, helpfully traces some of this development, providing along the way some general insights into certain sociological phenomena related to suicide.[21] Hecht herself is an atheist, and her goal in the volume—written, we are told, out of her own struggle with the suicides of some close friends—is to lift up the communitarian argument that, as we saw, is the second principle found in Thomas' list. What her survey shows, however, is that just this argument is bound up with the larger Christian notion of life's divine giftedness such that it is in fact difficult to extricate from the richer textures of the scriptural outlook. And Hecht's attempts to do so, at the end, do as much to underline the social dislocation that has occurred with that outlook's cultural eclipse as they serve to make her own more limited and dangling point.

For all the charges that Christianity, in its origins, was in fact a suicidal religion at its core, and that martyrdom and its valorization was a kind of social psychosis or communal "death wish," the church rather quickly made clear that suicide was against God's law (as did Judaism concurrently, and Islam later). This stricture against suicide was not accomplished through ecclesial law (despite frequently repeated claims to the contrary by even reputable historians): canonical prohibitions did not appear until the early Middle Ages and tended to be local in scope. Nonetheless, Christians generally saw suicide as "shameful," and the confusions over martyrdom and self-destruction made the topic concrete in many areas. One of them was North Africa, where Donatist Christians separated from other Christians over questions of moral rigor. Some Donatists, it seems, developed almost a cult of martyrial self-offering, and the results were seen by others, like Augustine, as incomprehensibly perverted and dangerous. Like other Christians before him, Augustine saw suicide as an assault upon the goodness of life. But he went further, articulating his views in scripturally legal terms and in a way that became classic (as Thomas makes clear): suicide is a sin against God, based on the Decalogue's prohibition of murder (*City of God*, 1.20–21). Biblical figures like Samson in fact committed such a sin and are faultless only because they received special and direct command from the Holy Spirit that therefore released them from liability. Furthermore, and on this basis, figures like Samson can never serve as examples for others. If Jesus "willingly" died, this too represents an element that is not translatable to normal human life.

With Augustine, the church explained her condemnation of suicides in terms of the sixth commandment, "Thou shalt not kill." To this were added elaborated elements: for instance, suicide forecloses the possibility of repentance, and hence despair ought never to be final, since, once dead, the soul's destiny is set (i.e., suicides destroy their own souls).

In addition, the "proprietary" rationale was also emphasized: suicide "steals" from God what is rightfully his. These kinds of arguments, however, mask extensive meanings, which historians have rarely pursued. For instance, the relationship of self-killing to killing "in general" is worth pondering. No one was unaware of the fact that killing went on all the time, and often that killing was deemed to be "licit." Thomas himself addresses this in his discussion. After all, capital punishment was viewed as permissible in defined circumstances, and certainly the violent pursuit of criminals and the destruction of their means of perpetrating "injustice," which often included taking their lives, was a standard part of social existence. What removed suicide from these accepted realms of killing? The answer, I believe, was the uneasy conscience of the church with killing altogether. That killing might be "acceptable" was in fact a euphemism, as it were, for the deeply troubling net of death that common human life had set us within. Whatever the justifications, everyone knew that "Thou shalt not kill" was a commandment whose violation had been nailed into the community's daily round. And the rejection of suicide became, perhaps, the reparative token of penitence for this quotidian daily failure.

Such a piece of speculation would at least help to explain the astonishing and troubling embodied revolt against the suicidal victim that evolved in Christian society. Hecht rightly enumerates the way that the Western church progressively attached to suicide penalties that must seem to us—as they do to her—grotesque: not only were suicides refused church burials, but their bodies were subjected to various means of horrific disposal like mutilation, drowning, physical dismemberment, desecration; finally, ruinous economic sanctions were taken against even the families of suicides. Reading about these responses makes one blanch. "Commonly the church enforced punishment of the corpses, which might be dragged through the streets, impaled on a fence and left to rot and be eaten by animals, or buried at crossroads with stakes through their hearts. More practically, the suicide's estate could be confiscated, further harming his surviving family."[22] Whether transference or not, this kind of reaction, which only developed over time, emerged from a deep and pervasive sense that in suicide something of the most profound and sacred quality had been approached and trespassed against.

It was not that people in medieval Europe were naïve as to motives for suicide. Terrible "sadness" in the victim was commonly noted. The crushing weight of horrendous circumstances likewise loomed large in what was said about a suicide: poverty, disease, debts, and the rest. While mental illness was not discussed in the same terms as today, obviously, "madness" was a category some suicides were seen as inhabiting. And, of course, demonic possession found a place in the list of causes. Thus, for all the brutal vigor of response to the bodies of suicides, in fact we know from the few accounts we have that these kinds of causes often were seen as mitigating the suicide's responsibility and, as has generally been the case, rendered ecclesiastical and communal response far more supple and nuanced than the stark condemnations formally articulated in canon law and elsewhere might indicate. There is, furthermore, every indication that suicides were routinely presented in official description as something else—victims of accident, illness, what have you—and, with the connivance of the authorities, were never recorded as self-murders in the first place. This was a difficult area in which to tread, and no one did so either lightly or consistently.

The sixteenth and seventeenth centuries do seem to mark a change, not in official rejection of suicide, but in the practical responses made to it. Or at least this is what we are told. As the Reformers addressed suicide, we see little change with respect to formal teaching. But historians wonder if, for instance, there was an upswing in the rate of suicide in seventeenth-century Britain—as some contemporaries claimed—due to the deep psychological pressures brought on by Calvinist predestinarian despair. Some historians have posited, instead, a growing individualist isolation due to urbanization and the economy behind it and have wondered if this might have stoked suicidal malaise. Robert Burton's celebrated 1621 volume *The Anatomy of Melancholy* treated suicide at length as a category of this newly emphasized disease of the soul, and, as we noted, discussion of suicide as well as questioning of its actual status began to be bruited about in literary circles of the time with a novel openness.[23] By the eighteenth century we see the beginnings of explicit rejection, here and there, of former arguments for prohibition. Most especially, the notion of anybody's "proprietary right" to our lives was increasingly disputed. This was the Baron d'Holbach's argument: if society cannot offer us a decent life, it has no "right" over us in any case. Thomas Hobbes had said something similar earlier about our allegiance to the state, whose purpose and duty is to keep us safe. The baron now applied such Hobbesian reasoning to the cosmos, not only to the civil polity. In this period we also begin to have evidence here and there (e.g., Stockholm, of suicide "clusters") moments when individuals seem to rush into imitative behaviors of self-destruction, bound by certain common social settings (e.g., poverty). Social documentation of these phenomena also begins to proliferate.

If the seventeenth century marks a rise of toleration for suicide—and that is not so clear—this is, in any case, bound up with many social and political factors, not just critique of religion (property, rights, individualism, etc.). Certainly I would not argue that attitudes to suicide are bound to the Great Transition, for instance. My purpose here is simply to stress how deep attitudes to suicide are significant indicators of theological truth. In fact, for all the legal changes with respect to suicide, self-killing remains deeply shocking. What *has* changed more recently are the attacks on this deeper truth that suicide somehow uncovers something fundamental of our lives that we dare not transgress. Changes in attitude here are sometimes related to deliberate intellectual claims; others, to shifting social contexts. But all these factors are in fact *lifted* on the tide of the Great Transition to our detriment. In our day, when in the United States alone there are over thirty thousand persons a year who successfully kill themselves (with eastern and central Africa, Korea, and countries of the former Eastern Bloc having yet far higher rates of suicide),[24] we simply do not know how to talk about this, even as we fumble for responses. Is it murder and rebellion? Is it the cruelty of the world, or is it the pressures of social injustice? Or, finally (as more recently), is it mental "disease," to be classed with cancer and diabetes? Hecht's *Stay* is a plea made in the midst of this situation of confused explanation and response: "Stay," at least for those who love you, she begs, for the mutual engagement of life that we all depend upon.

So Hecht takes up the communitarian strain: this is something all of us can understand. Beginning with Milton's notion that suffering can be borne for the sake of some unknown future in the service of others—"They also serve who only stand and wait" (from the sonnet "On His Blindness")—she traces the more modern argument for this communitarian obligation from Diderot to Rousseau (suicide is "larceny committed against mankind") to Kant.[25] She singles out, especially, the Kant of the *Groundwork for a Metaphysics of Morals*: our life is for others—parents, children, and colleagues: "To annihilate the subject of morality in one's person is to root out the existence of morality itself from the world as far as one can, even though morality is an end in itself. Consequently, disposing of oneself as a mere means to some discretionary end is debasing humanity in one's person." She ends her history with Victor Hugo, who,

> in *Les Misérables*, writes a few striking sentences about profound inner pain and our duty to bear it and live through it: "You want to die, I want that too, I who am speaking to you, but I don't want to feel the ghosts of women wringing their hands around me. Die, so be it, but don't make others die. . . . Suicide is restricted . . . as soon as it touches those next to you the name of suicide is murder."[26]

But the point Hecht makes—turning to Melville, Hemingway, and others—is that suicide affects others, "kills" always more than one, "solitary" though its enactment and end are meant to be. This becomes one of Hecht's main arguments for the book: suicide is contagious and imitative, especially for the emotionally vulnerable. So we must find ways, in our own vulnerability, to help others like us.

She is absolutely right in all this. The communal character of suicide—which makes the "free-will" and the "deterministic" legal responses secondary issues—reveals a crucial fact: life is filiated, in its fullest positive and negative modes. Hecht herself is an avowed atheist; yet in this discussion she lays out, almost despite herself, the thickly textured character of life in its "bondedness" genealogically, familially, and communally, in a way that snatches life's basic meaning away from individual will and lays it elsewhere. One wants to know where, exactly. One could simply say we do not know, and instead hold on to social interrelatedness as a kind of basic meaning, a good "in itself," but without real explanation outside from this intuitive and ultimately utilitarian thrust. This is Hecht's atheistic line: we must do everything we can to relocate the suicidal, as it were, within the framework of his or her mutual responsibilities, for the sake of the whole (for others, for you and me). But in fact, the communal character of life in its filiations points to something else: the fact that the "whole" is itself a gift. The responsibilities and filiations are not stand-alones but rather expressions themselves of the great receptiveness, in its miraculous presentation, that constitutes our existence. To *be filiated is to be created*. Yet to be created is to receive the responsibility of filiation. This is obvious on the most fundamental level of the ecology of life itself: consider the so-called microbiome that constitutes the thousands of microbes that inhabit a human body, for the sake of *health*, not disease.[27] It is not even clear, in this case, that a human life even "exists" apart from other lives in terms of its "as-such" character. But this material claim is applicable to the more specifically human aspect of relational filiation more broadly.

Responsibility, in any case, is probably not the best word for what constitutes the moral character of human existence. The notion of "responsibility" rightly implies the way that our lives as they are lived do so "in response" to that source of their being, to God. But the responsible life is not simply a "response" in the sense of an exchange, as some might understand it: as if God gives us life, and we, "in turn," respond to this life in a certain way, and in fact as called to do so. There is no "in turn" with respect to our lives. This is an important point, and it is one that, within the Christian faith, must differ radically from an atheistic viewpoint. Take for example, the debate over the work of the philosopher David Benatar. Benatar, in a book with the arresting title *Better Never to Have Been: The Harm of Coming into Existence*,[28] argues that pain is always bad, that existence is always painful, and that therefore existence is bad. To be sure, there is some pleasure in existence too, he admits; but depriving the world of pleasure, by depriving it of existing people, is no harm in itself. And since no people means no pain, then "better never to have been." He applies the argument then to the question of having children (he is against it—that is, he is an "anti-natalist"), of abortion (a good idea), and of species extinction (a rather systematic accomplishment of his purported "better world"). Some of the discussions over the book engage the complex logics of the pain-pleasure calculus Benatar deploys. And its deployment is inevitable, in some fashion, if in fact existence is simply a fact rather than an artifact. Creation *by God*, however—which contradicts not the "fact" of existence but only its "merely" factual account—means that the goodness of existence is intrinsically infinite in comparison with any humanly experienced pain or pleasure. For if "created," existence comes from, is a result of, and arises only because of God's own gift that it should be at all. Every creation is the invention of material goodness, which stands in a category completely other from that of pain and pleasure and from that which is measurable or exchanged.

The very fact of our lives, that we exist at all, is a *nonreciprocal* reality. Our existence lies outside of our hands in its bare metaphysical truth and in a way that simply cannot permit logically our attempts to understand its meaning by "getting behind" it so as to "figure it out." Nor can we order this meaning in any way beyond its already given form. Our lives are in fact "filiated": bound to an order of textured relationships and their genesis whose shape we can in fact influence through our choices or unthinking circumstances. And they are filiated because this is "who" we are, not "how" we choose to be. Thus, any choices we make are always limited and informed by this "who" that we are, from the beginning and even to the end. Who we are is not within our means of controlling. This is not to say that we are *incapable* of choosing births and deaths; we do so all the time, for children and for adults: in conception, adoption, medical treatments, war, economic policy, and even in the small relational engagements we pursue or end. These are all choices that mark, as they should, the most wrenching struggles of our lives and societies. We must also say, however, that these choices we make trespass onto the most sacred of precincts. They are ones we simply cannot understand and whose meaning must finally come to us as a tremendous gift or burden, freeing or crushing, in mercy or judgment. Christians rightly understand that our debates in all these realms of life and death, then, are not about maximizing goods or pleasure and about minimizing pain; they are about our ultimate relation to God who has made us. If we subject to death, to a death that even we can perform upon ourselves, it is only because we are not our own.

## The Impossible Concept
### *Thinking about Life*

The reality of suicide, then, unveils two aspects of this "who" that we are: life or living existence first, and, second, that life's givenness. While we may think of suicide as destroying life or giving it up somehow, and while we may speak of suicide in terms of "choosing" to do this giving up, and thus as an act of the individual will, there is a deeper reality that suicide unveils that actually contradicts these normal modes of speech we use about it. It "cannot be" that life is destroyed simply by an act of human will. This is not because our freely chosen killing is something we do not see with our own eyes happening all the time—this is what war is, and murder, and fatal negligence—but because suicide opens the door onto the chasm of being from which stares back the great prospect of life's *non*negotiability in being given to us at all. Suicide's unveiling of life's nonhuman givenness is a paradox, to be sure, but one that, I believe, long consideration resolves on the side of human passivity, as it were: we can do nothing in the face of the fact that we are at all. All of our attempts to do so thrust us not into nothingness but into the great chasm whose mystery is life itself. We do not leap to our deaths—though, in a sense, this happens all the time, from tall buildings to high bridges to steep cliffs—rather we discover, despite ourselves, that which we could not ask for, ever, because our being made is itself a truth without a question. Because we are alive, we know that we will always fall into the hands of God, for better or worse.

Many of these considerations can sound tortured. But this is inevitable as we reflect on the things we somehow come face to face with as we consider our own beings, simply because *our beings are not our own*. So Paul writes in 1 Corinthians 6:19-20, speaking in terms of redemption, though also, contextually, in a way that must apply more fundamentally to all persons in the very fact of their existence. Perhaps the philosophical approach that has best engaged these questions is that known as phenomenology. Phenomenology derives from the teaching of someone less known in common discussion today, the German thinker Edmund Husserl (1859–1938), but its proponents do include recognized names like Sartre and Heidegger. More recent phenomenological practitioners, like Ricoeur and Levinas, have also had a tremendous influence on contemporary thinking.[29] The goal of phenomenology, as the name suggests, is simply to *describe*, in the most detailed and thorough way, the character of the things of this world as we come to know them: *phenomena*, objects, actions, intentions, and, of course, human beings, including the human self and its activities—consciousness, relationships, and actions. Phenomenology seeks to answer questions like, What is going on when we "think"? (Descartes, in this sense, was—along with the Augustine he so carefully read—one of the first "phenomenologists.") What does it mean to encounter an object in the world before us? How do we engage and experience what we call "freedom"? Like all philosophy, phenomenology seeks to get at the inner dynamics of our "common sense," although in this case without questioning that "sense" in its actual claims but rather uncovering its often inarticulate details.

Phenomenology has proven specifically helpful in elucidating the character of human existence, or at least the human self's existence, as an experienced reality. Thus, what used to be called "existentialism," like Sartre's, derived directly from phenomenological study. And more recently, several phenomenologists have opened up connections with religious (and even explicitly Christian) categories that, although obvious from a distance, were rarely explored until now. Just here, the central subjectivist base that phenomenology shares with much modern philosophy has moved out to a new breadth of purpose and claim. There are two special elements from these studies that I would note here that touch on the two aspects unveiled by suicide: what we call "life," and, secondly, the "givenness" of being, of existence in its comprehensive as well as its detailed reality.

The late Michel Henry (1922–2002) pursued his reflections on the self to the point of identifying "life" as the fundamental reality that is both at work and apprehended by the conscious subject.[30] To *be* conscious as a self is not simply to be "alive"—a living organism as it might variously be described by biologists—but to engage and to *be* life itself. All thinking, all apprehending of objects, all intentionality and feeling, comes down to the self-expression of life—whatever this is—as its own outworking. Henry devoted enormous care to showing how we are not selves insofar as we look *upon* life—or survey a world that may here be alive and there dead or inert. There is no "external" set of realities of which we are a simple member and of which we just happen to be a "living" member. Life is not a quality of objects. Indeed, Henry engaged a long-standing and celebrated polemic against the "barbaric" elements of a scientific positivism that could propose and promote a world of objects to be encountered as discrete elements, including human selves among them. A culture built upon such purported externalized and hence basically quantifiable building blocks—objects, clients, citizens, organisms—was not a culture at all, Henry argued, for human cultures are actually the intertwining experiences of *lives*. Cultures constitute "life" as life itself engages, through the living apprehension of its self-expression or being, the lives of others.

But just because a human being comes down to "life"-in-being, Henry came to emphasize its "nonreciprocal" character: we cannot "look at" our "lives" from outside, nor can we look at other people's lives in this way. Life simply "is"; it is the "is-ness" of our being here at all. And this life that is—it is "alive" in our normal biological sense of the term precisely because it escapes the control of our attempts at externalizing it. I am who I am—a life—for no reason other than that this life is alive, and its living extension is what it means for me to see and think and relate. I cannot "respond" to my life any more than I can call myself on the telephone. Just here is my responsibility: that I acknowledge and engage the world as Life rather than as a set of things, let alone one thing after another.

Henry came, later in his career, to pursue these insights into the realm of Christian philosophy and theology. The life of the self, after all, is an embodied one, and Henry was not seeking to deny the materiality of existence in a way that would somehow disallow scientific inquiry. But even materiality, he insisted, is materiality-in-relation-to-life as its more fundamental ground and context both. There are no "dead stars" to be examined in the cosmos except insofar as life encounters them as such. Hence, Henry began to consider the meaning of "incarnation" as a basic element of existence. And from this he moved to the exploration of the relation between, if you will, the multiple incarnations of life that make up our world and something that holds these together. The life that is a human self, he concluded, finds its truth in the Life that makes possible and that *is* that which we, as selves, only somehow partake of or "come from" and "aim toward."

Henry, from his philosophical starting point in phenomenology, actually came to engage one of the central questions of scriptural theology: the relationship of the "life" of living creatures and Life itself, in the sense of the Life that *is* God (or so he concluded). It is not only the case that Jesus will say that he is "life" (the Greek *zoe*, as in John 14:6), in the specially redemptive sense that his followers understood (cf. John 3:36), but rather this life is always bound to God's own self (Rev 22:1; Ps 36:9). The phrase "life of God" is given only once in Scripture, in Ephesians 4:18, and here in any case may refer to the life God gives rather than the one he possesses himself. Yet God is called the "God of my life" (*chai*—e.g., in Ps 42:8; Deut 30:20) in a meaning that seems to elide the distinction of possession. The discussion in John 6 of the "life" that is bound up with the heavenly gift that resides in and actually *is* Jesus' own flesh—this life comes down from heaven yet is also offered to the world in his body—is a kind of parsing of this relationship.

Although the relationship of God's "life" to my own life is peculiar, its meaning has been pursued consistently around the edges of the Christian tradition. Most challenging have been the opening verses of Genesis, where we are told that, on the fifth day, God created "living" creatures in the waters and in the air; and on the sixth day God did the same with land animals. When it comes to human beings, Genesis 2:7 describes this in terms of an exchange of "breath": "And the LORD God formed man of the dust of the ground, and breathed into his nostrils the breath of life; and man became a living soul (*nephesh*)," a phrase used earlier for the "living creatures" made in Genesis 1:21. This transfer of "breath" for the purpose of "life" is a claim made elsewhere in Scripture and in a way that only further underlines the profound relationship of divine sharing that this implies. So Isaiah 42:5 repeats this, bringing together the *ruach* of God's spirit (42:1; cf. Gen 1:2) with the spirit that is bound to the "breath" granting human life. Something like Job 33:4 merely repeats this as a standard trope (God's breath gives *us* life).

The plants themselves, we should note, while not granted the title "living" in Genesis, are nonetheless placed in the category of those things that bear "fruit" and create "seeds." These, in turn, will be bound to the character of "life" that human beings themselves engage through "fruitfulness" and filiation (cf. not only the cognate terms in Gen 1:28 but the identification of the two in Deut 7:13: God will "love thee, and bless thee, and multiply thee: he will also bless the fruit of thy womb, and the fruit of thy land, thy corn, and thy wine"). Thomas Aquinas needed to sort this out when it came to the question of "murder" and whether the killing of plants (and other animals) was forbidden on account of their common status as "living." Are all things related in this way, and, if so, how is this common "life" bound to God's own? Ultimately, there are texts that give us pause in this juggling of referents: for example, Ecclesiastes 3:19, where the *ruach* of human beings and animals is equated and both are given over to transience and "vanity." But only two verses later, in 3:21, this *ruach* is suggested as moving in different directions at death, depending upon the creature thus enlivened: beasts settling into the earth (and presumably being lost) and human breath rising up, perhaps back to its origin with God. Perhaps—but Solomon wonders if maybe they all disperse to the same dead end.

The discussion here is rich and difficult. It is not a surprise that there have been deep differences as to the meaning of God's breath and its tie to our lives. The early Fathers struggled with the character of the "soul" and the "spirit," in part to balance concerns over the intrinsic character of living beings vis-à-vis human beings, especially in their "redeemed" status as indwelt by the "spirit" of God. Calvin will do the same, in his own way, trying his best to limit the reach of the words used in Genesis 1 and 2, so as not to make too complex theological matters relating to "spirit" that come up later, in especially the New Testament. One can see the challenges here, for the biblical usage seems to imply that living beings, or at least human beings, are somehow continuous in their beings with God. The notion of some kind of inner divine aspect in each human being—a "spark," for instance—became a prominent theme in

some gnostic groups as well as later Christian sects, including Quaker-
ism. It has reappeared in the contemporary renewal of pneumatology, as
efforts have been made to tie "life" to the Holy Spirit in a special way
that permeates created being.[31] Some have argued that our contemporary
trajectory simply marks the final attraction of the seventeenth-century
philosopher Spinoza and his unifying sense of God-as-Nature. Henry
himself did not, in the end, articulate responses to these questions that
succeeded in satisfying some Christian critics, much as the medieval
mystical theologian Meister Eckhart (someone Henry engages at length)
failed to do. I will speak briefly to the question of the human "soul" in
chapter 6. But for now, a better place to engage the distinctions of creation, without any uncertainties regarding pantheism, is in the Catholic
phenomenologist Jean-Luc Marion.

Whereas Henry stressed the self-manifesting character of life in the
human self, Marion has stressed the "givenness" of the world, including
human life and selves. Reality is not simply "there," before us.[32] More
fundamentally, there is a kind of directional presence we experience, not
only in what is around us, but in ourselves as well: we do not stumble
upon the world or self, nor does it merely "appear" before us and within
us. Rather, reality is "proffered," as if from another person. Nor can one
interpret this in terms of some kind of violent thrusting holy spirit upon
us, for our very selves, as we dig down, share the same character of "being
granted." At root, Marion argues, there is a context, even a dynamic, of
unimpeded freedom in the world's being and our relationship to it and
to ourselves that, as we analyze our apprehensions, is not so much arbitrary as comprehensively coherent in its unified aspect of presentation to
us. If we "discover" the world or ourselves, it is not by accident but by
reality's self-offering.

Marion's work has, like Henry's, been robustly positioned within
academic philosophy. But more than Henry, Marion has also engaged
quite explicitly in Christian theological reflection, and his ecclesial commitments and interchanges are part of his working self-identity. It is no
surprise, then, to see the personalist implications arise in his writing
almost immediately: what is "given" has, as it were, a Giver as its ground
and source. And the very language of "givenness" is saturated with
Christian resonances—gift, grace, and so on. Some philosophers have
critiqued Marion's use of this language as itself begging the question:
if we experience reality as "given," then too we experience its supposed
"giver" as "given" as well, and thus a kind of infinite regress without

theistic implications is set up, whose logic, in any case, is flawed. These kinds of criticisms have been couched in technical phenomenological categories such as "reducibility" and "irreducibility" and in whether one can articulate the most basic elements of phenomena in terms of this or that category. One might well wonder, some have said, whether even in speaking in terms of giver and gift, one does not, in the end, risk the same equation of Creator and creature that Henry has been accused of setting up in "reducing" being to "life."

Marion, however, has been vigorous in responding to these kinds of criticism. God cannot be an object subjected to phenomenological strictures the way other objects of study are. If God is the "condition" of being, then the infinite regress—and all of its ethical dilemmas—cannot be applicable. And in any case, the category of "givenness" by definition marks a refusal to cross the line between God and creation. If "being"—reality, existence, that which "is"—is "given" to us, then there is something that is "beyond being" from which reality derives. Further-more, "derivation" here cannot mean some kind of realistic continuity: the Giver is not the gift, except in the strangest and most impossible and metaphysically upsetting of ways. If there is life—and there is—it comes as something without any possibility of will, demand, control, or even intentional understanding from the side of life itself. But it may also be the case that "life" (*contra* Henry) is to be equated not with God at all but with the very nature of that which is given by a Giver who is "beyond life." That is, "life" may be a creaturely predicate altogether; and hence its connotations of mortality are always intrinsic to its meaning. Certainly, this is what I would assert. At the least, the continuity of our lives with the life of Christ does not take place apart from the absolute caesura of death; and the Holy Spirit as "life" exists on both sides of the caesura as including such a death, not as transcending it.

Marion uses as one instance the example of Abraham "sacrificing" Isaac, and in this way he connects, quite explicitly, the philosophical to the scriptural and theological. This scriptural-philosophical world is not one in which gifts are "exchanged" among analogous players, as if God were one being, granted the greatest being, among many, and human actors in their turn, like Abraham, were called to balance and calculate the weight of a relationship and its demands: I "give" my son over for the sake of another, more powerful, giver. Rather, Marion argues, Abra-ham's sacrifice displays or unveils the "givenness" of Isaac, the fact that his being is itself a being-as-gift. In Marion's reading of the Genesis 22 narrative, Abraham is not seeking to "get something" in return; nor is he even "obeying" the stronger and wealthier party to a contract of exchange among givers who, if not equal in measure, are the same in their fundamental functions. Rather, the divine command is the statement of a *fact*—this life belongs to God for it is God's to give; and in the command's fulfillment by Abraham, he acknowledges this fact in the form of worship, or sacrifice.[33]

As a story, the simplicity and lack of details in Genesis 22 regarding divine and human intention permit this kind of interpretation. Indeed, to enter into intentionality deeply would, Marion might argue, actually necessitate this kind of recognition, for it would press us into the self-reflection of Abraham to such a point that this kind of encounter with the God of his givenness—and his son's—would present itself inevitably. Surely this is precisely what St. Thomas would imply with his last reason given against suicide: it is unlawful, "thirdly, because life is God's gift to man, and is subject to His power, Who kills and makes to live."

Contemporary phenomenology, then, takes us back to the modern struggle with suicide. Most arguers against suicide in the seventeenth and eighteenth centuries always came back to this fundamental Thomistic reason, just as Donne did in his own obscure way. John Adams, an early respondent to Donne's published work, for instance, spends a chapter focusing on the question of God's "propriety" over human life. Adams avoids biblical arguments, seeking to engage the topic on the basis of "reason." So he simply compares human concerns over the transfer of property rights—the need for written contracts and witnesses—with the impossibility of approaching even such care over dumb objects with the need for guarantees that a divine "transfer" of rights over life to the self-killer itself must imply: "Propriety is of so nice and tender a Nature, that when it is to be made over, all the care imaginable is us'd," he writes.

> How much more reasonable must this Caution be where *God himself is the Proprietor*, so good, so gracious, so just, so powerful a Being! and where *Humane Life* is the thing in Question; in which so many Persons may be concerned, and which may be of such *unspeakable value to him* that has it; if the *end* of it were *faithfully observ'd*; for what can make Man more *Happy*, or more *Glorious*? What can exalt him higher above the rest of the Creation, or nearer to the Divine Nature, than the continual discovery of *Eternal Truth*, and the *regulating* of his Passions and Desires accordingly, than the *improving* of others by *Example* and *Information*, and being the *Help* and *Pleasure* of a great part of

Mankind. Life *is the opportunity of being all this*; shall that then be *rashly thrown away by Self-murther?*[34]

All the elements of nature and love are here gathered, but they are gathered in such a way as to underline their own place within the giftedness of God's generosity and also within the comprehensive domain of creative ownership that defines God in his relationship with us.

## Responsibility for Life

I stress this divine comprehension of life's giftedness, because it must finally set many of the goods we associate with a flourishing existence— love, relationships, thoughtfulness and laughter, sexual expression, food and drink, social pleasures and their forms—within the encompassing and fundamental reach of mortal life as God's creative offer. If, with Freud, we stare into the abyss of our interior drives, we see death mixed up with all the elements of our unsorted motives. But if we stare at our deaths, there in the midst of these motives, we also see all of our lives in their desiring intertwining, as bound to the God who grants such a life that death implies. The "fullness of life" is thus bound to the specific character of our beings as mortal creatures, shaped by the fundamental aspects of that created being and its context. One of the more fascinating discussions of and against suicide was written in the mid-seventeenth century by William Denny, a lawyer and poet, who died in 1676. Denny's work, *The Pelecanicidium; or, The Christian adviser against self-murder* (named after the pelican, speaks of life and death suffered for the sake of her children), is unusual just in the fact that it so self-consciously places the theological arguments against suicide, not novel in themselves, within an elaborated scale of the life span and its form.[35] The work is striking in that it is primarily a long poem, whose verse is justified on the basis that David calmed Saul's self-destructive passions by song rather than by logical discourse. And the poem, interspersed with homiletical urgings, and after an initial Christian exhortation to hope, is framed in terms of the "pilgrim's" passage through the "wilderness." It is an extensive journey that Denny takes the reader through, filled with trials and difficulties, dangers and temptations to despair. (One wonders at his own state of mind during this period, one in which his royalist sympathies led him to prison and poverty.) At each step, he seeks to offer consolation and hope to the Christian struggling to move forward toward the promised "rest" that will greet him or her at the end

of life. All this is straightforward enough. It is so well etched in its pilgrimage frame, in fact, as to have raised all kinds of literary questions as
to Bunyan's knowledge of it.

The most arresting aspect of the work, however, is the way Denny
offers the individual contemplating suicide, not a vision of what the
human life can be without trial, but a full depiction of these very trials,
in their extended and relational form, as the substance of God's gift of
life itself. Granted, this is the world of Adam's fall; and "pilgrimage" is
the nature of such a postlapsarian existence. But it is an existence bound
to God's grace in its very giving, as it moves through time to an end, and
everywhere attached to the gift of its being at all. Denny contrasts "life"
to death, not as the simple and joyous over and against the broken and
sorrowful, but as the deep and textured over and against the thin and
empty, just because of life's constituent fabrication upon the foundation
of nothingness and grace both. Death is seen as always wrapped up *into*
life, at least insofar as life is what it truly is for the creature.

Denny's is a remarkable response to the question of human life in
terms of its gracious mortal texture, although it is itself but a developed
form of the kind of thick discussions of human being that had been a
part of literary culture for some centuries. Petrarch's popular *De remediis
utriusque fortunae* (On the remedies for fortune and misfortune [1366]),
for instance, offered an analogous vision, through a long series of dialogues on how a person ought to deal with good and bad fortune alike,
given our mortality as creatures before God.[36] Petrarch even included,
among these dialogues near the very end of the work, one devoted explicitly to "self-murder"—but only one, embedded as it was in a long series
of existential events that are part of "prosperity and adversity."

One of the great ironies of the post-Transition world of the West is
the fact that we no longer understand what is happening when this constituent feature of our lives—its deep and textured, and often troubling,
mortal aspect of mutual engagement—is pressed upon us. The treatment
of suicides in the past, and in the West especially, horrifies us, as Hecht
has emphasized. But the visceral repugnance these sanctions embody
should not surprise us, since it is, after all, but the reaction of life cast
away in the face of its inexplicable gratuitous offering: suicide stands not
so much as a surd but as a violent self-contradiction before the foundation of all things, including the very possibility of contradiction itself.
Suicide is "blasphemy" in this sense, something that rises up as a destroying rebel. To be sure, we are *rightly* horrified by past sanctions against

blasphemy just to the extent that they themselves betray this sanctity and miracle of life as well. Still, it is the reality of such blasphemy that must be retained in our era, simply because it is the truth of our being. Compassion for the victims of suicide, for the profound assault upon their own spirits from which their actions arise, is hardly misplaced. These are assaults that, in this essay, I have no reason to question or any chance to treat, though the designation of the "demonic" is hardly wrong, once again, in its description of what at least is at stake. But such compassion, I would argue, cannot turn into permissive acceptance without slipping into a perverted allegiance.

This is, in part, what has happened in the progressive movement toward legalized or at least tacitly permitted euthanasia, including the very murky area we call "physician-assisted suicide." It is almost as if we have become fatigued with the creative energies of struggle that death has thrust upon us and woven into our living existence, so that a response to death's own unexpected incursion has become an inured kind of embrace. This resigned embrace, perhaps, *is* the result of the Great Transition in a rather direct fashion. As life spans increase, and death withdraws to a hidden distance (although in fact hardly very far away at all), the very gift that death can represent in its inevitability, its "isness" of our own lives, has been increasingly muted. The possibility of "keeping people alive" medically in all sorts of conditions that, until only recently, would have been the doorway to death but are now set out to be open-ended and indeterminate forms of extended suffering has instigated a kind of rebellion on the part of mortality itself. This is all understandable. And it constitutes the reverse side of the Great Transition's inversion of expectation. Petrarch, as I mentioned, treated suicide in the course of his discussion of the vicissitudes of human life. He was thoroughly knowledgeable of the Roman literary Stoic tradition of suicide, but he still rejected it resolutely. Suicide, he said, marks "a kind of furious forgetfulness of what thou art."[37] In our own time, we see such fury, all about us. Remembering who we really are, and whose we are, then, must bring with it a gracious peace.

# III

# Death and Filiation

I now return to Hecht's plea for the communitarian demands of life: "Stay!" she urges the despondent, "because we are all part of each other." What it means to be part of one another is the central concern of this chapter, in which I want to outline how mortal creaturehood is defined by its generative and ramifying context and responsibilities.

Hecht's plea is not wrong. Indeed, so strong is the intrinsic power of her claim that it bursts the bonds of her own atheistic commitments: we are joined to one another precisely because our lives, as given by God, join us to "life" and thus to other lives. Unless this were so, we would have no claim beyond too-frequently perverted instinct. And so I have stressed how this insight points properly to the "filiated" character of creation, those lines that draw us together. For Petrarch, Denny, and others, these lines are temporally extended in terms of the tensile pulls of relationship given particularly in generation: the parent-child-adult-infant-aging-heritage set of relations. Suicide can uncover some of this in a kind of primordial way. But there are other *exempla*, as it were, that do the same in a more concretely familial fashion. *Un*willing death, for instance, is far more explicit than suicide in this respect.

One can observe the letters of those about to be executed in the midst of war to see some of this, the positive side, as it were, that the despairing suicide only marks by reverse. There exist, in this context,

collections of such material, like those of young French political prisoners during World War II who were sentenced to die. Almost all these
persons awaiting their deaths turn to their families—their parents, their
siblings, their spouses and children, their uncles and aunts. A few even
turn to their priests. It is almost universal, this final reach back into the
filiated sphere of life.

"My dear parents, my dear little sister," begins one letter that is completely typical.

> Adieu, because I am about to fall where so many of my comrades have
> fallen. I have done my confession, and now I am leaving, provided for
> with the Holy Sacraments. Be brave, and be proud [censured]. Adieu,
> Papa: you who always showed me the path of honor and integrity. . . .
> Adieu, mother; you who brought me into the world, and who took
> care of me in my suffering. Be brave—you still have Vovonne [his sis-
> ter] to console you. And adieu to you, little sister, as well. I am entrust-
> ing our father and mother to you. Make them happy, make their old
> age pleasant. Take care of our mother especially, because this will be a
> terrible blow for her. And now, they are coming to take me away. When
> the sun rises, we will be no more. . . . Adieu to all my family and all my
> friends. Your son, your brother, who is about to die, and who sends to
> you his final kisses. . . . Julien Ducos [twenty-four years old][1]

Then there is disease, which also pulls back the covering that clothes our
filiated existence. Petrarch's own experience with the plague, and his
children's deaths, his flights from city to city to keep them safe, and the
challenges this involved is an elevated example. This kind of concerned
flight is but one of many ways that disease (and war) uncovers a central
aspect of created life. In our day, the story of AIDS offers an example of
this as well, but one parallel to euthanasia's deformed emergence from
suicide's compassionate apprehension. With AIDS, a new understanding of human worth, in this case of homosexual persons, forged in the
difficult circumstances of death's assault, led to an uncomprehending
encounter with the filiated character of human life that has since been
misunderstood in civil policy and ecclesial dispute.

The AIDS pandemic is one that opens up a landscape beyond the
simple fact of life, to the question of life's ordering, the shape of its particular form in time. This, in turn, must ultimately lead into the area
of generation. Henry's notion of "life" as a kind of ground for all phenomena bound to the self—that is, as the very ground of self, in all its
mystery—is powerful. But seizing upon life itself does not go far enough

in explaining who we are. Hence, to reiterate Marion's insistence, it is life's "givenness" that defines *this* or *that* life; and this givenness, or giftedness, always carries with it, as a very part of its form and being, responsibility. To encounter death, in the midst of our lives, is to become responsible for the givenness of life, our own and the dying or dead person's. We become responsible for the way our life in its relationship with the lives of others can retain its proper character, shape, or form. This shape is precisely the filiated order of life that is being given and handed over in the process of birth, growth, sustenance, family, friendship, and death. The process itself is the gift of creation that Genesis describes in terms of "fruitfulness" and "multiplication" (attached, as we saw, to all living creatures). If there is such a thing as compassion toward that which is "given," toward life—and there must be, insofar as compassion is a responsibility to life—such compassion, then, is ordered to the generativity of this or that life in particular.

This is a difficult concept to grasp. For someone like Denny, what we have called "skinfulness" in its scriptural figure amounts to a movement through time that is shaped by the intertwining challenges of lives: lives given, given over, and given for, within the limits of a mortality constituted by God's creation of these lives. The "pilgrim's progress" that Bunyan made of this movement is shot through with this divine precedence and finally welcoming form, not as a "given," but as a constant "giving." That is the moving force of human "progress" through time. Human beings receive and pass on within this matrix. And this constitutes their faithfulness, in the sense of life truthfully expressing who one is. Suicide, for Denny, denies this truth; it denies the coming-to-be as gift that a person is (concretized in birth) as well as the given-over-in-being that is the self's constant form (concretized in family) as well as other relationships geared toward the future. The movement of "from" and "toward" characterizes a human person, but *just in the forms* that the gift is given: birth, the struggle for life in love and in offering new life and nurturing it, and the passing over of life, through mortal limitations, to another generation. All the "testing" and "consolation" that provides plenitude or a properly understood "satisfaction" to this pilgrim life is wrapped with this, at least in Denny's quite traditional Christian reading.

Furthermore, this traditional reading indicates in part why a person-centered argument often used to decouple marriage from its procreative essence makes little sense. It is not the case that human beings are *either* a good in themselves *or* simply ordered to utilitarian ends, like having children. Within the kind of filiated universe that Denny describes as central to the Christian vision of divine givenness, *no* human person is "just" a person. Each of us is the child of parents, and the relative of a range of birth lines, all the way down and in the most concrete and also mysterious of ways. To this degree our personhood is essentially generational. If suicide can uncover our givenness, the history of the AIDS pandemic can provide, paradoxically, a localized unveiling of that givenness' filiated form.

## AIDS and the Inversion of Filiative Compassion

The paradox involved in the AIDS pandemic is one of unforeseen consequences—where love and life have fueled a countermovement against these very currents of filiated generativity. One instructive element of the AIDS pandemic, especially in the West, is that it provides an example wherein human skinfulness, pressed upon us, has resulted in a strange willingness to pursue its own *déshabillement*, its disrobing. And this has led to a yet more disastrous nakedness than Adam's potential setting out into the world unclothed in his shame. In the case of the AIDS pandemic, it was in fact the encounter with death and the desire to embrace life that drove the churches to act in a deeply compassionate way. But just so, as if exhausted by the effort, a misunderstanding of this very drive in the end overwhelmed the churches' intuition by the counterforces of uprooting. "Life"—as a kind of abstracted, though very personally concretized, thirst, driven to a wild cry—lost its bearings in the ordering of time: the pandemic was that disorienting. And since this story has been part of one of the most defining shifts in Christian understandings of sexuality, and thus of creaturehood, it is worth pausing to consider it. In what follows, I am proposing a history that is controversial not in its dates and figures but rather in the interpretation of its ecclesial effects, which are all about the character of this "life" whose donated reality is not something we have in our power, in fact, to lay aside.

First, it is worth saying something about the rise and expansion of gay rights, in civil terms, for the story, in its common telling, tracks with elements of the Great Transition that are still so misunderstood. The standard progressivist view of our historical moment, at least on the issue of gay inclusion, is fairly straightforward. It follows, in a delayed fashion, a similar kind of advance in civic and social rights taking place among African Americans and women. Some of the latter developments, in their gendered form, are tied to elements of the Great Transition.

The time line might begin—granted, in an arbitrary fashion for the sake of symbolic manageability—in 1924, when the Society for Human Rights in Chicago became the country's earliest known gay rights organization. Alfred Kinsey's landmark book *Sexual Behavior in the Human Male* was published in 1948 and told the public that homosexuality is far more widespread than was commonly believed. (As it turns out, not nearly so much as Kinsey claimed—but the notion of a "stable" percentage was now solidly lodged in public consciousness, with its connotations of biological necessity.) Other gay and lesbian rights groups were founded in the next two decades, and in 1962 Illinois became the first state in the United States to decriminalize homosexual acts in private between consenting adults. In 1969 the so-called Stonewall riots in New York's Greenwich Village turned the gay-rights movement into a nationally known phenomenon. In 1973 the American Psychiatric Association removed homosexuality from its official list of mental disorders, and there followed—in the 1980s, 1990s, and, of course, the past few years with the various state legalizations of same-sex unions—a range of legally recognized expansions of civil rights for gays, many of which are paralleled and even initiated in other Western countries. Same-sex "marriage" has now become a central feature of civil discourse, and in fact of civil life in some regions, upheld by courts and furthered by well-organized lobbying efforts and legal action.[2]

The chronological arrangement of these elements seems to bespeak a seamless move forward in the expansion of rights to gay persons, rightly or wrongly. If there is conflict in this (and there was, and still is, to be sure), it has had to do, from the progressivist perspective, with the lingering hold of tradition and prejudice, like that aimed against blacks and women. While one can be more or less tolerant of the conservative drag on developments, a drag it has been and remains.[3] From the traditionalist interpretation, by contrast, the successful movement for gay rights has had to do with an unrelenting and religiously intolerant manipulation of the political process by a larger liberalized academic and legal network set on destroying the foundations of established moral values.[4]

But there is another aspect to this history, especially within the Christian churches, that is not well integrated into the standard progressivist view (seen positively or negatively). This is an aspect we are still struggling with in terms of what it has pressed into our consciousness. I am referring to the phenomenon of AIDS-related suffering that transformed the search for gay rights into an imaginative reconstruction of human destiny. Perhaps already infecting persons by the late 1960s, but not yet recognized, the disease known as AIDS (Acquired Immunodeficiency Syndrome, caused by the Human Immunodeficiency Virus [HIV]) was identified in 1981 and tied to over two hundred deaths. By 2002 there had been over five hundred thousand deaths in the United States alone due to AIDS, and by 2003 twenty million deaths in the world. In 2004 over 3 million AIDS deaths were reported during the year, half a million of which were of children born to an infected parent. It is estimated that upward of 35 million persons are infected with the HIV virus today, twice as many men as women, and concentrated especially in Africa, Southeast Asia, and the Caribbean (e.g., Haiti). By 2012, furthermore, 35 million people had died from the disease. AIDS represents one of the great experiential pushbacks against the Great Transition, at least if numbers have any meaning. Yet even here, the ongoing breadth of this pushback has tracked well with the Transition's already established beneficiaries—that is, those in economically developed nations. And the disease itself, and more importantly the way we look at it, also seems to have slowly subsided back into the parameters of the Transition's general expectations.

Death rates among HIV-infected persons have begun to drop significantly since the turn of the century, for instance (1.6 million died in 2012);[5] and more importantly, the new infection rate has dropped over 40 percent since the height of the epidemic in the 1990s (2.5 million infected in 2011).[6] Why the improvements is another matter: the greater availability of retroviral drugs for those infected has clearly reduced the death rate; but also, possibly, there has been a "saturation" of the most susceptible populations as well—that is, the most vulnerable in various areas have already died. The most vulnerable in this case are children born to infected parents, young people who are sexually active outside of a monogamous marriage—whether heterosexual or homosexual—and those who were already ill. There have clearly been some key behavioral changes as well since the disease was first identified, the most important obviously being the reduction of sexual activity, especially among the young: this has been clearly documented in many parts of the world and in those countries where the rates have been reduced. Also, an increased willingness to engage in "protected sex"—the use of condoms, for instance—has proven important in many areas (although the entire question of "abstinence" vs. "protection" has proven an issue of intense, often politicized, debate).

One of the chief topics of discussion in public health policy surrounding AIDS has to do with the relative resources spent on treatment versus prevention education and, of course, what kind of education. It is still the case, however, that the average infection rate in much of sub-Saharan Africa is around 10 percent, which is astonishing and depressing when we realize this is an average where places like Swaziland, Lesotho, and Botswana have adult rates of close to 25 percent. By contrast, in the United States, infection rates may be around 0.6 percent, or as many as 1.1 million; and in Canada, 0.3 percent, or as many as seventy thousand are infected, a trend, however, that may be going up, not down—in part due to people living longer with the disease; but rates of new infections are somewhat up among gay men, young women, and aboriginal persons. In these countries there is perhaps a shift toward a larger proportion of cases being contracted, mostly by women, in heterosexual contact through gay or drug-using partners. Still, in developed countries certainly, we see that AIDS has receded back into the shadows of expected health for the population as a whole. This may not be helpful for public health, but it represents a kind of "settling of the dust," in more ways than one, for the moment.

This flurry of dates and statistics is a morally inadequate way to present a general picture. Still, it is necessary at least as a preface to a consideration of how AIDS affected the course of gay-inclusion history within the church. This last story has not yet been told, nor certainly is it well understood. Hence my reflections here can be tentative at best. But there are some aspects that we can already identify. First of all, the AIDS epidemic initially brought a new media spotlight on gays in, for example, the United States, in all sorts of ways, positive and negative. Second, it galvanized gay political groups and put them in coalition with a broad range of other political, health, community, and religious groups seeking to combat the disease and alleviate suffering, thus "mainstreaming" the movement across the board. Yet at the same time, as a result of this new public exposure, something else took place that proved a kind of unexpected disclosure that profoundly altered the social self-awareness of many people. Brought to light now was a whole array of explicit sexual practices that until the advent of AIDS was barely known publicly, and certainly not generally mentioned: the average number of partners gay American men had sex with (over three hundred in a lifetime), forums of sexual encounter (baths, bathrooms, etc.), the mores of sexual relationships, and the differing meanings of sexual experience held by homosexuals and heterosexuals within various subcultures.

This unveiling of until-then hidden behavior was not, however, just a matter of new public knowledge about homosexual practices. For in the discussion about AIDS, sexual practice in general became a topic of popular examination, since AIDS had begun to spread in the heterosexual community as well, both among drug users employing infected needles and among those involved in bisexual and then multiple sexual encounters. The whole topic of sexually transmitted diseases suddenly gained far more interest and research. But so did the sense that sexual activity was bound to life-and-death matters whose navigation, especially among the young, was not something to be taken for granted and instead was defined by a host of moral, cultural, and religious commitments and realities. Even though Freud's particular theories had been rejected by the general public by this time, his insight regarding the deep connection between physical passions and mortality refused to disappear. "The body" as a matter of moral and theological concern became a new focus among people of all political persuasions. None of this was possible forty years ago. The result was a growing sense among some groups that ordered sexual relationships, among the young and older population, demanded attention and encouragement. This realization, tied to changing demographics in divorce rates and the number of two-parent households—all matters at least related to the Great Transition—represented a synergistic revolution of interest and concern.

Finally, the pandemic of AIDS in places like Africa, which could not afford the resources necessary to control the disease medically, focused the matter—at least initially, in the late 1980s and the 1990s—on behavioral change, among heterosexuals as much as anything: that is, fidelity within marriage and abstinence outside of it was seen by many as the only mechanism capable of controlling the disease. Uganda proved a great example, initially cutting infection rates by over half, through campaigns aimed primarily at abstinence education and the encouragement of marital fidelity.[7] In this the churches took a leading role, having a set of moral teachings that cohered with what were viewed as sound health demands.

What all these responses and changes did was to rearrange, and in fact invent, the pieces with which people made sense of their sexual lives as persons embedded in cultures of formation, expectation, and free self-construction. The rearrangements and inventions, furthermore, were never given respite, let alone resolution, once they began to tumble out in the 1980s, under the shadow of the disease. They are still taking place, in a context of very high biological and moral stakes. Yet they are taking place in a context in which the reality of mortality was very quickly repressed in favor of the dynamics of temporally unimpeded individual self-assertion whose dynamic the Great Transition has fed. Indeed, in the most recent period, the significant advances that have been made in the AIDS fatality rates, pressed often by unrelenting political demand, have simply furthered the notion—perhaps mistaken—of AIDS as a controllable illness. It has become like many other illnesses and thus subject to the technical dynamics of the Transition's ideological consequences.

None of this came about without experiencing the sounding of the clock, which demanded that creaturehood be addressed in the AIDS crisis one way or another—as it turns out, in a way that produced ironic results. It is hard to say where the "gay rights" movement might have gone in the churches had AIDS not appeared. But however we might speculate, the whole dynamic of AIDS and its cultural apprehension injected into the question of "gay rights" a growing polarization of religious morals that was fueled not by insouciance to creaturehood in its existential truth but by the deepest concerns over life and death, often experienced personally and with enormous agony by people of every commitment. Conservatives and liberals, gays and straights all expended love in the most extreme and exhaustive of ways in the course of confronting and grappling with this disease and the people ensnared by it. Friends, lovers, and even strangers found their deepest energies given over in care and, too often, mourning. Among the most powerful places this was evident—and certainly from a later legal, civil, and ecclesial policy point of view among the most socially influential—was among the family members of gay victims of the disease. Mothers and fathers, siblings, and sometimes children of men whose sexual orientation they had rejected or distanced themselves from experienced transformative relations of care now that they were enmeshed in the mortal fates of their flesh and blood. There were, of course, many cases where these relationships were repudiated as well, often with heart-wrenching results. Yet there is no question but that the suffering of gay AIDS victims turned many hearts of parents to their children, and children to their parents. Though these efforts became swallowed by the policy dynamics that Great Transition life has understandably spawned, they remain telling testimonies to the textured character of genealogically filiated existence.[8]

And it was into this mix that the specifically religious questions regarding sexuality within churches in North America began to arise. In the United States, the Episcopal Church was, for instance, a leader in some of the initial coalitions to fight AIDS, and thus it aligned itself with a range of pro-gay groups. There has always been a disproportion of gay members within Anglican churches in general, for a number of unconfirmed reasons. Also, because of the high education rate and low birthrate of Episcopalians in the United States, the denomination did not suffer the devastation of AIDS within its heterosexual population as much as some other denominations did that were more demographically diverse. Thus, the negative "moral reaction"—complex and ambivalent in many ways—to varied and confused sexual mores did not grow within Western churches all to the same degree or to the same extent as within non-Western Anglican churches. Indeed, just the opposite took place: as many Western churches responded to AIDS, compassion and engagement, as with the case of suicide, tended to sweep all before it. It was just this that proved easily transformed into an inured acceptance of a now reduced realm of creaturely existence, wherein the specifically genealogical—something that had spurred initial concerns and involvement—was gradually let go of as a necessary part of human definition. Gay rights was played off, and inevitably so, the "procreative" character of human existence. It is impossible, furthermore, to extract a work like Benatar's, mentioned in the last chapter, from this developed context: when life is reduced to a calculus of relative suffering, generative existence inexorably becomes expendable.[9] The horrendous irony of the AIDS pandemic is that from the emotions of love that were kindled by generative compassion for the ill and the dying emerged a new ethic of sexual life in which procreative identity was no longer essential or even central.

Not all Christians in the West, of course, accepted the evolution of attitudes exemplified in large swaths of the Episcopal Church. Furthermore, unlike some other denominations, churches like the Episcopal Church or the Lutheran Church (not to mention the Roman Catholics) were parts of large worldwide communions, where the largest and fastest-growing churches—far dwarfing North American denominations—lie in Africa and some parts of Asia. This is precisely the part of the world where AIDS has been deadliest and where the sense of sexual self-control has been seen as most vital and necessary and easily located within religious teaching. In fact, that teaching was

reapprehended by younger churches as part of their original bequest
from the West. "Conservatives" in the Episcopal Church, for instance,
thus found themselves aligned with the so-called Global South in a
struggle for moral clarity and, as they saw it, a battle, however confused, to regain it. These were the lines drawn in the late 1990s, as the
push for "same-sex" blessings took on a high-profile public image and
as American Christian leaders were increasingly viewed as "dangerous"
to faith and public health in Africa and elsewhere. Thus, alignments
between the Global South and conservative Western Christians were
quickly cemented, although often ignoring other differences. All this
is part of the current ecclesial struggles of the present, within Roman
Catholicism now as much as elsewhere.[10]

Given the way I have laid this out, the story of these struggles seems
to be all about politics. But if this is the case, I want to stress that it is the
politics of creaturehood that is at issue more than the politics of the civil
society. This means that the struggles over sexuality, and same-sexuality
in particular, will not go lightly toward resolution. For with these politics,
death itself has hidden in the background, not absent but simply crouch-
ing by the door. Anyone who thinks that this revolution of concern over
the body and Christian faith has emerged from even its initial phases
is, I believe, deeply mistaken, precisely because the revolution's deeply
textured creaturely context has barely been faced, let alone engaged. The
debate and struggle over AIDS prevention and abstinence (as well as matters touching other sexually transmitted diseases and abstinence) has only
just begun in the health field, despite the sense that the battles are already
long and bloody. Religiously, the reexamination—a very cursory affair
thus far—of the radical notions of procreative experiment, of family refor-
mulation, and of the relationship of marriage and divorce to the reality of
family and mental health has also only just begun, constantly overtaken
by new technologies, creative legal constructions, and political strong-
arming. While questions of divorce and remarriage might seem settled in
a permissive direction within many churches, this seems unlikely to persist in the long run. In fact, divorce and remarriage has emerged as a topic
of the greatest importance within the present sexuality debate. There has
certainly been theological work around these issues, but far less than one
might expect, and certainly far from anything that might cohere into a
recognized tradition that is disseminated among the faithful.

In any case, the outlined story as I have presented it drives toward a
profound inference. This inference is so obvious that its restatement seems

almost tautological. But it is also one whose need for restatement thus underlines the cloud of misunderstanding—rather than of direction— that has risen up and enveloped our passage through the wilderness. The inference is this: not only does the question of mortal life have something to do with sexuality, but sexuality cannot escape being defined as something that moves toward and out of genealogy. Sexuality is, just as it has traditionally been viewed as being, bound up with procreation in its culturally enmeshed and temporally extended forms and meanings. If suicide unveils the character of life, that character—unveiled in many ways, including by AIDS—is saturated with a procreative meaning, which rises up within the frame of mortality in such a way as to overshadow death itself. Few who have read the book can forget the miraculous ending to the late P. D. James' prescient and profound novel *The Children of Men*. In James' tale, an unexplained and universal onset of male sterility has doomed the world to a politics of euthanasia and violence, as the aging population of the rapidly extinguishing human race quickly overburdens the dwindling numbers of younger persons. In the midst of this setting of death, an unexpected and endangered pregnancy marks redemption. Yet this single and unanticipated pregnancy proves a threat to the now entrenched regimes of death that have taken hold of society. Their determined quest to exterminate the pregnant woman and her friends expresses their complete incapacity to deal with a new life, once all they have come to expect is their own personal and corporate disappearance. James' open Christian claims in this case—the child is born and then is secretly baptized by the beleaguered Christian community that has survived the disintegration of civil society—only press the point theologically.[11] Her larger argument is clear: a society that has lost its central genealogical vocation is not only doomed; it becomes inhuman. Hence, divine grace must move in an opposite direction.

## Generative Filiation

AIDS is not a parable. It is one major human tragedy, among many, that has been caught in the dynamics of human choice and social drift, in this case those of the Great Transition. The parable, if there is one, lies in how we frame the story of filiative procreation more broadly within our Christian self-understanding, taking seriously the events, choices, and currents of human life. Here, we have had some recent debate that has stressed variety and multiplicity of views over time, such that a single or overarching Christian self-understanding has been rejected by many as historical wishful thinking. I would question the conclusion here, however. To be sure, there have been varieties of local law, custom, and permission within Christian cultures with respect to sexuality over the past two millennia. But the basic lines of discussion have been stable, and they point in a relatively stable direction of filiative value, even if it is one that has been contested at times.

It is true that generation or procreation's informing centrality to life, as a created gift, has not gone unquestioned in the Christian tradition. Paul, as we know, laid out rather difficult instructions in 1 Corinthians 7, which, to this day, both challenge and confuse. Most of us wonder today if it is really "better" to be single, as Paul might seem to imply in verses 8 and 28. Yet he knows he cannot forbid marriage, nor does he. And much of 1 Corinthians 7 is in fact devoted not to singleness at all but to marriage with the assumption of children (e.g., v. 14). By the later letters, as in Ephesians and the epistles to Timothy, it is clear that families with children, and the relationship of these children to their parents, is at the center of the church's life. There are, furthermore, good reasons, understood already in the early church, to think that Paul himself had once *been* married (and was now a widower), with all the struggles, like Augustine's later, that this might involve.[12]

Still, we also know that a debate over the place of marriage and procreation emerged within the church by the fourth century at least, bound up with the rise of monasticism and wrapped up in developing theologies of the human body that tried to make sense of both Scripture (Paul especially) and current philosophical perspectives. We have seen this already in interpretations given to the skins of Adam as mentioned in Genesis: many commentators believed that the skins represented the passions of fallen, mortal flesh, somehow bound negatively to the course of experienced human life spans. On the one hand, spectacular disputes like that between Jerome and the monk Jovinian erupted, which led to Jovinian's official condemnation in Rome in the late fourth century. Jovinian was accused of "heretical" claims regarding the equality of the married life among baptized Christians with the celibate life of virginity. On the other hand, councils like Gangra, a local provincial gathering of bishops in northern Turkey (c. 340/350), felt bound to pronounce that the married life was to be valued like the ascetic life, largely because Scripture itself presents it as honorable. The council, in fact, openly opposed the "arrogance" of some ascetics in raising themselves above the ordinary and "simple" life of married persons.

Augustine himself joined the debate, eventually opting for a kind of qualified affirmation of the married life and its procreative center.[13] Certainly, the procreation was an indispensable condition to getting married, as it was for the ascetic life, whatever the second-best character of marriage might be: we must be born in order then to have a vocation. Augustine struggled to make sense of the Genesis story on this score, finally accepting its assertion that male-female sexual distinction as well as generative purpose was at the root of God's vision for human life. What troubled him was the issue of sexual passion and its uncontrollable forces, and this pressed him to valorize the celibate monastic existence he had himself later embraced. Still, Augustine's own life was conflicted on all these scores, bound as it was by a deep loyalty and debt to his mother's personal faith and influence, by a regretful yet, for all that, happy life over many early years with his legal mistress, and finally by the sheer joy of his son, Adeodatus—the name means, literally, "given by God"—whom he raised with a personal care and tenderness that is notable. Adeodatus' death as a teenager is barely mentioned by his father in his writings; yet the very subtlety of his reference to the beloved boy's demise, in the midst of so much described delight, bespeaks an aching poignancy.[14] Augustine's engagement, late in life, with the whole question of infants who die, and the question of their original sin and baptism, is thus not theoretical or abstract but deeply wrapped up with his own uncertain notions of what a human life comes down to in this world. And if his notions are "uncertain," it is just because the issues are so extraordinarily real to him. He remains amongst the most textured Christian thinkers of creatureliness, whose sometimes unpleasant reputation is based on the caricatures of cut-and-paste quotation. More than any other theologian of the early church, Augustine *struggled* with the meaning of mortal life that is given within the filiated context of parents and family.

For all that, in the West especially, sexual existence became divided by the church into two spheres: the higher sphere of the celibate clergy and religious orders, and the lower sphere of the ordinary population, where procreative sex was permitted but hedged about with prohibitions against pleasure and the constant teaching that there was a "more perfect" path that avoided sex altogether. Even if the reality of the church's life on the ground was far more complex than the official teachings admitted, the popular modern notion that the church long promoted a culture that denigrated sexual life is not off the mark. At the least, the Western church's official theology, geared toward the values of a monastic anthropology, never developed the tools to engage procreative existence. Modern rejections of procreation on the basis of concerns over population, as well as theodicy—the world being too evil a place in which to bear children—have, in their own ways, built upon some of these deeply embedded, if unconscious, judgments that the church itself bequeathed to popular imagination.

Of course, the lower sphere of ordinary life was insistent and could never be repressed, even in terms of self-definition and promotion. We have seen this already in the way that suicide unveils the filiated sphere in general for many early opponents of self-murder. Something similar with respect to sex is evident in people like Chrysostom, in the fifth century, whose marriage sermons provide a window onto another, less prominently displayed, Christian tradition. Chrysostom's Christian vision could see the life of the family as a central figure and location of the Christian church itself, in its presentation of *redeemed* humanity "in Christ." In addition to such formally presented documents, small openings to the powers and breadth of filiated affection incarnated specifically in family terms are provided by funerary inscriptions, from, for example, the Catacombs:

> "Flavius Crispinus to Aurelia Aniane, most worthy wife, who lived 28 years. We were married for 9 years with love, and she never gave me cause for pain. Farewell, my dear. Be at peace with the holy souls. Farewell in Christ!" (ICUR, IV, 12566)
>
> "To the most beloved husband Alexius, a most sweet soul, lector in the title of Fullonica. He lived with me for fifteen years. He was united with me in marriage at the age of sixteen. Virgin to a virgin from whom I never had any grief. Rest in peace with the Saints, with whom you have deserved (to live). Buried on 15th December." (ICUR, IV, 11798)
>
> "To Stephen and Generosa, most sweet parents, who lived long without ever quarrelling. The most unhappy Drusus made this tomb for the finest of parents." (ICUR, III, 9170)[15]

No one should doubt, then, that the Reformation's reversal of publicly articulated values—with respect to celibacy and the order of "perfection," led most persuasively and iconically by Luther himself—represented an ecclesial revolution of sorts.[16] In an instant, quite literally, marriage and child-rearing became, among Protestants, an ultimate Christian virtue within the temporal existence of human creatures. This open claim was certainly experienced as revolutionary, as it touched the lives of thousands of priests and then particularly of monastics, not only among those who left their cloisters in droves but among the many who were forcibly driven out and hardly without cruel pain. But it is also true that this grand reversal was deeply powerful precisely because it bespoke an already existent set of commitments and understandings and certainly lived realities that the culture of monastic perfection had only glossed over within the lives of the church's people. And, arguably, the Reformation's recasting of procreative marriage back into the center of human Christian existence had as its ultimate consequence the Catholic Church's own final shift, in the nineteenth century especially and then into the present, toward a procreative culture (despite the claims to the more perfect life still being made).

Thus, the weight of the Christian claim to male-female procreative existence—the human family, generated from the joined created lives of men and women—simply overturned efforts to limit it. That is a positive historical observation, for which critics of the Christian tradition, explicit and subterranean, who favor a nonprocreative reading of the gospel, need an answer. Certainly, the present culture of sterility is one of a neo-anti-Jovinianism, and rereading that particular controversy is a useful tonic. We might also call the present culture a new Marcionism. (The second-century heretic Marcion infamously considered the bodily fluids, like sperm, to be pure "filth" and the fetus "a repulsive coagulated lump of flesh, nourishing in this same slime for nine months.")[17] Certainly, our present Western culture is related to previous attempts at segregating the Old Testament from the New Testament as well as to modern Christian anti-Judaism of a familiar kind, now couched in the politics of sexuality. Given this contemporary anti-Judaic strain, which also infects many of our churches, we should turn quite explicitly to the Old Testament to see how the generative and genealogical character of life is in fact laid out as bound to its created center, in a way that simply resists the post-AIDS embrace of childlessness. In what now follows, I will try to tease out some questions regarding creation and sexual identity. And in doing this, I will use key texts from Leviticus, as much as an example of a commitment to the proper Christian reading of the entire Scripture—the Old Testament here—as of anything. There are other places one might just as well go, but Leviticus is a wonderfully clear challenge in this regard, and it encourages the kind of larger contextualized reading of Scripture, and of human life, that I have argued is necessary for our faithful thinking about human life.

## Divine Creation, in Its Filiative Mode

In the last chapter, we looked at the mysterious character of life's presentation to the self, as the self. The language of phenomenology proved a useful way to talk about this. Let us now ask what constitutes Scripture's own way of talking about these matters. The traditional Jewish and Christian doctrine of *creatio ex nihilo* (creation out of nothing) is not treated by the Scriptures in any elaborated or focused way and is even somewhat blurred at the opening of Genesis. The teaching is nonetheless present and emerges as a central feature of the scriptural understanding of God. Paul writes that God "calls into existence the things that do not exist" (Rom 4:17), and he ties this aspect of God to God's most glorious work, the resurrection and the "new creation" associated with it (2 Cor 5:17; Gal 6:15). Throughout the Bible, creation stands toward God as that which has no standing apart from God and from God's mercy and gracious will in letting it be at all (cf. Isa 40–48; Ps 104:29-30). At the core of creation's being, in fact of *anything* created, is the reality that it is distinct from God. Indeed, one way of describing "createdness" *is* "distinction." Not only is the creature distinct from God, but since it comes from nothing and is utterly God-derivative, the creature's being arises in a completely *asymmetrical* relationship with God. We can define "life" as that which maintains this asymmetrical relationship; and because it is asymmetrical, it is only God's own self that can give it. So, "distinction" is a biblical way of speaking about fundamental giftedness.

The implications of this kind of asymmetrical distinction in God's creating are enormous. It means first that God, who is "all in all" (1 Cor. 15:28) and the Alpha and the Omega (Rev 22:13; and cf. Isa 48:12), makes something *other* than himself. This is an incomprehensible affirmation, although it is a necessary one. In human terms, God creates space, room, distinction, particularity, difference, and differences—a world apart from what is, in fact and fundamentally, all that there is, God's own self. God lets there be something other than himself, and in so doing God allows an alteration to the *whole* of reality, to the very reality of his own being. There are all kinds of aspects of this claim that deserve theological attention and have received it in spades: the question of Trinitarian "difference" in the actual life of God understood "apart from" creation and its relation to difference in creaturely terms—God's relationship with "metaphysical possibility" and action itself. I do not think it mistaken, however, simply to speak of creation as a miracle, not only from the perspective of historical consciousness (which is the kind of conundrum that touches upon issues of evolution). Far more profoundly, creation is a "miracle" in a metaphysically foundational way—the invention of metaphysical possibility as we are able to name this—because it represents God opening himself to what is "not-God," to something that, by all logic and all truth, should not be.

Creation, then, constitutes the most essential "difference" or "distinction" of any conception, and it lies at the root of all things that are not God. In Genesis and elsewhere in the Scriptures, notably Leviticus, this character of distinction that underlies creation is described in terms of "separation," the separation, for instance, of the "lights" (Gen 1:4), the separation of the creatures into clean and unclean (Lev 10:10; Lev 11; Lev 20:25), and the establishment of particularity through "naming" (Gen 2:19-20). For human beings, of course, this fundamental distinction is also given in terms of the male-female difference that is representative of the creative and created otherness that God establishes by placing something over against himself: "she shall be called Woman because she was taken out of Man" (a word that implies a distinction now made from what was once less distinct) (Gen 2:23).[18] Although the "image" and "likeness" that human beings maintain in relation to God has often been attributed to the diversity of the Trinitarian divine reality (Gen 1:26-27), it may also more accurately reflect the creative distinction and separation of being that male and female express from God's own act of bringing into existence. God's name of "I am," only because of this creative work, now implies an "I am not" with respect to something new and other. The world now, from the hand of God, is made up of "this" and "not that," or of "this" and "that," where neither are identical.

## The Historical Character of Life's Embodiment
### *Reconciliation and Fruitfulness*

Before we focus more specifically on the sexual aspects of this reality of created distinction, we can observe some of the ways it plays itself out in the larger scope of God's redemptive love. On the one side, the character of *creatio ex nihilo* means that the lapse *from* distinctive separation of beings is equivalent to the lapse into nothingness. "Dying" is a movement into the erasure of distinctions, and death is the simple reality of disappearance of that which is other than the other things that exist. This dynamic explains, in part, the reason why Leviticus perceives skin disease of the kind described in Leviticus 13–14, mentioned in our first chapter, as an element opposed to God's creative purpose. As the

normal human skin disintegrates, the very texture of created being—
the skin itself—dissolves in its specificity and turns the human body
into an image of something not yet fully formed (hence the comparison
of a leprous person to "raw" meat [Lev 13:14ff.] or to a stillborn infant
[Num 12:12]). To have skin is to be a distinct creature; and to have one's
skin fall apart is to dissolve as a living being. Skinfulness is about being
a living creature. Sin, in this context, is analogously death dealing—it
presses human life into a movement away from created distinction into
"sameness" and "commonality," vis-à-vis all "other" humans and creatures, making them "like the beasts that perish" (Ps 49:12).

We can pursue this line of thinking in terms of sin's opposite. If sin
drives the creature into dissolution—moral and material—that which
is "of God," God's own creative being, drives the creature into new
existence and toward the formation of new existence. This is generally
described in the Bible in terms of "fruitfulness": creative being or existence according to its intrinsic purpose from God is "fruitful." By the
same token, the repair of sin, its lapse into the indistinction of nothingness and death, is a renewal of difference in a way that is fertile and fruitful itself. In scriptural terms, this is called "reconciliation." Christianity
in particular parts ways with many other religions in understanding the
repair of sin not in terms of the disappearance of difference (vs. Gnosticism) but in understanding created distinction as something that does
not bring death but rather embodies in itself the life God invents. The
final fulfillment of all things, according to Paul, is not the "return" (*redi-
tus*) of difference into the undifferentiated Divine Being but rather the
"reconciliation" of all things in "subjection" to God (1 Cor 15:25-28;
Col 1:20). Hence, the nuptial vision of the end of Revelation (chap. 19)
is distinctive and distinguishing both. Subjection, of course, presupposes
difference, and hence reconciliation is the maintenance of created difference, not in a static way, but in a way that "bears fruit." Fruitfulness itself
is one of the marks of reconciliation—the "fruit of the spirit" and the
"fruit of the resurrection" (1 Cor 15:20; Gal 5:22-23). The relationship
of names and naming to this reality bears out the connection: names are
given to new creatures at their birth and becoming; similarly, those who
are redeemed and reconciled to God receive a "new name" (cf. Isa 62:2;
Rev 2:17; 3:12), which marks their existence as "new creations."

It is this larger and more final character of reconciliation that is
reflected within the embodied lives of creatures within time: they are
made for the fruitfulness of procreation and generativity. Hence, God

speaks to the creatures in Genesis and says "Be fruitful and multiply!" (1:22)—and to human creatures in particular—and commands them to do the same with a kind of force (Gen 1:28; 9:7). Much of the Levitical legal material dealing both with human relations and with the animals and plants of the earth is shaped by God's creative purpose for the sake of fruitfulness and multiplication. For instance, the discussions of planting trees and gathering their fruit in Leviticus 19 are drawn in parallel to human sexuality, as the trees are left fallow for several years as an image of "uncircumcision" (19:23). It is an odd locution except as one understands the act of circumcision, with its drawing of "blood" (the "life" of the creature [Lev 17:11; cf. Gen 9:4]), as a sign of deliberate seed giving and fruit bearing. Plants, like human beings, demand the maturity that makes fertility possible; yet fertility is the purpose of growth and maturity. In this context one can explain the prohibition of mixed breeding (Lev 19:19): such failure to live according to distinction means that life itself dissolves through the dead end of sterility.

The distinction between "clean" and "unclean" animals (and concomitant foods) derives from the separating aspect of created life. While the specific purity categorizations given in the Bible remain mysterious in their rationale, the fact of such difference does not represent contrasts in moral conditions. Rather, the distinction between clean and unclean stakes out a world in which Israel learns and lives the truth of difference, for the sake of the world's own life. Declaring all foods "clean" (Mark 7:19) was not so much a repudiation of these differences by Jesus as it was an act of reorienting Israel to this truth and its vivifying purpose. So, the New Testament asserts that food is for the sake of the hungry, moral integrity (the "heart") for the sake of mercy and healing, the Sabbath for the sake of created fulfillment ("made for man" [Mark 2:27]), the Jew for the sake of the Gentile's life and vice versa (Rom 11:11-32), and both for the life of the world (Jesus' own contradiction of the law, for the sake of the law's purpose of life—"cursed is everyone who hangs on a tree" [Gal 3:13]). In this framework, "neither male nor female" (Gal 3:28) is thus given for the sake of the proper or greater fruitfulness of each and both together, their flourishing as "Abraham's seed" (Gal 3:29).

The orientation of the Law to the creative purpose of life itself, then, with all of its differences and distinctions, is precisely what keeps the sexual character of male and female difference so stable in scriptural discussion: food is for life—the life even of the poor and the hungry; sex is also for life, the life of children. In both cases, this life comes into being through the suffering of difference for the sake of new life—that is, through love itself. Such suffering of difference for life is at the root of all refracted images of love within the world of space and time. This includes, even, God's love in creating anything at all and in "sending his Son": "God so loved the world that He gave His only Son" (John 3:16). God's love is a suffering love because God first made that which could be loved and love in return; he made, that is, something distinct and other than God. It is probably mistaken to inject this dynamic into the Trinitarian life of God, as if God is "distinctive" to himself (although internal "generation" has been attributed to the Godhead in just this way, not unreasonably). "God is love," we are told; but we are also told: "this is love, not that we loved God, but that God loved us and sent His Son"(1 John 4:10). Hence, divine love (which is what love is, John says) is that self-movement out from God toward that which is other than God.

Similarly, Paul draws into sacramental comparison the great image of the Bible for God's love as a creative love: human marriage between a man and a woman. The comparison is based on the utter distinction of Christ and the church, for which Christ gives his life as for "his own body," a body that is "his" based on the sexually rendered unity visible in the marriage of male and female (Eph 5:21-33). The oneness between the two, their "identity," is actually founded on their distinction that is suffered in a certain way and direction. The shape of this love is death itself—a life given for another life (cf. Rom 5:7ff.; John 15:13). But this gift is not simply a principle of action or an ascetic experience; it is for the sake of new life. And the death experienced is thereby never final. Indeed, it is a death that derives from the suffering of difference in love—the Righteous for the Unrighteous, God for the Ungodly (1 Pet 3:18; Rom 5:6)—that marks the extreme distance taken by creation itself vis-à-vis God. Male and female, in their sexual coupling as "one flesh," is the human embodiment of such love. Furthermore, this love bears fruit. "For unless a grain of wheat falls into the earth and dies, it remains alone; but if it dies, it bears much fruit" (John 12:24).

It would be wrong, therefore, to equate the distinction of male and female with the distinction of clean and unclean as both being matters that are somehow "overcome" by the New Law or the gospel brought by Jesus. For the issue is not distinction itself, which is bound up with the very relationship of God to his creation; it is rather with the context in which distinction is properly oriented toward the creation and sustenance of new life. The distinction that undergirds creation remains affirmed in the gospel, and distinction's reconciled character is precisely that which gives life, and the giving of life that created distinction provides is that which represents its reconciling power. When Jesus speaks of the life of the resurrected as "neither married nor given in marriage" (Mark 12:25), the point here is not the disappearance of male and female particularities—any more than when Paul speaks of there being "neither male nor female in Christ Jesus" (Gal 3:28). Distinction remains, as when we hear of the voices of "many tongues and peoples" praising God (Rev 7:9ff.): they now work together, not against each other, as did Cain and Abel, and the very nations of the world and Israel, until Jesus "brought those who were far near" (Eph 2:13). Just so the "wolf shall dwell with the lamb" (Isa 11:6), not because wolves and lambs are not different in their heavenly or eschatological transfiguration, but because their difference is now one that bears the fruit of peace, God's creative intention from before time.[19] It is *as* lambs and lions that true life is lived. Hence, the differences of creation do not stand as a metaphor for a principle. Rather, the differences are exactly those things and forms by and within which the particular life-creating work of God is given.

Reconciliation and "new creation," therefore, are not matters of new or reordered couplings, both physical and moral. They are matters of couplings whose procreative force—unlike the mule—is now unleashed in the power of love.

## Defining Fruitfulness in Terms of Filiation

It is now possible to place the explicit prohibitions of certain kinds of sex found in the Bible within their textual location, as informed by this broader understanding of creative existence, distinction, and fruitfulness—all of which describe the very reality of divine love. The argument is often made, for instance, that the Bible's attention to homosexuality (e.g., Lev 19:22; 20:13) is, even if accepted as such (and most scholars now do), extremely limited in extent. Thus, one might rightly wonder how the topic could take on such an important role in current debate and prove such a scandal among our churches' common life. For some, it seems as if this focus elevates a minor scriptural concern out of some kind of irrational fear. But we can no more dismiss Scripture's and Judeo-Christian tradition's sexual concerns here than we can allow a modern compassion toward the suffering of battered selves to lessen our concern over suicide and euthanasia. For the argument just outlined above is one that must necessarily heighten the importance of homosexuality as a religious stumbling block because it places its scandal smack in the middle of one of the central claims of the Christian faith: *creatio ex nihilo* as the act of love that manifests God's true being. We can see this by briefly noting three discussions of sexual life that are prominent in Scripture, all from Leviticus, wherein the reality of homosexual acts must necessarily prove problematic and even—as the text itself states—contrary to the nature of God. All three examples touch on the reality of generative genealogy.

### Bodily Fluids (Leviticus 15; cf. Leviticus 12)

These texts have long been the source of a certain prurient humor (and they were, in the nineteenth century, often printed in Latin, even within English Bibles, because of their potential for stimulating undue interest among the curious young). From Calvin on, there has been an explicit perplexity over the fact that Scripture's Law is so focused on bodily fluids, at least in this book, which is almost ignored in modern life. Within the category of bodily fluid, of course, we find not only a woman's menstrual flow but male semen, the fluids of childbirth, and finally blood itself. This last provides the clue to the entire category's meaning: "blood is life," we are told, and it is so in a kind of primordially creative way (Gen 9:4; Lev 17:11). Blood marks the reality and also the giftedness of life as coming from the hands of God, and therefore blood's spilling upon the ground and seeping away represents (and is in fact) the dissolution of existence that is God's alone to give and take. (This connects to the later question we examined regarding divine "proprietary" ownership of human life.) In this light, Abel's blood, "crying from the ground" to God (Gen 4:10), gives voice to life's own passing, in this case at the willful hands of a rebel creature, turning against his own being, Abel's blood brother.

The "uncleanness" associated with bodily fluids in the Law derives from this reality of creaturely existence dependent upon God's own will and love. The loss of fluids upon the ground, flowing outside the body, displays the limitedness of life itself, and it reveals the strange fragility of its continuance as something at God's command. Indeed, life's continuance is tied to a certain form of fluidic continence or containment within the flesh and among the bearers of flesh. The flowing of the body's inner liquids—and semen was, from a male's point of view, related to blood in its life-giving and procreative force—constitutes the functioning of life; the outflow of these fluids is the risk of life's creative purpose, ever bound up with its created mortality. The wasted outflow, finally, is just that—a throwing away of what is precious enough only to be expended in love. "Waste" in this context is specifically located. Even the leper's sores, "running" with the fluids of a human body's life, stand as a slow wasting away. But so too does the loss of fluid during the sexual act (and by implication, in deliberated autostimulation or coitus interruptus). All these wasted outflows partake of death, even as they ironically, if briefly, luxuriate in the flow of life. Water itself, as a source of life (not of hygiene, in any medical sense), is fundamental to the scriptural outlook, even while later developments in the Christian West eventually came to view water as a source of danger and disease, to the point, as we know, of some cultures, like France's, for five hundred years avoiding bathing altogether, at least from a medical point of view.[20]

There is no question but that homosexual sex is problematic in this fluidic context. Among homosexual males, the fluids of the body are at best expended, in a focused way, on what cannot, intrinsically, receive and give birth. Among homosexual women, the cycles of the inner flow of life take place without ever being granted their interior engagement with the sources of procreative offering given by the male, and the menstrual outflow takes place, so to speak, in the loneliness of purposeless expenditure—the dissolution of life. While one may well identify, in the sexual acts of both cases, experienced feelings of affection among partners, as few would deny, such affection is intrinsically unequal to the risking love of God's own creative self-offering given over to that which is other than himself. Such divine love, Scripture repeatedly reminds us, is in fact given within the specific interactions of distinct sexual beings, male and female. It is given over for the life of a creature, a life intrinsically mortal because not God's own, and thus a life that is permeated with risk simply by being a creaturely life at all.

Before the Great Transition, this was all well known: mothers died in childbirth or during pregnancy, babies died then or later, and fathers, in their own way, faced the onslaught of mortal threat at every turn. To procreate was, quite simply, fraught with danger, but with a danger that was bound to life's giftedness itself. In this context, the potential of sterility in human heterosexual union, by contrast, is not a contradiction of life in the same way as embraced sterility. Sterility is in fact an expression of the ever-present power or potential of the creature, made by God, to display its own origin, simply because it is "other" than God. Sterility in heterosexual couples marks their limit from God and constitutes the creature's finiteness, mortality, and freedom bound up as one. Yet a sterile coupling of male and female is still love, and not sin, because such unions *risk* procreative generation from the start, which is the very nature of creative love.

### Genealogy: Sex and Heritage

Much of the Law's sexual injunctions are either explained by or wholly bound up with lines of relationship along which intercourse is permitted (cf. Lev 18 and 20:10ff.). The degrees of permitted consanguinity—later elaborated and often altered in the Christian West—and the areas of prohibited familial sexual liaison are matters of intense interest to the Law. As with the scriptural focus on bodily fluids, post-Transition readers are often puzzled as to why. Modern social-political analysis has generally explained the Bible's interest in who can marry whom in terms of the control of property along identifiable and limited lines. And there is truth in this explanation. But the reasons for exercising control over the channels of heritage derive from the ordering and hence support of families and their offspring and generations. "From generation to generation" is the expression of the power of creative filiation-in-fruitfulness to sustain itself through God's grace. And the scriptural definition of relational rights, honors, and prohibitions, given in terms of distinctions and differentiations, speaks to the provision of procreative stability and even abundance. Genealogy, within Scripture, is a sacred icon of divine creation and its purpose in time. Hence genealogy initiates the entire gospel of Jesus Christ (Matt 1:1ff.). That the genealogy of human salvation, in both Matthew and Luke, proceeds from the insertion of the God-Man into the human chain of generation by a kind of sui generis miracle, however, does not deny the inevitability of the chain itself. Rather, it submits the miracle to filiated reach of God's creation.

Confused, broken, or, in some cases, nonheterosexual sex is most clearly something that stands outside the dynamic of scripturally defined heritage. Sterility, as a *natural* function rather than the challenge met within a risk of love, undercuts the architecture of human history as embodied in the Savior's lineage—which is to say, it undercuts the purposes of God "from before the foundation of the world" (John 17:24; Eph 1:4; Rev 13:8). It is true that there are today technical means by which, for instance, homosexuals can provide the physical components necessary to human generation within a medical process involving several persons. The fact that children of such techniques are still born of a distinct mother and father, but have had that reality masked and in some cases wiped away from record, ought to be a deeply troubling permission and practice within modern societies, for it constitutes a deformation of life's own shape. Even more so is the possibility of multiply parented embryos, which some governments have now permitted. The adult individuals involved, after all, cannot either conceive or give birth to children as partners. They do so, essentially, as "uncoupled" individuals, for whom the risk of creation, which is bound up with the nature of divine love, is excluded as an intrinsic element of action. The result is that there are no homosexual genealogies of an integral sort, unless heterosexual coupling intervenes. Yet even Jesus takes as his bride the church—and from this union are many "children" (Rev 21:2). It is this heritage through which the nations are brought to Zion, and the courts of heaven are filled (Isa 66:7-11; Ps 128).

Furthermore, we should note that Leviticus and the Law as a whole are deliberately sensitive to the reality of childlessness but that they place this experience within the genealogical framework by offering means of sustaining it through adoption or other familial adjustments. Genealogy, then, is not *simply* biological, as advocates of adoption rightly note. Genealogy is also about ordering the human community's transfer of life in familial ways that are bound to one another coherently. Indeed, the "virgin birth," and Jesus' adoption by Joseph into his lineage, and the notion of "adoption" in Christ as its parallel for us, represent the way that this kind of generativity turns back to the ex nihilo character of fruitfulness in the first place, whose absolute ground is divine grace. This hardly makes adoption a norm, however, as some Christian advocates of same-sex marriage assert; rather it underlines the way that natural genealogy is itself always supernatural, always intrinsically gracious. And it explains why marriage itself—although it can be explained in covenantal terms as a humanly initiated act (two persons exchanging vows)—can never be reduced essentially to a matter of human covenantal willing (again, as some advocates of same-sex marriage insist). In marriage, two people are given to one another, as God gave Adam to Eve and vice versa in Eden. Each is thus a "gift," ordered to the divine act of gift giving (progeny), for which no humanly grasped covenant can ever prove adequate.

As we have argued, the divine purpose of fruitfulness, while it extends far beyond the physical forms of procreation, is embodied necessarily within these forms. The mortal aspects of any created fruit, furthermore, are also embodied in just these physical forms, simply because these are the forms in which God gives life and takes it away. Hence, the family, in Scripture and the Christian tradition (and even despite the byways of monastic celibacy and its valorization), has proved a central basis for the metaphors of spiritual formation. The family, in fact, has proven to be the actual realm of spiritual formation's enactment (e.g., Col 3:18ff.; 2 Tim 1:5; even 1 Cor 7:14 on the inestimable gift of sanctifying children). It is not the case that a morally more basic ascetical premise makes use of marriage as a metaphor. Rather, scripturally speaking, all metaphors move out from the existential fact of human marriage. Hence, marriage itself is never simply about two persons, understood apart from the families from which they come and to which they are given over; rather, two people derive, in their creative being, from the lived reality of marriage.

### Jubilee and the Social Sustenance of Heritage as Genealogical Justice

One of the favorite texts of Christians interested in the political reordering of social life according to defined principles of justice is chapter 25 of Leviticus, with its injunctions regarding the sabbatical years and the Jubilee. Little is said in this Levitical text that touches upon sexual relations. In fact, this is one of the arguments of those seeking to marginalize traditional Christian teaching on sexuality: the important biblical demands of moral justice from the Old Testament (embodied in the Jubilee, and perhaps bound to Luke 4:16ff.) that still impose themselves upon Christians simply do not include worries over sexual behavior.

But, to take the Jubilee texts as a case in point, the concerns over the regular "return" of property and land every fifty years, as well as the forgiveness of debts, are all carefully intertwined with the character of family and heritage, which the book as a whole has intricately laid out. Jubilee is not about justice "in general." Instead, Jubilee represents the "justice of genealogy" in particular, whereby the maintenance of family resources can be renewed at least every fifty years, for the sake of continued fruitfulness. In fact, fruitfulness stands at the center of the Jubilee regulations, since Israel is asked to live off the divine provision of the fields for two years running, that of the sabbatical year and that of the Jubilee Year. This marks an experienced submission to the fertile creativity of God's own love, embodied in the land itself and in his choice of Israel. Like marriage and its risk of procreation, the Jubilee year constitutes the procreative risk of Israel in her relationship with God, the outcome of which is given in the reassertion of the human family's solidarity and historical continuance.

The argument from justice, at least with respect to the Jubilee, simply cannot assimilate alternative sexual patterns in this case. If anything, the Jubilee commands point to a kind of social imperative through which justice is at least partially defined in terms of its support for generative family life, wherein parents, children, and descendants are held together in a clear legal and divinely provided fashion. Filiation here is granted a divinely legal basis. Similarly, any of the injunctions in Leviticus 19, often viewed as the center of the righteous demands of holiness, make sense, not on the basis of an abstract justice, but on the basis of the specific needs of families and the responsibilities due them. The extraction of the Jubilee, by some theologians, from its Levitical context constitutes a profound scriptural distortion.

It is true that the Transition has inevitably blurred these contextual meanings of Leviticus. Some modern historical critics, constrained by the experiential marginalization of mortality, have thus found it more plausible to assign Levitical concerns with procreation and genealogy to earlier agrarian patterns of economy. The biblical texts, in these kinds of readings, become exemplars of social stages of development. In fact, though, the New Testament is fully consistent with Leviticus on these matters. The suffering love of fruitful self-offering within created distinction is fully epitomized in the incarnation itself, according to the New Testament, and, in this, the "fruitful" demands of genealogy are extended, not set aside. So we begin to see, in the course of the development of the New Testament's understanding of the human creature in light of Christ Jesus, the ways that slavery is as much an assault on created life as is homosexual behavior (which cannot inherit the kingdom of God [1 Cor 6:9]): the slave, it turns out, is in reality a family member (a "brother" [Phlm 16]); and the practice of slavery is a destruction of the human soul (Rev 18:13) that is the root of created life—that is, it is murder, in the same manner as Cain's murder of Abel, the spilling of blood upon the ground and the consignment of bodily fluid to uselessness.

Jesus and the New Testament in fact continue to stress the embodiment of love's self-offering in family as the expression of created life: children are healed on behalf of and in response to the love of parents (Mark 9:14ff.; Luke 7:11ff.); salvation is given to whole families and households (Acts 16:33-34); households are themselves ordered for the sake of divine love's receipt and demonstration (Eph 5:21–6:9); and all of these kinds of particular implications of the fruitfulness that flows from the risk of reconciled distinction finally give way to eschatological fruitfulness and the fullness of the kingdom (neither taken nor given in marriage, as in Mark 12:25) of the pure bride (Eph 5:26-27; Rev 19:8). The character of the "true family" ("who is my mother?" [Matt 12:48]) lies not in the dissolving of families but in suffering their bonds for the sake of love. Without this ground of familial genealogical constraint, there would be no meaning to the moral struggle involved against turning back to bury one's father (Luke 9:60), the pain of a faith that ends by dividing families (Matt 10:35), or the horror of those who betray their own blood relations (Luke 21:16). None of these would *hurt* were it not for their fundamental stability, whose breaking up floods them with life, not with the relationships' disappearance.

Unveiled in the New Testament wrestling with procreative genealogy, of course, is the cost of true fruitfulness that goes even beyond human families and that touches the very reality of God's self: the Father has a Son, and the Father "gives up" the Son through the Spirit. There would be no sacrifice without the love assaulted by such a gift. Only thus is abundant life established as the foundation of the world.

In all three of the scriptural topics noted above—fluids, genealogy, and the justice of genealogy in Jubilee—we see how nonheterosexual, nonparentally tethered, and unstable partnerships whose procreative directions are either stymied or disoriented are unassimilable within the scriptural description of God's creative purpose. They are, in a Thomistic sense, "unfitting." Even apart from any explicit discussion of homosexual behavior, this fact appears obvious; and given the few explicit references to such behavior, their brief articulation when it *does* occur can be seen not as arbitrary but rather as expressive of a necessary (if not always dominant) aspect of human life as "creature." There is no way of arguing otherwise except by rendering the coherence of Scripture itself fictive and by divorcing the knowledge and discussion of God as "Creator of Heaven and Earth" from the Scriptures altogether. The deep unease that many Christians feel over post-Transition-constructed sexuality, thus, is partly tied to the sense that it does indeed constitute a kind of attack upon Scripture itself in its foundational authority for the created world's order.

Describing nonheterosexual, nonparentally tethered, and unstable unions as "unassimilable," rather than simply "prohibited," is an important choice of terms here. For it is not immediately clear how the "sin" of this kind of sex may or may not differ from other related frustrations of God's creative will. These frustrations could take the form of physical infertility among heterosexual couples, the choice or circumstance of singleness and celibacy, masturbation, or other nonprocreative ways of living and engaging sexuality. Furthermore, we are well aware of virtues that are and have been embodied in homosexual love and partnerships—devotion, care, even sacrificial self-offering. This was one of the great unveilings of the AIDS pandemic, so powerful as to disorient hitherto common assumptions. But sacrifice is not a general principle, and it comes in many forms. It is the nature of creative risk that it be bound to the character of differentiated fruitfulness and hence mortality. This is how Scripture consistently presents the sacrificial character of procreative filiation in particular. It is in this sense that nonheterosexual coupling is *not intrinsically orderable* within the scriptural form of created life.[21] That is to say, although much is mysterious about the scriptural form of male-female sexual life, homosexual relationships cannot be positively adjudicated publicly within the grid of God's will for the church within the world, as revealed in Scripture and in the tradition of the church's reflective and prayerful life.

We have not been given a divine creative grammar—including that grammar's propositional content—through which to make sense of such divergent forms of relationship as nonprocreative filiation. The biblical discussions of "marriage," as everyone agrees, testify to this lack: God talks about marriage a good deal in the Bible (perhaps more than about any other human relationship), with an exclusivity that is disconcerting to present preoccupations. Polyamorous or homosexual relationships are, quantitatively, abnormal to this discussion; they remain culturally "odd" and "strange" to the society of the body in which God has called us as we understand and experience our existences, both individual, relational, and corporate. Thereby, these nonheterosexual couplings are also some-how "foreign" to the origins and meanings of marriage as these are given in the creation framework of Scripture. God simply has not given us the tools, scripturally, to take the phenomena of nonprocreative, nonhetero-sexual marital relationships and to distill them into some set of least common-denominator principles or realities that can then be compared with other recognizable goods of the church. For if the Bible *has* given us principles by which to approach our sexuality—and the word "principle" is one, I believe, that is misleading to scriptural theology in general—they are all expressive of a creative fruitfulness in risking differentiation that has no logical room for nonprocreative filiation, precisely because it is about the fruitfulness of life in a very particular way. While vows of celibacy may be celebrated in the church, infertile marriages never have been, nor should they be. They are suffered—and their suffering is virtuous, holy, and, in one sense, a participant in the redeeming work of the cross, which itself is a reality "bearing much fruit." The signs of Abraham and Sarah—and of many others like them afterward, not to mention the virgin childbirth of Mary, with all of its fluidic outpourings—are demonstrations of this redemptive suffering, whereby the actual risk of loss in the offering of procreative liquid is granted divine blessing. But the sterility or parental/genealogical confusion of other kinds of unions does not fit this form, because their condition is intrinsically directed toward infertility or genealogical disruption and chosen on that basis.

## Filiative Creation as a Concrete Reality

We should be clear that the present argument regarding sexuality as derived "from creation" is not an argument based simply on natural signs and biology. It is not as if "looking" at the shape of the human body, or analyzing patterns of sexual intercourse among animals, or tabulating statistics on the social correlations of differing forms of sexual activity could, in themselves, demonstrate the "way we are made to be" by God or "should be."[22] Just as the practice of reducing suicide to the observed social patterns of life ending is ultimately a barbaric response to suicide's reality, so too is the reduction of human sexuality to an encyclopedia of human practices. However interesting such exercises may be, they do not cohere with the character of life as it is contextually lived within the Adamic movement of skinful wandering. As Michel Henry argues, the "statistics" of the scientist tell us nothing about the actual character of "life," something that can be gotten at only as it is lived by this or that person. But just because of this, human life can never be simply about "nature" in general, as if we could look at a world, fallen in many basic ways, and pick and choose those aspects that we see that affirm our sense of God's will (or our own). Thus, it cannot be the case that the experience of this or that "inclination" or attraction could be defined as "natural" simply "because it is there." For this particular element that "is there" is one that one *chooses*, for any number of reasons, to signal out. It is too often a personal choice that determines what we consider "natural." Instead, any argument "from creation," in a Christian sense, is first of all about the shape of God's own nature and historical will, which is revealed in the forms of Scripture.

Arguments "from nature" or from sociology on the question of sexuality are misleading, unless subjected to the scriptural figures of created existence. Such arguments "from nature" often end up by elevating abstractions and essences that are descriptively alien to Scripture and hence to the rich substance of created human life. These abstractions include the notion of "complementarity" between males and females in psychophysiology. Some Catholic and Evangelical theologians and ethicists have claimed to be able to extract the principle of complementarity from the Bible itself, even though the whole conceptual framework of this kind of discussion is absent from the scriptural texts that talk about creation and about men and women in particular. "Complementarity" as a term that simply means two different things going together is one thing, and certainly a quality that describes the creation of men and women in a broad way. But apart from the basic action of procreative filiation, the term cannot gain a consistent particularity of definition, nor should it. We find out what women and men are by living through the fortunes of their coupled filiation through time. This is something that is described in the Scriptures, but the scriptural account does not constitute a genetic blueprint of sex-based personality types and capacities.

It *is* possible, to be sure, that there may be a natural symbolization to the kind of intrinsic orderability heterosexual marriage offers, in contrast to other forms of partnership. And it is indeed here that the procreative risk of heterosexual marriage comes to the fore. We should not disregard the historical fact that a unique social scaffolding is provided to marriage, despite its range of cultural expression, through the normal concomitance of biological children. The historical reality is that children are not "asked for" in marriage—and here the *Pirke Avot*'s claims about individuals, formed, born, grown, dying "perforce" by God, apply to their parental conception—but instead "given" through the miraculous effects of sexual coupling, which mirror an entire range of extraordinary life. Unasked for, yet given according to grace, this reality of filiation mirrors the inexplicable order marriage presses upon the church, and through her, upon the world, through God's gracious and mysterious provision that is most fully embodied in the gift of the incarnate Word, even unto death on the cross.

Creation, then, is shaped in its particularities by difference, by the cost of difference, and by its own fertile sustenance through the ongoing risk of distinction, which is governed entirely by the grace of God's creation. Understood in this sense is the ground within which the love of God emerges and takes hold of all things. Creative distinction and its suffering, however, are not "principles" but the *actual material of salvation's form.* Hence, the "moral" life of families, apprehended and experienced in its framework of male-female coupling and procreation, is a universal command and grace, insofar as humankind—Adam—has populated the earth. Generation *is* a part of the skinfulness of human life. It is not an add-on that arose from the aleatory encounters of a human species drifting through time.

As human creatures, we are *something*, something distinct, and something peculiar. Donne, in one of his great sermons,[23] notes how so many of us wander through our lives as if we are "nothings," without distinctiveness, and thus without calling to the distinctive time and place of our life within the one "Body" that is God's "universal creature":

> [T]hou commest from him [God] into this world, as though he had said nothing to thee at parting, but go and do as thou shalt see cause, go and do as thou seest other men do, and serve me so far, and save thine own soul so far, as the times, and the places, and the persons, with whom thou doest converse, will conveniently admit. Gods way is positive, and thine is privative: God made every thing something, and thou mak'st the best of things, man, nothing; and because thou canst not annihilate the world altogether, as though thou hadst God at an advantage, in having made an abridgment of the world in man, there in that abridgment thou wilt undermine him, and make man, man, as far as thou canst, man in thyself nothing.

Donne wonders how it could be possible that God created us with no distinctive purpose and hence without distinction at all. It is, he says, inconceivable that the whole of the universe's being, utterly at God's disposal to bring into being or not, should be so vague as to lack any particular order:

> [A]s though that God who when he was pleased to come to a creation, might yet have left thee where thou wast before, amongst privations, a nothing; or if he would have made thee something, a creature, yet he might have shut thee up in the closs prison of a bare being and no more, without life or sense, as he hath done earth and stones; or if he would have given thee life and sense, he might have left thee a toad, without the comeliness of shape, without that reasonable and immortal soul, which makes thee a man.

God might have left us as a toad. Yet a toad is not a man! While this is a matter of nature, we say, it is more basically a matter of God's grace, not wielded against toads and insects, sheep and trees. It is rather a matter of this particular grace that is the ordering of a human life in such and such a way, while ordering others in this or that way, separating and arranging each. This is Scripture's reach, which happily embraces the leaping frogs of Exodus as much as all other creatures, yet so that they might remain the particular creatures of his mercy.

"Particular," however, does not mean autonomous or solitary and unrelated. Part of God's creative mercy is given in the procreative filiation that is peculiar to human beings, and it is in the network of this filiated dynamic that the particular human creature exists as such. We can take as a striking example of this the case of child killing. One of the strange realities of the human history of infanticide is the way that it was rarely treated, even in Christian contexts, on the basis of seeing the children involved simply as individual beings. Indeed, children rarely had stand-alone "rights" as they do today and even as various adult individuals did in the past. But infanticide has nonetheless proven a universal and persistent tragedy (and usually a crime of sorts). As with suicide, evidence for particular rates and experiences in this or that period and culture is rare until the modern epoch, and even more recently the reality is subject to much deliberate misdocumentation. But what is interesting is how, despite intense disapproval, the killing of one's own children has been subject to conflicted and often deliberately self-limited responses. The causes of infanticide, especially at the hands of mothers (and it is almost always infant children involved), seem to be consistent to the present:[24] a mother's shame, for example, at illegitimacy; her isolation, desperation, feelings of revenge, jealousy; her poverty; and some psychiatric issues (debated, especially those around parturition and lactation). These causes, furthermore, have been generally acknowledged by societies and authorities across time. But they have also often elicited a kind of leniency that seems to fit poorly with the deep repugnance most cultures have felt in the face of child murder. Finally, this leniency seems to have grown in official terms, certainly since the eighteenth century— that is, until very recently. The conjunction of repulsion and leniency is puzzling.

The reason for the conjunction, however, goes to the character of procreative filiation itself. Infanticide in the past, as well as its highly inconsistent response, was never evaluated simply in terms of the child's self. It was, in fact, better understood within a different set of *ramified* familial relations, bound to creaturely life itself. The fact that a child was a part of some larger familial set of bonds was part of the reason that responses to infanticide were far more nuanced than one might expect. It is possible that children gained a new standing, vis-à-vis late antique culture, within the Christian church's anthropology; hence, their status as "en-souled" creatures became authoritative by the fourth century. But this contrast between Christian and pagan attitudes is debated. Less contested, though, is the change that took place in Christian culture with respect to children's family *relationships*: all historians note how novel was the responsibility that Christian parents took for the formation of their children in morals and faith, for instance, and for the integrity of their future lives. Children were deliberately nurtured by parents so that they did *not* become the drifting "nothings" of Donne's description. This linking of generations in common duty for particular creative purpose also rendered the child, not a simple individual, but a player within the genealogical train of grace. Life is not just a person, in this view, but a person whose subjecthood is wholly enmeshed with others in filiative engagement.

Even as our contemporary culture struggles unsuccessfully to support this deep insight, it has nonetheless begun to understand that we are constituted as persons only to the degree that we are also persons in relation to an "other," another person whom we face. What is less obvious to modern culture, however, is that this "other" is not just someone exterior to my being, with whom I have to do, but that, as Christian (and Jewish) religious claims make clear, this "other" person is the other-who-is-my-being, who is part-of-my-flesh. Hence, a prominent Jewish interpretation of Genesis 2:24—"they shall be one flesh"—reads the text not only in terms of two persons who are joined but in terms of two persons whose joining generates a third, another person that proceeds from them. That the man and the woman become "one flesh," according to Rashi on the Talmudic tract *Sanhedrin* 58a, refers to the *child*, not to their own marriage and sexual act (these are presupposed). The man and the woman become one, not in the sexual act itself, but in the fact that this act *gives rise* to the "one flesh" that is the new human life that they generate. In this case, we must understand that the character of sexuality, in its marital orientation, is *always* triadic, even if that triad is only a hovering presence (or absence). The modern notion that sex is about "what two people do" is thus fundamentally mistaken, and destructively so, unless what they do is bound to generation.

Modern Christian theologians have been slow to pick up on this dynamic (although Jean-Luc Marion has embraced Rashi's interpretation).[25] Instead, the cultural press of human recognition for children moved in the direction of granting them increased "rights" as individuals. This provided the basis, thankfully, for ever-growing interest in children's welfare and for their legal protections. (Oddly enough, though, violence among children and perpetrated upon them in developed countries like the United States—including adolescent suicide—has steadily increased over recent years.) But the development of "children's rights" has also had the effect of disengaging children from their filiated identity.[26] The "rights" of children in Western societies today pertain to their individual persons, not to their familial relationships. Indeed, in many contemporary social settings, parents have become presumptively suspected agents of violence, before they are assumed to be bound by "one flesh." And hence children do *not* have a right to a father and mother, preferably their own (nor do parents have that reciprocal duty in any comprehensive way), in societies moving to embrace alternative parenting arrangements. Yet such relationships are bound up in the parents' and children's identity as creatures who are born, one flesh from two flesh, and who, in turn, become fruitful.[27] Created mortality is characterized by filiative fruitfulness; the two cannot be separated. The haunting and now famous story of Danilo Kiš, "The Encyclopedia of the Dead," describes this with a kind of awesome horror: Kiš imagines a project to record every single human death since the French Revolution, one in which the volumes for a single letter become seemingly innumerable.[28]

In the Great Transition, the entire filiative breadth of human creaturehood has become obscured, even as the means of procreation have become, as it were, technologically facilitated. As the sociologist Paul Yonnet has argued, the essential giftedness of life has today become instead the product of human will: children are conceived, brought to term, and then given life in the world, according to schedules and means ordered by the parents, and not necessarily through the physical engagement of the biological mother and father of the child. Thus, to be a child is now legally defined by being "desired" rather than by being "given."[29] This shift is critical and deeply subversive of fundamental Christian truths of creaturehood, which, because they are defined by the quality of mortality, are ever bound to the divine gift. For in fact "desire," by this or that adult or parent—or desirability—can never define a child's life and the filiated realities and responsibilities built into it. "The Lord gave, and the Lord hath taken away," Job says (2:21), stating the character of human life precisely in the face of the way its constituted reality supervenes upon human desire. This supervention is the experience that lays out Job's transformative engagement with God. But if human existence is indeed filiated in this sense, it only shows, as Yonnet argues forcefully, that a culture that is ordered around "desirability" must always crumble in the face of actual human life, a life always given, and given out, lived with as given, and let go of as such.

The point of human life is not just to produce babies, of course, but to order life itself within the limits of its created form. And procreation is not, of course, the central "theme" of the Bible. Scripture works figurally, not thematically: the people involved, and their situations, are what is the core of both Scripture and human history. Yet just these people are the people of a procreative genealogy, and this is the net of Scripture's temporal extension. Hence, David and his wives become a key procreative figure: there is the genealogy from David to Christ; but there are also the difficult elements within David's family tree that also emerge as figures of life, of its vulnerability, and of its threats. Modern readers of the Bible often misunderstand this and see David's behavior as proof of Scripture's inconsistency and of the church's bad faith in picking and choosing which elements of human behavior depicted in the Bible it likes. There is, however, neither inconsistency nor bad faith involved: the figures of David's life hover over all human existence as both threat and context, as it moves into Christ. The fullness of experienced, not abstracted, promise requires this.

From these figures, synagogue and church have been able to identify elements whose ordering of life is fit within the pressures of creaturehood, for ethics is nothing else than such a living fit within moral life. So, for instance, monogamy becomes a key element in the Jewish and Christian traditions, just as Leviticus itself indicates with its aim for clarity and stability within procreative relationships. The Christian church can "deal with" divorce and so on, not because divorce does not matter, but because God found a way to deal with David; but the judgment upon divorce, as upon other forms of relational life outside of the stable marriage, is also part of the church's dealing, just as judgment's forms emerge within Scripture's display. Historical permission, seen throughout the Scripture's stories, is finally judged scripturally, through the outcome of its people's own genealogy.

In the end, procreative filiation carries along with it the order of human temporal existence. And since that order is scripturally rendered, we can follow it along to see who we are. The scriptural order of procreative filiation takes in Hagar and David, plagues and wars, technologies and cultures, AIDS and mourning. The great Christian poet Charles Péguy, killed in World War I while still a young father, wrote at length about the "holy innocents," those children murdered at Herod's command when Jesus was born, in an attempt to rid Palestine of a potential rival messiah (Matt 2:16). To be an "innocent" in this case, Péguy claims, is to be a human being "not yet" molded by the sorrows and sins of the world; hence, to be an "innocent" is to be "simply" a human being. To look at these young children slaughtered in Bethlehem, then, is to see "who we are" in some kind of unadorned reality. So Péguy writes of them, taking God's voice, comparing them to other saints and martyrs:

> [These children, who] alone could sing that new song, what had
>     they done?
> Wonder now at the order of my Grace.
> They had done this, They had come into the world.
> One thing, that is all, or to put it otherwise,
> They had done this, to have been little new-born babies.
> They were a group of little Jewish sucklings.
> Boys and girls.
> Their mothers said as in all countries in the world: Mine is the
>     prettiest.[30]

Generation and genealogy become the perfection of heaven.

# IV

# The Arc of Life

The murdered children of Bethlehem, Péguy wrote, each represent a human being who is "simply" alive. Yet, as Péguy himself acknowledges, there is, in fact, no "simple life," if it is life at all. The "holy innocents" can stand as a kind of foil, conceptually, for what life is meant to be. They can even stand as an image of hope. But in either case, foil or hope, the meaning of these dead children's "innocence" is apparent only in relation to life as it is *actually* lived by most people. And all such actual life is shaped by its temporal passage. Skinfulness presses forward, along a path that, however uncertain, follows to an end that properly determines the passage itself.

Péguy goes on and explains seven reasons why God loves the children of Bethlehem for whom "Rachel weeps" (Matt 1:18). With the last reason, he hints at a kind of subversive reading of all that he has said above. "They remind me of my Son," God says, "[a]s he would have been" had not his own passage to the cross, over those several decades, been accomplished. There is no "Jesus as he would have been," however. It is but a fantasy, and an ultimately hopeless one at that.

> They remind me of my Son.
> As he would have been if he had not changed since then, as he was
>     when he was so beautiful. If that stupendous adventure

Had stopped there. That is why I love them, God says, above all oth-
 ers they are witnesses of my Son.
They show me, they are as he was, if only
He had never changed. Of all the imitations of Jesus Christ
Theirs is the first and it is the freshest; and it is the only one
Which is not in any degree
Which is not even a fraction
Of an imitation of some brand and some bruise and some wound in
 the heart of Jesus.
Theirs is a total ignorance of outrage and affronts,
And of injuries and insults.
They are only aware of murder, and of having been killed, which is
 nothing.
They were never turned to derision.
That is what I love in them, God says. That is why, for what I
 love them.
They are for me children who have never become men.
Lambs who have never become rams.
Or sheep. (And these follow the Lamb wherever he goes).
Infant Christs who will never grow old. Who never grew up.
 While mine grew
in wisdom, and in age and in grace
and in favour with God and man.
I love them innocently, God says. And that is the seventh reason.
(It is thus you must love innocents).
As the father of a family loves his son's friends
Who go to school with him.
But as for them they have not moved since that far-off time.
They are the eternal imitations
Of what Jesus was during a very short time
For he grew, indeed. He grew up
For that enormous adventure.[1]

"Adventure," in today's English, may not rightly translate Péguy's French
of *aventure*. By "adventure" Péguy had in mind the sense of that which
life thrusts upon us, that which "comes" to us, in terms of the unexpected givenness of our histories. The notion of going forward through a
period of time is central to such an adventure, just as it is central to what
a human creature's life must engage.

## The Extended Character of Life in Scriptural Terms

Scripture describes this extended adventure that is human life in several ways. There is first of all the reality of the life span itself that Genesis 1–3 describes:

> [Gen 1:26-29 KJV] And God said, Let us make man in our image, after our likeness: and let them have dominion over the fish of the sea, and over the fowl of the air, and over the cattle, and over all the earth, and over every creeping thing that creepeth upon the earth. So God created man in his [own] image, in the image of God created he him; male and female created he them. And God blessed them, and God said unto them, Be fruitful, and multiply, and replenish the earth, and subdue it: and have dominion over the fish of the sea, and over the fowl of the air, and over every living thing that moveth upon the earth. And God said, Behold, I have given you every herb bearing seed, which [is] upon the face of all the earth, and every tree, in the which [is] the fruit of a tree yielding seed; to you it shall be for meat.

> [Gen 2:21-25 KJV] And the LORD God caused a deep sleep to fall upon Adam, and he slept: and he took one of his ribs, and closed up the flesh instead thereof; And the rib, which the LORD God had taken from man, made he a woman, and brought her unto the man. And Adam said, This [is] now bone of my bones, and flesh of my flesh: she shall be called Woman, because she was taken out of Man. Therefore shall a man leave his father and his mother, and shall cleave unto his wife: and they shall be one flesh. And they were both naked, the man and his wife, and were not ashamed.

> [Gen 3:15-23 KJV] And I will put enmity between thee and the woman, and between thy seed and her seed; it shall bruise thy head, and thou shalt bruise his heel. Unto the woman he said, I will greatly multiply thy sorrow and thy conception; in sorrow thou shalt bring forth children; and thy desire [shall be] to thy husband, and he shall rule over thee. And unto Adam he said, Because thou hast hearkened unto the voice of thy wife, and hast eaten of the tree, of which I commanded thee, saying, Thou shalt not eat of it: cursed [is] the ground for thy sake; in sorrow shalt thou eat [of] it all the days of thy life; Thorns also and thistles shall it bring forth to thee; and thou shalt eat the herb of the field; In the sweat of thy face shalt thou eat bread, till thou return unto the ground; for out of it wast thou taken: for dust thou [art], and unto dust shalt thou return. And Adam called his wife's name Eve; because she was the mother of all living. Unto Adam also and to his wife did the LORD God make coats of skins, and clothed

them. And the LORD God said, Behold, the man is become as one of
us, to know good and evil: and now, lest he put forth his hand, an take
also of the tree of life, and eat, and lie for ever: Therefore the LORD
God sent him forth from the garden of Eden, to till the ground from
whence he was taken.

There is a range of realities here that define the life span: creaturehood
as utter dependence upon God for our being and identity; male/female
distinctions as somehow fundamental to that dependence, origin, and
relationship; sexual relationships (nakedness) as bound up with this
dependence; generation (multiplying) as well as the movement from
family to family, described in terms of leaving parents and joining a new
generative one-fleshedness, whether this is in the coupling or in the children conceived from the coupling. All this is located within the paradise
of Eden's precincts, and does not represent the consequences of sin, as
many in the early Christian tradition supposed.

The Genesis account goes on, however, and expands this vision
through the reality of the first disobedience. The so-called divine "curse"
of Genesis 3:14-19 translates these fundamental aspects of life, including
their sexual components, into a new and more difficult realm. This realm
contains the deep antagonisms and fears of creaturehood, seemingly
shared among all creatures (woman, serpent, and the earth); abusive and
unequal relationships; the toil for survival, binding human beings to the
earth; the afflictive quality of mortality; as well as the divinely gracious
meaning of its suffering (e.g., the skins themselves).

Life span is the extended matrix of creaturehood. Filiative genealogy, however, marks the extending matrix of creaturehood. Genealogy
is implied in the garden with the command to multiply and to leave
parents and join together into one generative and generated flesh. But it
is only explained in chapter 4 and then becomes a central feature of the
first few chapters of Genesis and occasionally at other points in Scripture. The centrality of genealogy is often lost on readers whose focus
on the act of creation obscures the definitive importance of creation's
temporal outworking within the Scripture's discussion. The genealogies
of Genesis actually *name* the process of generation and then extend it
through the ongoing passage of human beings, derived from Adam and
Eve, through history. Thus, the sexual conception, birthing, and raising
of children capture the life span for the whole span of human time. Filiative genealogy becomes the recapitulation of Adam and Eve as history,
with all of its beauties and desperate challenges.

The initial literary genealogy of the Bible follows the blessing and curse of the first human couple. It is filled with toil, survival, conflict, love, grief, bitterness, and struggle:

[Gen 4:1-4, 16-26 KJV] And Adam knew Eve his wife; and she conceived, and bare Cain, and said, I have gotten a man from the LORD. And she again bare his brother Abel. And Abel was a keeper of sheep, but Cain was a tiller of the ground. And in process of time it came to pass, that Cain brought of the fruit of the ground an offering unto the LORD. And Abel, he also brought of the firstlings of his flock and of the fat thereof. And the LORD had respect unto Abel and to his offering. . . . And Cain went out from the presence of the LORD, and dwelt in the land of Nod, on the east of Eden. And Cain knew his wife; and she conceived, and bare Enoch: and he builded a city, and called the name of the city, after the name of his son, Enoch. And unto Enoch was born Irad: and Irad begat Mehujael: and Mehujael begat Methusael: and Methusael begat Lamech. And Lamech took unto him two wives: the name of the one [was] Adah, and the name of the other Zillah. And Adah bare Jabal: he was the father of such as dwell in tents, and [of such as have] cattle. And his brother's name [was] Jubal: he was the father of all such as handle the harp and organ. And Zillah, she also bare Tubalcain, an instructer of every artificer in brass and iron: and the sister of Tubalcain [was] Naamah. And Lamech said unto his wives, Adah and Zillah, Hear my voice; ye wives of Lamech, hearken unto my speech: for I have slain a man to my wounding, and a young man to my hurt. If Cain shall be avenged sevenfold, truly Lamech seventy and sevenfold. And Adam knew his wife again; and she bare a son, and called his name Seth: For God, [said she], hath appointed me another seed instead of Abel, whom Cain slew. And to Seth, to him also there was born a son; and he called his name Enos: then began men to call upon the name of the LORD.

[Gen 5:1-32 KJV] This [is] the book of the generations of Adam. In the day that God created man, in the likeness of God made he him; Male and female created he them; and blessed them, and called their name Adam, in the day when they were created. And Adam lived an hundred and thirty years, and begat [a son] in his own likeness, after his image; and called his name Seth: And the days of Adam after he had begotten Seth were eight hundred years: and he begat sons and daughters: And all the days that Adam lived were nine hundred and thirty years: and he died. And Seth lived an hundred and five years, and begat Enos: And Seth lived after he begat Enos eight hundred and seven years, and begat sons and daughters: And all the days of Seth were nine hundred and twelve years: and he died. And Enos lived ninety years, and begat Cainan: And Enos lived after he begat Cainan eight hundred and fifteen years, and begat sons and daughters: And all the days of Enos were nine hundred and five years: and he died. And Cainan lived seventy years, and begat Mahalaleel: And Cainan lived after he begat Mahalaleel eight hundred and forty years, and begat sons and daughters: And all the days of Cainan were nine hundred and ten years: and he died. And Mahalaleel lived sixty and five years, and begat Jared: And Mahalaleel lived after he begat Jared eight hundred and thirty years, and begat sons and daughters: And all the days of Mahalaleel were eight hundred ninety and five years: and he died. And Jared lived an hundred sixty and two years, and he begat Enoch: And Jared lived after he begat Enoch eight hundred years, and begat sons and daughters: And all the days of Jared were nine hundred sixty and two years: and he died. And Enoch lived sixty and five years, and begat Methuselah: And Enoch walked with God after he begat Methuselah three hundred years, and begat sons and daughters: And all the days of Enoch were three hundred sixty and five years: And Enoch walked with God: and he [was] not; for God took him. And Methuselah lived an hundred eighty and seven years, and begat Lamech: And Methuselah lived after he begat Lamech seven hundred eighty and two years, and begat sons and daughters: And all the days of Methuselah were nine hundred sixty and nine years: and he died. And Lamech lived an hundred eighty and two years, and begat a son: And he called his name Noah, saying, This [same] shall comfort us concerning our work and toil of our hands, because of the ground which the LORD hath cursed. And Lamech lived after he begat Noah five hundred ninety and five years, and begat sons and daughters: And all the days of Lamech were seven hundred seventy and seven years: and he died. And Noah was five hundred years old: and Noah begat Shem, Ham, and Japheth.

Filiative genealogy is what sexualizes the life span in its fundamentally created form. Sexuality, broadly conceived, becomes the vehicle of human history through the genealogical adventure, which is given in these terms of generation, and in terms of the movement of generation *to* generation. To define sexuality biblically, therefore, necessarily involves the notion and reality of creaturely "passing on," of passing on life, of passing on truth, of passing on worship and relationship—of "tradition" in its fullest sense. Sexuality implies tradition as something that binds persons, times, cultures, and realities together rather than pulls them apart. "Tradition means learning and teaching," Gilbert Highet once wrote about Bach.[2] The music of Bach was not the outpouring of a "solitary soul," Highet insisted, but the prism through which the wisdom of the past could be both crystallized and also passed on to others. Bach spent countless hours copying and learning the music of others. His own sense of music making had at its heart the sharing and passing on of its form to others (including, famously, his family). This is related to a more basic reality, articulated in the famous aphorism attributed to Hippocrates, the full version of which goes like this:

> Life is short, art is long, opportunity fleeting, experience deceptive, judgment difficult. For (as a physician) one must not only do the right thing, but also see to it that the patient, the people around him, and the whole context collaborates with him.[3]

"Life is short, art is long." The "art" in question here is the *techne*, the knowledge that is built up intricately, through learning from others. Physicians, in the context of which Hippocrates speaks, can help in the healing of vulnerable human bodies only with the support and engagement of the patient's families and friends. Genealogy is directly implicated in a humanly and historically networked form of knowledge, because knowledge that is useful to life's extension cannot itself be achieved in the short life of a single individual. The skins of Adam and Eve are garments of salvation in part because they are passed on to others in a divine movement that overcomes Satan's cynical claim of "skin for skin" (cf. Job 2:4).

The extended adventure of human life involves a third component, wrapped up in life span and genealogy as its formative core. If something is passed on from generation to generation, the tradition exists for a purpose and for a purpose whose fulfillment is variously accomplished, for good or ill. This "ethical" aspect of filiative existence reflects the way such a life "fits" with the pressures of creaturehood. Life is extended over time among human beings in ways that are good and bad, such that a life itself constitutes a "probation" of sorts, a testing for the future, in which learning becomes the basis for growth. The eighteenth-century Anglican theologian Joseph Butler,[4] among others, was emphatic about this: temporal existence is not exhaustive of our life's meaning, but it always prepares for something literally beyond itself. Traditionally, this has meant that our life "here on earth" is laying the groundwork for eternal life; it is a "probation" or testing that leads through time into eternity. "For we must all appear before the judgment seat of Christ; that every one may receive the things [done] in [his] body, according to that he hath done, whether [it be] good or bad" (2 Cor 5:10). Probation, in fact, captures that range of explicitly "moral" elements that arise in physical creaturely life, including our sexuality: the way our ordering of our time forms our character, the decisions that shape us through time, the things we do with the time we have, what we pass on to others, or how we leave them. What kind of person we "become" is determined by our probative existence, such that we move toward our death as a certain *kind* of person who can rightly receive something with our death that goes beyond it.

At the end of Genesis, the fruit of this long genealogical book is given in the final blessing of Jacob upon his sons. Jacob's blessing sets out a set of probative life spans for his children, each of which acts as a prophecy for what they will become through time. To be born from parents and to give birth in turn to other human beings is to live as a certain kind of person and to be a person who is ultimately shaped in order to be judged:

> [Gen 49:1-33 KJV] And Jacob called unto his sons, and said, Gather yourselves together, that I may tell you [that] which shall befall you in the last days. Gather yourselves together, and hear, ye sons of Jacob; and hearken unto Israel your father. Reuben, thou [art] my firstborn, my might, and the beginning of my strength, the excellency of dignity, and the excellency of power: Unstable as water, thou shalt not excel; because thou wentest up to thy father's bed; then defiledst thou [it]: he went up to my couch. Simeon and Levi [are] brethren; instruments of cruelty [are in] their habitations. O my soul, come not thou into their secret; unto their assembly, mine honour, be not thou united: for in their anger they slew a man, and in their selfwill they digged down a wall. Cursed [be] their anger, for [it was] fierce; and their wrath, for it was cruel: I will divide them in Jacob, and scatter them in Israel. Judah, thou [art he] whom thy brethren shall praise: thy hand [shall be] in the neck of thine enemies; thy father's children shall bow down before thee. Judah [is] a lion's whelp: from the prey, my son, thou art gone up: he stooped down, he couched as a lion, and as an old lion; who shall rouse him up? The sceptre shall not depart from Judah, nor a lawgiver from between his feet, until Shiloh come; and unto him [shall] the gathering of the people [be]. Binding his foal unto the vine, and his ass's colt unto the choice vine; he washed his garments in wine, and his clothes in the blood of grapes: His eyes [shall be] red with wine, and his teeth white with milk. Zebulun shall dwell at the haven of the sea; and he [shall be] for an haven of ships; and his border [shall be] unto Zidon. Issachar [is] a strong ass couching down between two burdens: And he saw that rest [was] good, and the land that [it was] pleasant; and bowed his shoulder to bear, and became a servant unto tribute. Dan shall judge his people, as one of the tribes of Israel. Dan shall be a serpent by the way,

an adder in the path, that biteth the horse heels, so that his rider shall fall backward. I have waited for thy salvation, O LORD. Gad, a troop shall overcome him: but he shall overcome at the last. Out of Asher his bread [shall be] fat, and he shall yield royal dainties. Naphtali [is] a hind let loose: he giveth goodly words. Joseph [is] a fruitful bough, [even] a fruitful bough by a well; [whose] branches run over the wall: The archers have sorely grieved him, and shot [at him], and hated him: But his bow abode in strength, and the arms of his hands were made strong by the hands of the mighty [God] of Jacob; (from thence [is] the shepherd, the stone of Israel:) [Even] by the God of thy father, who shall help thee; and by the Almighty, who shall bless thee with blessings of heaven above, blessings of the deep that lieth under, blessings of the breasts, and of the womb: The blessings of thy father have prevailed above the blessings of my progenitors unto the utmost bound of the everlasting hills: they shall be on the head of Joseph, and on the crown of the head of him that was separate from his brethren. Benjamin shall ravin [as] a wolf: in the morning he shall devour the prey, and at night he shall divide the spoil. All these [are] the twelve tribes of Israel: and this [is it] that their father spake unto them, and blessed them; every one according to his blessing he blessed them. And he charged them, and said unto them, I am to be gathered unto my people: bury me with my fathers in the cave that [is] in the field of Ephron the Hittite, In the cave that [is] in the field of Machpelah, which [is] before Mamre, in the land of Canaan, which Abraham bought with the field of Ephron the Hittite for a possession of a buryingplace. There they buried Abraham and Sarah his wife; there they buried Isaac and Rebekah his wife; and there I buried Leah. The purchase of the field and of the cave that [is] therein [was] from the children of Heth. And when Jacob had made an end of commanding his sons, he gathered up his feet into the bed, and yielded up the ghost, and was gathered unto his people.

In this way, Israel herself is given a life span, a genealogical form, and a body that is tested, shaped, and probed. Much of the Old Testament constitutes the account of this life of an entire people.

The New Testament picks up, carries along, and reshapes these elements of life span, genealogy, and probation. How it does so is, of course, crucial to our interests. But that it does not *discard* these elements is also crucial: from a New Testament perspective, creaturehood remains a critical reality and not merely an eschatological castoff. The Gospels themselves begin with genealogy; they provide a life span that is then revisioned into a form of probative existence, as Joseph must struggle with a profoundly difficult relational decision. From this decision, the rest of the narrative tumbles out like a load of fruit from huge basket:

[Matt 1:1-25 KJV] The book of the generation of Jesus Christ, the son of David, the son of Abraham. Abraham begat Isaac; and Isaac begat Jacob; and Jacob begat Judas and his brethren; And Judas begat Phares and Zara of Thamar; and Phares begat Esrom; and Esrom begat Aram; And Aram begat Aminadab; and Aminadab begat Naasson; and Naasson begat Salmon; And Salmon begat Booz of Rachab; and Booz begat Obed of Ruth; and Obed begat Jesse; And Jesse begat David the king; and David the king begat Solomon of her [that had been the wife] of Urias; And Solomon begat Roboam; and Roboam begat Abia; and Abia begat Asa; And Asa begat Josaphat; and Josaphat begat Joram; and Joram begat Ozias; And Ozias begat Joatham; and Joatham begat Achaz; and Achaz begat Ezekias; And Ezekias begat Manasses; and Manasses begat Amon; and Amon begat Josias; And Josias begat Jechonias and his brethren, about the time they were carried away to Babylon: And after they were brought to Babylon, Jechonias begat Salathiel; and Salathiel begat Zorobabel; And Zorobabel begat Abiud; and Abiud begat Eliakim; and Eliakim begat Azor; And Azor begat Sadoc; and Sadoc begat Achim; and Achim begat Eliud; And Eliud begat Eleazar; and Eleazar begat Matthan; and Matthan begat Jacob; And Jacob begat Joseph the husband of Mary, of whom was born Jesus, who is called Christ. So all the generations from Abraham to David [are] fourteen generations; and from David until the carrying away into Babylon [are] fourteen generations; and from the carrying away into Babylon unto Christ [are] fourteen generations. Now the birth of Jesus Christ was on this wise: When as his mother Mary was espoused to Joseph, before they came together, she was found with child of the Holy Ghost. Then Joseph her husband, being a just [man], and not willing to make her a publick example, was minded to put her away privily. But while he thought on these things, behold, the angel of the Lord appeared unto him in a dream, saying, Joseph, thou son of David, fear not to take unto thee Mary thy wife: for that which is conceived in her is of the Holy Ghost. And she shall bring forth a son, and thou shalt call his name JESUS: for he shall save his people from their sins. Now all this was done, that it might be fulfilled which was spoken of the Lord by the prophet, saying, Behold, a virgin shall be with child, and shall bring forth a son, and they shall call his name Emmanuel, which being interpreted is, God with us. Then Joseph being raised from sleep did as the angel of the Lord had bidden him, and took unto him his wife: And knew her not till she had brought forth her firstborn son: and he called his name JESUS.

The life span of Jesus rewords these elements and shapes them, as he follows the path that leads him from innocence, in Péguy's terms, to the adulthood that constitutes his "life" in its own probative form. And in doing so, Jesus engages in his own divine generation, his "passing on" in a filiative way that becomes the church, though only because the church is first given in and as Israel:

> [John 19:13-18, 25–30 KJV] When Pilate therefore heard that saying, he brought Jesus forth, and sat down in the judgment seat in a place that is called the Pavement, but in the Hebrew, Gabbatha. And it was the preparation of the passover, and about the sixth hour: and he saith unto the Jews, Behold your King! But they cried out, Away with [him], away with [him], crucify him. Pilate saith unto them, Shall I crucify your King? The chief priests answered, We have no king but Caesar. Then delivered he him therefore unto them to be crucified. And they took Jesus, and led [him] away. And he bearing his cross went forth into a place called [the place] of a skull, which is called in the Hebrew Golgotha: Where they crucified him, and two other with him, on either side one, and Jesus in the midst. . . . Now there stood by the cross of Jesus his mother, and his mother's sister, Mary the [wife] of Cleophas, and Mary Magdalene. When Jesus therefore saw his mother, and the disciple standing by, whom he loved, he saith unto his mother, Woman, behold thy son! Then saith he to the disciple, Behold thy mother! And from that hour that disciple took her unto his own [home]. After this, Jesus knowing that all things were now accomplished, that the scripture might be fulfilled, saith, I thirst. Now there was set a vessel full of vinegar: and they filled a spunge with vinegar, and put [it] upon hyssop, and put [it] to his mouth. When Jesus therefore had received the vinegar, he said, It is finished: and he bowed his head, and gave up the ghost.

All of these elements have been profoundly obscured in the cultural alteration of the last century. Nonetheless, their details have not been rendered obsolete. Quite the contrary: we still die; we still come "from" other sexed creatures; we still inescapably pass on—often poorly—the gift of life and its form to others; and thus we still live lives that inform our ultimate destinies. It is simply now the case that most people, the church included, no longer realize this in general, nor therefore do they think of their creaturely existence as given primarily in the ordering of these elements. Instead, the creaturely elements of life span, filiative genealogy, and probative existence exert their force surreptitiously, dragging

down our fondest social hopes and our misdirected desires into realms of
unappeased dissatisfaction.

By contrast, procreative filiation presents an extended life that actually involves a limited, if rich and often disconcerting, set of interactions
with others. And here we find the kind of probative purpose that properly drives creaturely existence.

## The Shape of Wisdom

Having a limited and mortal life span means that a human creator is,
literally, defined. In general terms, this definition points to the donative ground of human life. Divine love offers this life as a gift, and God
finally takes that life to himself. Hence, the limits of human life also
define the nature of divine love as we know it. If God loves us, it is
because God gives himself, which gives himself over to his own creatures
in the face of and within the limits of mortality (cf. 1 John 4:10).

The Christian tradition, from within the New Testament, has
described this in terms of the cross. But it is important in this context
to note how "the cross" is not only a historical denotation or a theological concept. It is also a material object, with a physical and experiential
shape. Hence, the cross quickly took on a pictorial character in Christian
iconography, verbal and visual—as in the poems of Fortunatus, or in the
mosaics from San Clemente (Rome), according to which the cross itself
exhibited the realities of birth and death, through images of fertile life
emerging from its beams or around it: flowers, green leaves and trees,
animals. The cross "of life," then, was seen as a font of fruitfulness, in the
Levitical sense, and became the site of generation.[5]

This traditional iconography of the cross is significant. It points to
the fact that the human creature's life has a *shape* as well, defined in
advance by its maker's self-giving. One can speak of a "figure" in analogy with, say, a statue, where a mass of stone is worked on such that "out
of it" a shape emerges. In this case, created life emerges, not from brute
matter, but from the mysterious purposes of God; yet, like a statue, that
life gains a particular form over time, even as, from the start, it is already
a particular shape. Thus, created life is a living figure, something that,
beginning with its initial form, moves, changes, develops, but nonetheless is a single thing. It is not so much that this figure that is a human life
is itself a "cross"—but rather that the cross, because it became the object
of God's donative being with respect to human creatures, can somehow
depict this figure as a whole.

Because human life has a shape, it can symbolically represent the integral form of a complete reality. Human creaturely existence is not only the agglomerated set of all that creature's individual temporal moments. Rather, an entire human life marks the sum of the probative aspect of filiated existence. Paul speaks of this in terms of a certain kind of becoming—becoming "like Christ" through the process of "conformance," a very shape-oriented word, whose Greek, *morphe*, points to this clearly. Thus, Paul will speak of his hope of "one day" becoming like Christ, through suffering (cf. Rom 8:29), through the passage of faithfulness, through the slow process of simple struggle in life (Phil 3, ending at v. 21). The issue here has to do little with debates over justification but rather more specifically with the shape of a life itself (cf. 2 Cor 3:18–4:18). The "perfect man," toward whom we move, is the "whole" person of the second Adam, the skinfulness of our lives being the vehicle of this movement.

In the post-Transition world, we have a hard time locating the wholeness or purposeful "shape" of such a life, in conformance with Christ. This is largely because we have lost a constant sense of our mortal definition as creatures. Obviously, the cross is a central place to look in identifying what it means to have "lived well." Paul himself goes further, by linking the faithful Christian life to the cross' figure in a specific way: the cross has its own "wisdom," as he puts it in 1 Corinthians. The "wisdom of the Cross" is an interesting conjunction of terms, and not just for its theological paradox. Wisdom, for Paul, as for us, is precisely the fruit of the life span, at least one that is well ordered. Thus, the shape of a life over time is one aimed at wisdom. Wisdom's association with time is crucial here. Péguy himself focuses on this as he draws the contrast between the "innocents" who are "simply born" and the form of Jesus' own and actual existence: the children killed in Bethlehem "never grew up. While *mine grew in wisdom, and in age and in grace*" (here he quotes from Luke 2:40). To live the life of Christ, which has the shape of his cross, not of the innocent without need of him (if such could ever by the case), a human being must grow in wisdom.

"Wisdom" is bound to "age" and "grace." Within the phrase of Luke 2:40 we can discern the character of a life's "shape," one that is ultimately conformed to a cross that proves Jesus' own descriptive life span. In most cultures, wisdom has been linked to experience of a sort. In English, the word itself, in its root meaning, has to do with seeing forms or shapes (as in the term "in such and such a wise," where "wise" means "manner").

Most traditions have seen wisdom as bound up somehow with that experience that involves the encounters a person will have with a multitude of shapes and forms over time. "Experience," in this context, itself points to a certain kind of "testing," in the sense of seeing what happens to something in this or that encounter. Wisdom in most cultures is associated with old age because it demands a multiplicity of forms, of things, of encounters, of trials and errors, and thus of testing over time.

Just living a long time, just "seeing the world," is not, however, the goal of the *Christian* life. In Jesus' case as well, the extent of his life span, although it was more or less "average" for his era, is only important in that it permitted "experience" at all. Jesus was saved from a child's death, which is a very important point. Nonetheless, Scripture claims not that "old age is the beginning of wisdom" but rather that the "fear of the Lord is the beginning of Wisdom" (Prov 9:10; Ps 111:10). "The fear of the Lord," furthermore, is quite specific in its ground and focus. "Fear" is something *creatures* have; that is part of what it means to be a creature. In respect to God, creaturely fear has to do with the fact that we realize that all the things we come upon and that come upon us—experience, the world—are not ours; they are instead "given." They are, like our own selves, offered to us. The final wisdom must, therefore, be some kind of utter receptivity, much like the child's in Péguy's presentation, yet now immersed in experiences that themselves betoken creaturehood's most substantive forms—that is, their filiated and generative challenges. Wisdom, along with its ground in creaturely fear of God, is a *knowing*; it is somehow taken up by will, and thus, given its temporal location, it is learned.

The wise Christian has learned that all things come from God and thus that "all is grace," in the words of the cleric in Bernanos' *Diary of a Country Priest*, whose hard, if Jesus-like, life span has pushed him into revelatory encounters regarding his own life and that of others.[6] Learning, in just this way, that all is grace *is* wisdom. But it is wisdom only because it comes through the process of "experience," of bit by bit having things come upon us—literally, "adventure"—of having things be given and then taken away, of learning to love. Experience becomes wisdom in this way because it learns to take on hope and self-giving. In this kind of experience, we grow in awe and reverence for the very center of our existence. When we look at ourselves and finally say, "Oh, this is my God!" (Isa 25:9), literally, we will have reached the place of God's "fear" and wisdom.

There is much to say about learning in the course of the life span and about the "divine arithmetic," as one writer described the art of "numbering our days" (Ps 90:12). But before one can examine these realities, one must reflect on the more basic fact that "life" is itself "learning." In Henry's rich discussion of human subjectivity as the self-revelation of life, this self-revelation is always "life-among-other-lives"—which is to say, encounter and adventure. Cognitive scientists and others have engaged, and will continue to engage, in difficult reflections on the actual processes, neurological and social, that are central to human learning. But almost all agree that learning, including language learning, is wrapped up with a complex set of *interactions*, by which children most basically, but all ages in a broader way, encounter external realities. Only in these encounters do we engage in a process wherein sense making, pattern forming, and sign indicating are worked out, internalized, adjusted, and shared. Whatever genetic predispositions we may have, there really is no learning or language without such interaction. The child *must* be with other people: with parents, adults, and other children. Everything depends on this.

Thought, in other words, develops out of the taking in of external experience that is then formatted and shaped by speech, which can be shared and reshaped in turn, over and over.[7] Obviously, this process is quite complex. But we know that children can only progress in their learning insofar as their encounters and engagements provide them with material they have no choice but to apprehend, internalize, re-form, and then express. This follows an order, even if we are still uncertain as to its exact shape or possible shapes. But the process itself is also dependent on external realities: the world, social groups, individuals, parents. This is why context and environment for children is so important to their learning.[8]

The fundamental point regarding creaturehood is this: I am able to think because *I am put into the world*, and the world comes at me. Other people, furthermore, are the vehicles of this world that I encounter. Speaking, thinking, learning are all part of a process of constant adjustment, rearrangement, and then appropriation that takes place at every new instant and whose larger shape is given over time. While such a claim must seem commonsensical, the veiling of the clock has meant that often we act as if learning is *not* the visage of our life spans, or that our life spans are not the very particular boundaries of our learning. Our fascination, since the seventeenth century, with tales of "feral children,"

supposedly raised among the beasts in the woods or wastelands of a
dehumanized landscape, represents less a deep acknowledgment of these
claims than, as with tourists gazing on Strasbourg's great astronomical
timepiece, a kind of vestigial but fleeting sensibility that wisdom has
slipped through our fingers like dripping water.[9]

The Christian view of wisdom is deeply implicated in this veiled
common sense. This view tells us that we learn as we, creatures that we
are, navigate the passage of our lives among other creatures, in such a
way that we encounter the gifts of God and learn their gifting and their
grace. Learning happens, that is, as we recognize that this and that is
*from God*, all of it: it is God who has made us, and we are his (Ps 100:3).
How we recognize this is critical. Well we know that many persons reach
the end of their lives and, granted the chance for reflection (which not all
receive), they shake their heads and say, in a kind of numbed perplexity,
"I don't know. I just don't know; it doesn't add up at all." How lives "add
up" remains, for many, a stone upon which they stumble. We also know
those who, in simple bitterness, mark out a list of wretched elements: my
father was a drunk; my wife died; my daughter does not talk to me; my
job was lousy . . . Now what? Mortality in this case is nothing but death,
whereas its actual purpose is to frame our lives and bound them into a
shape. A central Christian vocation is to grasp an answer to the question
of how one learns from life in a way that leads neither to confusion nor
to resentment but to fear and to praise. That answer is given, in Christian terms, only as I see and engage these realities of my life as a *creature*
whose experiences turn me toward my creatureliness in God's hands.
Only in this way will the Christian find his or her life to be a path to
wisdom rather than to simple dissolution.

A life that learns for the sake of wisdom, then, is one whose experiences have been ordered to a shape, ultimately the shape of Christ Jesus
himself and the form of his own "wisdom." There *is* such a thing as an
"unfinished life," in this regard: undifferentiated, blurred edges, much
like the skin that Leviticus was so interested in healing from its crumbling and corruption. It is not only Leviticus but its substantive topics
that we have a hard time talking about in our era, largely because our
own vision has taken on the character of this dissolving film of formli-
ness: our anxieties and disappointments are all mixed up in a kind of
oozing stew, whose place in our lives is irresolvably uncertain. Curiously,
we have developed critical sophistication on matters of narrative and
"plot" that should help us see at least the intrinsic power of shaped lives.

Yet at the same time, we distrust such theories' application to (or, better, their necessary derivation *from*) our actual lives. We prefer to leave the latter to desultory self-construction.

But human lives *have* a shape, whether we like the shape they have or not. That shape is given in their birthedness, their dying, and the traversal between the two that is directed by the forms of filiated existence over a few short years. It is not a question of constructing metaphors for our existence that somehow offer a variety of possible overlays to this foundational shape. Rather, Jesus' own scripturally articulated life—as figurally given in the whole of the Scriptures, Old and New together—is the form our often frayed threads, tied to the basic shape of skinly creatureliness, will be pulled into. That is the "promise" of our creation.

In a real way, critical theory about narratives—Peter Brooks comes to mind—can truthfully describe our lives to the degree that we accept their variety as graciously effective retellings *by* Jesus of his own life offered to us. Thus, when the medieval monk Aelred writes a devotional work on "Jesus at twelve years old,"[10] he is not trying to offer Jesus' twelve-year-old experiences, as recounted by Luke, in the form of various spiritual metaphors; he is, instead, digging into the power of the New Adam's existence to provide its promised form to the shape of our created existence, which *must* include the passage of childhood into adolescence, at least if we live long enough to traverse it. Into this place, mothers and fathers, families, knowledge, generations, and learning are laid out, in Christ's own form, as the meaning of our creaturely destiny. Similarly, stages of developmental life, whether understood physiologically or psychologically, have their normative status defined in terms of Christ's own figural personhood—one that encloses Israel as well—and not primarily in some independent biological or cultural process. With that prioritizing of meaning in mind, we can learn much from the research and theories of thinkers like Erik Erikson, or Piaget and Vygotsky. More recent studies of "course of life" issues, often worked out in the context of gerontological psychology, very reasonably make use of narrative theory, and in particular the work of more Freudian-influenced writers like Brooks, because of the need for the elderly and dying to understand their lives. Those who are approaching their deaths, after many years of living, often engage in the repeated practice of trying on different shapes to their autobiographical retellings. This late-life self-reflection resembles the way readers allow their own lives to "try on" the meanings unfolded in a novel, until bit by bit some kind of resolved and articulated meaning seems to "fit" a person's sense of self and history. Among the very old, this is often done by telling stories about oneself to others, such that reminiscence becomes central to aging.[11] The fact of creaturehood, however, uncovers this observed process of aging and narrative meaning-construction for a life span as a *response* to a "given"—that is, to the basic ordering of Adam to Adam that marks the great traversal.

It is this "given" that must finally distinguish the Christian life-course from any other narrative project. Life is all givenness, not simply a set of covenants and contracts, as Hobbes would have it. The freedom of human agency lies not in countering or overcoming such givenness—something that results in the impossible strivings of the suicide—but in giving thanks for it. To arrive at such thankfulness requires its own kind of choices and strategy. Achieved thanksgiving is an almost purely moral set of choices, which aim at "seeing" the truth of the given, not at transforming it. The moral act, the act of freedom in this case, is, in Iris Murdoch's terms, the work of coming to apprehend the "world as it really is."[12] Here is the place of "tragedy," whose assaults can some-how keep us honest in our attentions and our loves, much as Mur-doch's own tragic descent into dementia exposed the love she shared with her husband.[13] The "world as it really is," of course, is not simple to discern. Certainly, it is not the individual's world of self-fabrication in the midst of otherwise limited objects.[14] But Christians can at least describe its ultimate form: the "world as it really is" is, in the end, the scriptural Christ (or Christic Scripture) as the final "given," exposed in the fact "that in the dispensation of the fullness of times [God] might gather together in one all things in Christ, both which are in heaven, and which are on earth; [even] in him" (Eph 1:10). The "meaning" of a human life is "given" just in this final divine purpose. All meaning flows down from this source—Christ's scriptural form—like falling waters cascading upon the naked figures of human bathers standing in a pool beneath a great cliff.

The "wholeness" of a life, then, has to do with distinctions that are drawn together over time into a definable shape. Beauty is given in form; and form is given in proportion, and proportion in relationships of dis-tinction. The Catholic theologian Hans Urs von Balthasar and others have stressed what some have called the "analogy of natality" when it comes to understanding human life and, we must add, with respect to just this extended shaping that learning involves.[15] Life takes its rise from birth, obviously, and thus is founded on this initial gift; but the gift of birth itself, once granted through a man and woman's sexual coupling, is given in a relation that grows out of child and mother first, and then father, and then others. Without question, the initial maternal relationship is fundamental to learning, as most cognitive psychologists recognize. Seeing, smiling, touching, sucking, "mirroring" movements and emotions, being led, receiving, and offering all constitute this creative blossoming. The infant grows from a perspective of grace received and leading *toward* grace. For Balthasar, this "analogy of natality" stands as the foundational turn toward God himself, even if it is not quite conscious. As the limits pressed upon this turn also intrude (one could argue they do so immediately, in pain, hunger, and incapacity—as Freudian students of childhood such as Melanie Klein understood), the child slowly gains a sense that there is a *shape* to her or his life. It is a shape filled with endings and beginnings of their own, and, at the last, with a final ending.

Before the Great Transition, this was all made obvious, in a world where parents, siblings, neighbors, and relatives died often in the child's own experience. Yet whether obvious or not, it is in such a fashioning of experience that the shape of life achieves its wholeness.

## Wisdom's Arc

Ordering that wholeness in its proportional meaning has always been a central part of Christian life, and of human life more generally. The link between learning and form, and both with experience, was usually presented in terms of various "ages" of human existence within the life span. This is, in fact, a universal human perception regarding our lives. Every culture has had its own generally similar ways of periodizing the movement from infancy to old age. Early Christians borrowed these frames from their own surrounding culture. Many ancient Greek thinkers, for instance, spoke of the "seven ages" of human life, viewing the number as symbolic of perfection and wholeness itself. Others elaborated this movement more precisely, although keeping to the seven-stage image, and seem to have addressed this to quite specific developmental patterns: the first age involved a person's initial seven years, which ended as one's "baby teeth" were replaced; the second period was brought to an end by puberty, at fourteen years; for men, the next seven years were devoted to the "beard's" full emergence by age twenty-one; there followed the time of "strength," to twenty-eight; then came a time for marriage and child rearing; then adulthood and "developed character," to age forty-two;

followed by "wisdom" for at least fourteen years; at sixty-three came the time of decline and senility, leading to the average time of death for those who were able to survive that long, at age seventy.[16]

By taking seriously the fact that our lives follow a pattern, whose proportion, movement and interrelation of parts gives it beauty, we can be faithful to its creatureliness. This ordering, even if it comes in many different ways, is an expression of wisdom's particular learning, because such ordering is about how we encounter and engage the rest of creation on our progress through life. Other cultures and times divided the life span into three ages or four or five. And, as these kinds of reflections took on rooted assumption in the West,[17] they were elaborated in terms of local cultures—French or German, Jewish or English. In the same way, the stages of the life span have always, in all cultures, assumed slightly different shapes for men and women. Scripture speaks variously of this as well, obliquely and explicitly, in Proverbs, Ecclesiastes, and the Psalms, among other places. At least five distinct "ages" can be identified in these books: those of infancy, childhood, youth, adulthood, and old age, and perhaps even the dotage of the almost dead. (For if the skin of lepers, as the Scripture indicates, represents a return to the uncertainty of life's formation, its translucent dissolution to a fetal condition, so too the skin of the very old begins to thin and reach the fragility of the infant's emergence from the boundaries of nothingness.) One should probably add as separate stages motherhood and fatherhood, which, although not completely age specific, are generally related to adulthood.

> Yet thou art he who took me from the womb; thou didst keep me safe upon my mother's breasts. Upon thee was I cast from my birth, and since my mother bore me thou hast been my God. (Ps 22:9-10)

> Train up a child in the way he should go, and when he is old he will not depart from it. (Prov 22:6)

> The glory of young men is their strength, but the beauty of old men is their gray hair. (Prov 20:29)

> You shall rise up before the hoary head, and honor the face of an old man, and you shall fear your God: I am the LORD. (Lev 19:32)

> Remember also your Creator in the days of your youth, before the evil days come, and the years draw nigh, when you will say, "I have no pleasure in them." (Eccl 12:1)

> For thus saith the LORD concerning the sons and concerning the daughters that are born in this place, and concerning their mothers that bare them, and concerning their fathers that begat them in this land. (Jer 16:3)

To texts like these, we should add as well the discussions of generational relations in the New Testament, in the so-called "household codes" of Ephesians 4, or 1 Peter 2 and 3—likewise, the discussions in Titus 2, so frequently deployed today in Evangelical circles.

The New Testament, in any case, seems to have made use of the categories of the Greek "seven ages," using terms that fit realistically into significant age groups, distinguishing infants, children, youths, adults, mature adults, and the very elderly by their normal Greek terms. These stages of life properly ordered, and in a deep way that is not usually explicit, the framework of human relations as they are applied in more theologically oriented texts, where metaphor colors important exposi-tions according to well-understood creaturely forms (e.g., believers as "children," or Paul as "father," and so on).

Beyond scriptural texts that speak generally of the ages of human growth and decay, we should, continuing with Péguy's appropriate lead-ing, probably look at the life of Jesus especially to gauge the kind of age-related experience whose order and shape became part of Jesus' own "growth in wisdom." In this case, we can note an array of "ages" through which Jesus passes— for example:

> *Birth*: And so it was, that, while they were there, the days were ac-complished that she should be delivered. And she brought forth her firstborn son, and wrapped him in swaddling clothes, and laid him in a manger; because there was no room for them in the inn. (Luke 2:6-7)
>
> *Infancy and circumcision*: And when they had performed all things according to the law of the Lord, they returned into Galilee, to their own city Nazareth. (Luke 2:39)
>
> *Infancy and flight with family*: When he arose, he took the young child and his mother by night, and departed into Egypt. (Matt 2:14)
>
> *Family*: And he went down with them, and came to Nazareth, and was subject unto them: but his mother kept all these sayings in her heart. (Luke 2:51)

*Adolescence, in the temple*: And it came to pass, that after three days they found him in the temple, sitting in the midst of the doctors, both hearing them, and asking them questions. And all that heard him were astonished at his understanding and answers. (Luke 2:46-47)

*Adult with family*: There came then his brethren and his mother and, standing without, sent unto him, calling him. (Mark 3:31)

Is not this the carpenter, the son of Mary, the brother of James, and Joses, and of Juda, and Simon? and are not his sisters here with us? And they were offended at him. (Mark 6:3)

*Adult*: Ye men of Israel, hear these words; Jesus of Nazareth, a man [*aner*, a mature man of strength and character] approved of God among you by miracles and wonders and signs, which God did by him in the midst of you, as ye yourselves also know. (Acts 2:22)

*New family, at the cross*: When Jesus therefore saw his mother, and the disciple standing by, whom he loved, he saith unto his mother, Woman, behold thy son! Then saith he to the disciple, Behold thy mother! And from that hour that disciple took her unto his own [home]. (John 19:26-27)

(*Old man*: Moving beyond the New Testament, it is worth recalling the wonderful encounter of Justin Martyr, told in the Prologue to his *Dialogue with Trypho*, with an "old man" by the sea, who brought him to a knowledge of Christ. That this "old man" was Christ Jesus himself is well argued by some; and the layers of theological and anthropological meaning in this are, in any case, worth pondering.[18])

We defer as well as refer to this pattern, if somewhat loosely, in common prayers we utter, like the well-known birthday prayer from the Book of Common Prayer: "O God, our times are in your hands; look with favor, we pray, on your servant *N.*, as s/he begins another year; grant that s/he may grow in wisdom and in grace, and strengthen their trust on your goodness all the days of her/his life."

It is true that many of the roles attached to these ages are, in their particularities, "socially constructed," in the sense that their forms in their distinctive details vary according to the expectations cultures have developed around behavioral norms associated with age and, of course, with gender as it too is molded by age. We can easily see traces, in many cases, of how these forms change and evolve: forms of address and protocol between generations, the demands of defined lines of authority, based on respect, social roles, and experience. Such cultural evolution demands, for instance, that Catholic and Evangelical appeals to the "natural" complementarity of the sexes must be tempered by rigorously critical historical and sociological work.

Still, as Luke writes, Jesus "grew in wisdom and in grace." The key point is that the order given in a person's life represents the way that person learns "wisdom," and that this is done relationally, according to one's placement within a developing stream of given interactions. The notion of an arbitrary shape, or of an equivalence and even equality of significance for this or that point in a person's life, is intuitively nonsensical. The significance of a given event for a child is utterly distinct from the same event's significance for a teenager or adult or elderly man or woman. Our modern era has preferred to talk, when we have wished to talk about all this at all, in terms of a person's "character" and sometimes of a person's character formation: there is, we assume, a *continuity* of shape that defines a person's life, perhaps somewhat malleably, but in a steady fashion over time. Often, we even speak in terms of a person's spirit with which they are "born" and that they then "live out" in certain ways. Modern notions of continuous character deal with desires, passions, and emotions as elements to be deployed in the expression of a person's identity. The more venerable tradition of the "ages of man," however, suggests that what is important is less this continuous character that people "take with them" through life, slowly building in this direction or not, so much as the periods of a life itself—its times and days—and the way they relate one to another. What is important, that is, is the overall "figure" constituted by the events and responses of our aging. Emotions and feelings are not unimportant to this overall figure, nor is the character that emerges from their successive pull. Each aspect is deeply formative of our perceptions and to some extent defines them.[19] But continuities of character and emotional identity are less definitive of our lives than are the constellations constituted by the movements of encounter we experience through time.

In the shadow of creaturely mortality, therefore, emotional life and desire—so dear to contemporary discussions of sexual identity—are only secondary aspects of that identity. Emotional makeup and the strange elements that drive our emotions, including sexual arousal, suffer enormous change; they vary over time and are intrinsically murky and unfathomable. Attempts—often quite concrete and practical in their demands (for example, in cases of predatory pedophilia)—to sort these out in psychological and neurological terms have demonstrated how murky they really are. It is probably impossible to apply a coherent template of emotional life to creaturely existence, which is why the "ages," or temporal forms, of human life are more revelatory of who we really are. Among other things, our contemporary science has identified some of the enormous physiological and biochemical differences among the distinct ages of life, from hormones to the way organs function. This was already well known by earlier thinkers (within the framework of their own science) who generally imagined the different ages of life as being governed by the differing interplay of the internal bodily fluids that every person has in various proportions. Early modern interest in human health was based on the fluids of the body as they proportionalized themselves in different ages, influenced by specific circumstances.[20]

The physiological perspective on stages of life is not the only one. It has always been known that each age has its virtues and characteristics that are precisely honed by the time of the individual person's life, within its span, and that is shaped as well by the experience of its adventure. These virtues, and often their mirroring vices, achieve their profile within the specific context of a person's encounters as they follow one another. Each age's character is, therefore, always dependent on the other ages and the experience of their ordering, and thus, unless there is an understood *interdependence* of a certain kind among the "ages," there is no learning and there is no wisdom. The great challenges of countries that have gone through destructive civil war include those of upsetting the generational balances that shape the character of growth. Where the average age of a society is very low—often the case after wars, especially in countries where the Great Transition remains something barely grasped—not only are expectations weighted by the clustering generational desires, but politics and moral formation are wrenchingly skewed. Conversely, as societies, especially those of the Transition, as in the West, grow older on the average, and older ages come to predominate, the proportions of interdependence shift, often away from the integrated concern for the early end of the life span. The deepest challenge here lies in the form of wisdom that can thereby be learned. If we speak of the fact that every generation is needed within a given society or culture—or church—it is not simply for diversity's sake but more importantly for the sake of wisdom and responsibility, beauty, and especially that love that undergirds creaturely existence. In many modern post-Transition societies, the loss of a sense of and commitment to the ordering of our lives in this way, let alone their *right* ordering, has seriously undercut our ability to love in a way coherent with our creaturely condition. We may still have tools to make the world a "better place" in certain material ways; but we can no longer apprehend the truth of who we are as creatures of God made in love and for love.

One way simply to reintroduce ourselves to this orchestrating framework of the life span is to take a well-known instance of its articulation and follow it through. By the seventeenth century, in fact, the periodized life span was presented in the form of a sturdy genre of *memento mori* moralism: thinking of our progress toward death as a spur to a sober life before God. In a piece entitled "The Weeke," for example, the poet Edward Browne offers a synopsis of the life cycle that is meant to steer us toward God:

> For he divides the life of Mortall men,
> Into sev'n parts, till threescore yeares and ten;
> And therein I will show how pretious time
> Is vainely spent, each age in one short Rime.
> The first tenne yeares man is a harmelesse child,
> And as a Lamb his life is meeke and milde;
> But after that (Goat-like) he skips and Joyes,
> In foolish vanities and Idle toyes,
> And so till thirty man's an untam'd Colt,
> Heady, and from all goodnes doth revolt;
> And untill forty hee's a sturdy Bull,
> His limbes are strong, with blood his veines are full,
> But after that, his courage will not faile;
> For as a Lyon then he will prevaile:
> And then at fifty hee's a crafty Fox,
> And Lawyer-like gets money in his Box.
> And so till sev'nty by Industrious paines,
> Woolfe-like hee's greedy to increase his gaines;
> But after that he feeles his bones to tire,
> Therefore much like the Dog he loves the fire,
> And keeps at home like to the wyly Cat,
> Where he delights to sit, to prate and chat;
> Thus doth the Carnall man waste his lifes weeke,
> And seldome doth after true Riches seeke;
> I meane the wealth, which beyond Age will last,
> And still endure after this life is past:
> Therefore the Sages, That did first ordaine
> And gave unto each day It's severall name,

Did well at first the nimblest Planet place,
And last of all that of the slowest race,
To shew that man in youthfull blithfull plight
In Grace and vertue should take most delight:
For painfull age cannot so well hold out
As lusty youth, yet still should goe about,
In vertues race, and not out of it start,
Till death doth strike him with his deadly dart;
Therefore I'll pray, that with the glorious sun,
I may rejoyce in vertues Race to run,
And with old Saturne therein persevere,
So should I well conclude the weeke and yeare.[21]

Far better known than Browne, however, is Shakespeare's own version of the genre. "All the World's a Stage," from the play *As You Like It*, is a brief soliloquy that has etched in English-speakers' minds the passing of the ages in each person's life span. Deliberately cynical in presentation, this poem is meant to bring a knowing, though somewhat painful, smile to our lips.[22] His analysis provides us with the basis for a quick overview of age ordering, to which I shall add aspects of Augustine's own discussion of the topic for some more serious counterpoint.[23] Augustine takes the seven ages of life and places them in connection with the seven days of creation (hence Browne's focus on the "the week"). He links them, as well, with the seven ages of "the world" or of history, the fulfillment of which means that, effectively, there are only six early ages to a person's creaturely life, the final one awaiting consummation. It is nothing but an image, of course, but a brilliant one in showing how the creature and creation are bound to time and to their Creator. Following Shakespeare and Augustine together, we can get a sense of what was in fact not only a Christian but a widely shared human grasp of the way of wisdom as it was ordered before the Transition.

## The Stages of Life

All the world's a stage,
And all the men and women merely players:
They have their exits and their entrances;
And one man in his time plays many parts,
His acts being seven ages. At first, the infant,
Mewling and puking in the nurse's arms.

Infancy (*infantia*): Infants regurgitate frequently, but there is much more to their lives than that. Augustine likens infancy to the first day of creation, the formation of something out of chaos. This is the miracle of our birth, the foundation of our existence upon grace. Babies are sacred in world culture, and they should be: they mark the deepest connection we have to our creaturehood's origin. On this day we behold, just as we ourselves were, something thinking and feeling, come from nothing, except God. For Augustine, however, infancy is something related to the ground of our being, even as it is also forgotten, like the age before the flood, lost in an oblivion, yet hidden behind all we do. Like the inner workings of a mysterious machine, they are there, but we cannot ever get to them or understand them: our thinking and feeling "emerge" in our memory; we do not make them. Receptivity is the driving nature of this age just as is dependence.

Infancy marks the first encounter we have with the world, and as such it is an almost pure encounter. It is all about touching, seeing, listening, receiving, the intimacy of literal physical presence with parents and family and with surroundings. Everything is close by and immediate; nothing is far away. Our earliest life, furthermore, continues to lurk in a hazy availability to our later consciousness, in that our more mature thinking involves a cognitive and willing grasp of reality that we take to ourselves and form, building on these primal discoveries and habits. Every study that has been done of infancy tells us that a child's physical interaction, in affective warmth, with a parent—a mother especially— will predict later personalities: empathy; the ability to share, give, and receive affection as a child or adolescent or adult; how information is taken in and processed in a relational manner.[24] Since reception is the foundation of all learning, once the artifacts of God's creation are a given, human life is handed over to impoverishment to the degree that there is nothing to receive.

Infancy is foundational, therefore, in the sense of being an image of the rest of our lives; we are simply *given* things, over which we have little control: food, warmth, and affection itself. We also have it simply taken away: this remains an issue for the whole of our life spans, as we suffer illness, accident, hostility, and betrayal. We are infants in this regard all our lives, but we also grow in learning how to order our lives within this condition that is ours: ultimately, we are driven to learn to love others, such that the love that surrounds us as infants, and as pure grace, might be shared. Although human creatures might know something about the loss of a parent as a young person, unless they have learned from this a deeper language of love and forgiveness, they have not grown. Although in a sense we are called to rediscover the innocents of Bethlehem who precede our faith, Péguy's Christ must thus surpass them if he is to be the Son of Man.

> And then the whining school-boy, with his satchel
> And shining morning face, creeping like snail
> Unwillingly to school.

Childhood (*pueritia*): Here we enter into "formation" in its true sense, hence "the school" of our human creaturehood. The notion that childhood is a modern and especially bourgeois invention was much in vogue in the last century but has now been pretty much debunked. Likewise, the idea that "schooling" is a modern fabrication linked to the rise of the nation-state is also a myth. Although the institutional structures vary and have changed, the special formational character of childhood is indeed universally identified.[25]

The most precious things of our learning are first set in motion and given articulate foundations here. Like the second day of creation, things are "separated out," the grids of our behaviors are laid, and the basics of morals (which refers first to the shape and manner of our living) are offered. For Augustine, this corresponds historically to the age of Noah to Abraham. Childhood is the time of our first "memories," hence its rooted hold on our beings. No one doubts that families and societies, just as each of our individual beings, rely on what happens in our childhood. The moral and social imperatives are so great, and obvious, here that one wonders how we have gone so wrong in our contemporary culture by casting childhood to its own devices, subjecting it to free-floating pressures of the world. For it is always a school time, no matter what kind of school a child is in. Our societies are ordered by what our childhoods have left to the world.

The learning that takes place in childhood is of a certain kind: pressing boundaries, determining consequences, self-consciously beginning to think about loss (which is a kind of limit that frames a life). So, children are rightly focused on learning the elements of order: what the lines of demarcation in behavior and expectation are (going to bed, crossing the street, doing chores and homework, addressing others). The disciplines of writing, which we associate with formal schooling, turn out to be crucial since they involve, physically, small motor skills as well as neurological nuances of connection—so too music hearing, singing, playing; the mastery of tools; the relational care of writing letters. More broadly, childhood provides a person encounters of limits or obedience with the world of relation and subordination. This is important to learn, not cruel: the human creature has its love disappointed and sometimes even ruined; it also has the capacity to rethink, reorient, and rebuild. Unless one can learn about this, through the encounter with and ordering of limits early, a person is left bereft of basic skills by which to navigate or traverse the world.

Childhood is also a time that is adult oriented in many ways, something that modern life, since the eighteenth century increasingly, has moved away from, as the independent world of the child has been not so much invented as cast off on its own and allowed to expand and bloat. For children to learn in a way appropriate to the human life span, they need constant monitoring and engagement with adults. They need also to be left with themselves, to work out for themselves the practical meaning of what they are learning. But children cannot learn alone, without adults, for older persons provide the shape to the limits children must learn to run up against and creatively engage.

> And then the lover,
> Sighing like furnace, with a woeful ballad
> Made to his mistress' eyebrow.

Until recently, this stage was called "adolescence" (*adolescentia*): For Augustine, who dwelled in a pre-Transition age, adolescence involves the first sexual engagement and the actual conception of children. And for Shakespeare too, it seems, the "lover" is the adolescent. The increasing delay in marriage in modernity has shifted matters enormously, and we are now in the West deeply confused as to the character of what we still call "adolescence." We are not sure what is supposed to happen at this time as well as whether or not some kind of further stage should be inserted after it before the transition into adulthood's forms.

For Augustine, however, adolescence is a time of fertility, the dry land emerging for growth in the history of the world's conception; the covenant with Abraham and the giving of the Law—Israel and her children—in the history of the human race. Here we encounter the press for ordering, struggling for obedience, engaging—much like childhood in a way, yet driven by new freedoms and desires and by a new demand for willful order for just this reason. From the point of view of social history, in our post-Transition era in comparison with the past, we have increasingly allowed adolescence to remain infantilized in many ways. We should, however, try to imagine what it would be like if this were not so or if greater effort were made so that adolescents might assume responsibility and express generativity, as in former times.

We should pause over this question. Adolescence stands as a cross-roads of sorts into adulthood. Before the Transition, many individuals, in any case, never passed across it but died on the near banks of the river of childhood. What we have been seeing in the developed West, to varying degrees, is a clear movement away from sexual formation that is based on the ordered life of generation and genealogy. Children are brought up, increasingly, without (many) siblings, without two parents, in some cases deliberately without their own biological mothers and fathers, and without grandparents as part of their lives. The resulting dynamics, writ large, constitute a loss of deliberate and communal order-ing for developing children and youth, which will obviously touch upon the construction of sexuality in particular and of many other related ele-ments of creaturely wisdom. If there is to be construction of a life form, it will increasingly, and especially at the crucial time of adolescence, be left to the undeliberated constructions, what some have labeled the "void," of drifting, untethered experiment. In many post-Transition societies there is little left to tell me who I am and am meant to be or become, as a sexual and as a more expansively reaching human being, when I navigate my youth. It is critical to identify, then, what it is that has taken over the formational space left when the "arc" of the life span, in its communal form, has disappeared.

A number of elements and dynamics have ended up filling this space, and they vary from place to place, person to person. But one thing that is held in common in the developing West and elsewhere now is the gradual (or rapid) "designifying of sexuality" altogether that has come to characterize adolescence, and the culture of those who are grown from this modern form of life. Once shorn of its communally ordered shape, sexuality in contemporary adolescence is left to its default, but semanti-cally thinned out, basis as a physical-emotional experience and force. "The sexual," in post-Transition cultures, emerges at a certain time in an individual's life, which could come between ten years to fifteen or six-teen. (There are continuing cultural changes afoot here as well, toward the earlier, as human physical development has become more rapid due to debated nutritional and hormonal shifts in economically abundant societies.) Whatever the exact year of its emergence, the sexual simply appears: a sense, a set of bodily changes, new and mysterious arousals, accompanied by other new and disorienting cognitive and emotional perceptions. But the actual contours of this emerging sexual existence "signify" nothing beyond these experiences and forces. Most state-based educational curricula through which adolescents are introduced to a self-conscious discussion of their growth focus upon biological realities, open-ended questions, the structuring of "choices," and the options for nongenerative sexual intercourse. Hence, the rise of sexuality as a "pleasure" principle, which stands not only as a wax nose of meaning but as one well past the melting point. "Healthy development," within a fully transitioned communal context, is understood as the way adults support adolescents in discerning and engaging their arousals without guilt, such that an "identity" can be claimed without pressure.[26] But even if the new desires of adolescence do not simply enter into a realm of uncontrolled urges, sexuality nonetheless is often culturally driven largely by immediate personal and contextual forces that may well have little to do with the adult "health" field today. These forces engage mostly those primordial urges, filtering them through peer and media-shaped pressures and images.

It is not clear that it makes sense to completely deconstruct "sexual identities," as a point of simple reality: adolescents, male and female, gradually assume a self-understood place, as sexually informed creatures, within the human community. But such identities are rightly now beginning to be understood, by both sexual "progressives" and "conservatives," as bound no longer to intrinsic or genetic fatality but to the force of social ordering itself, something that, in any case, research on adolescent identity shows.[27] One of the inner dynamics of a life span ordered by its "ages," and ordered in the relatively stable way it has been for generations (and for the purpose of generative and generational coherence), was that someone and something has always taught individuals what it means to be a woman or a man. Such teaching and learning was a part of the identity of a *generated* individual. At this point, and in a crucial way, adolescence was always seen as a particular point in creaturely formation wherein the Adamic character of male and female expressed itself in ways that could now be extended temporally through mortal filiation. The ecclesial joining of "confirmation" liturgical rites with adolescence eventually focused this element of formation as the moment for a deliberately conscientious apprehension of creaturely identity and vocation, in a way that mirrored many other non-Christian traditional cultures.

Around the same time as Freud was engaging his own studies in sexuality and the pervading forces of the unconscious, the French ethnographer Arnold van Gennep produced his seminal study on "rites of passage" (1909, and reprinted many times since).[28] Van Gennep articulated, in ways that are still used, the widespread structures of such rites around the world, especially those associated with the passage to adulthood. Most cultures, until the recent rise of atomized individualist societies like our own, have utilized such rites to both shape and symbolize, among other things, the character of sexual identity and meaning. Adolescence was the age at which this separative shaping found its formal enunciation and enactment. These rites of passage have generally followed a common structure, even across cultures. This structure, often divided into three phases, has been described as follows: separation from childhood links with parents; liminal passage, though which the adolescent confronts some symbolized form of death and passes through, if not death itself, at least its dangerous confrontation; and, finally, some kind of rebirth or creative reestablished existence within this now apprehended truth of creaturely life. The first stage places the young person into a condition of disassociation from the past, the second puts him or her into a place of trial and often pain and sacrifice that marks the transition into a new identity, and the last affirms that new identity with new powers and responsibilities.

We know rites of passage today mostly in terms of Jewish Bar Mitzvahs or hazing customs in certain peer groups, including gangs. In some societies highly pressured educational exams at this age perform this function in a way. But all this is limited, thinned out, and the very notion of an age of formal development whose shape is to be socially ordered has dissolved, however universal in human culture it has been until recently. Attempts have been made at inventing adolescent rites of passage anew, within groups of parentless inner-city children for instance, just as we have seen composed limited religion-based curricula and programs based on rites of passage ideas. But these have proven weak vessels, largely for their lack of lateral support within cultures and families.

Although adolescence, as a time not only of sexual engagement but literally of conception and generation, is something we no long encourage in Western societies, nonetheless we can and probably must imagine and put in place some analogue. Expressive interaction, after all, stands as a central element of such fertile generativity. And if adolescence is a time to learn commitment, the keeping of promises for the long term, the balancing of internal passions and external roles and responsibilities, it is possible to place these elements centrally into the lives of this age group in the form of nonsexual human intercourse. There are those who believe that teen sports has proven and remains so important (especially in its physical aspects) just because it functions as this kind of space for adolescent expressive interaction. This is the case too for theater, orchestra, or other corporate activities.

At the same time, adolescents are deeply dependent on adult mentors and guidance, and on this basis they learn to give life to others who are younger. Here is where interactions from infancy emerge in their fluency or halting character: the ways in which trust, affection, and empathy have been learned earlier now express themselves concretely with force. Adolescence marks one of the last ages in which most people can still naturally grow in these areas. And every interaction will be oriented to this somehow, for good or ill, consciously or not, such that the shape of the world to come, the landscape of skinful passage, is wrapped up in the form of life that emerges from adulthood's bud. After it run all the angers, lusts, resentments, or hopes and brave mercies of the future.

> Then a soldier,
> Full of strange oaths and bearded like the pard [i.e., the patchy colors
>     of a leopard],
> Jealous in honour, sudden and quick in quarrel,
> Seeking the bubble reputation
> Even in the cannon's mouth.

Youth or young adulthood (*iuventus*) was often associated, among males, with the age of arms, of soldiery; among women, with the full duties of administration of the family. For Augustine, youth is the pinnacle of the arc of life, which he compares with the reign of David the king: strength, valor, integrity sought after—if often lost—and creative oversight. From the vantage of divine invention, it stands as the fourth day of creation and embraces the lights of heaven that order time itself. Youth is like noonday, hence the measure of our rise and fall in its structured, because inevitably defined, movement. From Augustine's point of view, we are talking about a person's late twenties and early thirties—what today we would view as the prime of a professional athlete's career. This pinnacle is understood both physically and cognitively.

The traditional aspects associated with young adulthood obviously center on physical characteristics, bound to the body's health. Historically, young adults were those whose energies shaped cities and empires, tearing them apart or (less frequently) dragging them together. Without young adults, cultures would decline, unable to sustain their energies. This is something that the aging societies of the post-Transition are beginning to wonder about. But also, without the ordered movement of young adults integrated within a larger generational framework, societies destabilize themselves by failing to focus the energies of their young adults. One of the great predictors of civil unrest for so long has been the employment level of this age and unemployment's contribution to the civil turbulence associated with "youth bulges."[29] The fact that, at least recently, this dynamic has been belied in many places of Europe indicates perhaps an evisceration of the age's own inner strength. As Francis Bacon described it, the virtues of youth center on their energetic execution of new ideas: "Heat and vivacity in age is an excellent composition for business. Young men are fitter to invent than to judge; fitter for execution than for counsel; and fitter for new projects than for settled business."[30] And as the old hold on to power at the expense of the young, they must be careful not to do so in a way that simply robs younger adults of their capacities. This merely extends their adolescence, so that focused energies are left to ramble about in the desultory fashion of the unordered teenager.

Most government statistics (e.g., those used by nations or the World Health Organization to track disease or mental health and violence) have age categories that go to age twenty-four and then lump together persons from age twenty-five to around fifty or even more as a single period of adulthood. There is some rationale to this, having to do with university education as well as the extension of physical health. But it makes no sense in a basic way, given that a host of cognitive and physical capacities, including fertility, change steadily, and in the direction of decline mostly, by around thirty-five. That is, at least biologically, the period from age twenty-four to thirty-five *is* a distinct one. Hence, we do not have good lateral as well as historical information on, for instance, young adult mental health. Interestingly, there is evidence, but insufficiently detailed, that in areas like suicide, violence, and psychosis, the risk rate for young adults goes up. At the same time, the environmental influences during this period seem to be far stronger than therapeutic interventions can alter: for example, ten years of widespread mental health services and interventions in Norway has done little to alter the suicide rate among young adults, which seems far better correlated with family, economic, and other cultural identifiers.

One of the great shifts in the lives of young adults in Western countries is precisely their marginalization from a vigorous integration within the patterns of generativity, to which probative existence has been linked: marriage, children, family, and work. Modern post-Transition tendencies like the significant delay or abandonment of marriage, delayed and reduced fertility, attenuated family density, and uncertain employment and material sustainability have all altered, if not radically hollowed out, the kind of practiced mutual responsibilities that in the past were, by this age, well honed, at least in their material challenge. Elements of this are inevitable, given the changes of life span. But the major issue that has simply not been faced is how young adulthood properly coordinates with other ages. That is, one of the things that these shifts in identifying, describing, and furthering young adulthood demonstrate is the way that this age—as with any age, but especially here—is best examined, not in its discrete tenor, but as part of an interacting network of ages and of generations. So Bacon will go on in his essay "Of Youth and Age," precisely in a way that brings younger and older adulthood into profile in relation to the other:

> Certainly it is good to compound employments of both; for that will be good for the present, because the virtues of either age may correct the defects of both; and good for succession, that young men may be learners, while men in age are actors; and, lastly, good for extern accidents, because authority followeth old men, and favor and popularity youth.

Here, the question of tradition also arises, in Highet's sense, as learning is given and passed on in a very particular relationship, now of a certain necessary symbiosis of power. At issue in our era is the kind of learning and the particular traditions that are engaged. Obviously, young adulthood, as we are describing it, is the age of Jesus' own ministry and death. (Ironically, it is this age group that, in Western churches, has been most absent the ecclesial participation.) If Jesus' ministry constitutes the "prime of life," however, then we should observe its form as particularly revelatory of young adulthood's proper focus (cf. Isa 53:8, where being "cut off from the land of the living" is viewed as a sudden intrusion into the midst of strength; cf. also Isa 38:10; Ezek 17:22, where the "sprig" [NIV] is the means of power). What is given in Jesus' young adulthood and thus in this time of the New Adam is the gift of self for the sake of the world (cf. Rom 8:32). Just this becomes the focus of perfection in the form of "perfect love" (John 3:16; 1 John 4:10, 18). Jesus' ministry is the time of the divine love of the divine adult, received and given. Yet, the corollary of this is that if this strength of adulthood is itself deflated or dissolved, it cannot bear the heavier clothing, the skins of sacrifice. Jesus is the adult whose energies are most vigorous, most inventive and out-spilling—"grace upon grace" (John 1:16 RSV), a cup "running over" (Luke 6:38). As a human being, Jesus is able to do this insofar as he draws his life energies from adolescence's own passage into adulthood and orders them by wisdom's cumulative movement that pulls him forward from the place of aging. He dies and is resurrected as a full adult, even as his adulthood defines and judges our own.

> And then the justice,
> In fair round belly with good capon lined,
> With eyes severe and beard of formal cut,
> Full of wise saws and modern instances;
> And so he plays his part.

Maturity, or *gravitas*, now takes form with the aging adult. Shakespeare rightly makes this the generation of the judge. Physically, the arc of life is on its downward decline, but wisdom is at its zenith: the rigors of childhood, the fruitfulness of adolescence, and the experience of young adulthood are now complete, and sober-minded and clear-thinking vision can now give proper counsel and restrain ignorance from destroying life. The mature human being aims now at upholding the foundations of this graceful realm of creaturely existence.

To be sure, as Shakespeare hints, hypocrisy and rot can also have set in by this time, leadened by the veniality of fatigue and laziness. These are the perverted products of aging. But their proper fruit lie elsewhere, in the gifts of human maturity: counseling, judging, correcting, reconciling. We can note how, after the arc of adulthood has reached its upper height, the orientation of human encounter, and for that matter of human challenge, turns "backward": those who are mature and older have become the inter-actors with the younger: it is the only generative way that the young can engage and learn. So tradition reaches backward, as a means not of preserving the past but of sharing the present across the generations.

Maturity, in this traditional series, comes as physical vigor begins its gradual ebbing. Maturity is not, however, the sole possession of those close to death, since all of us are close in this regard, at whatever age. Rather, it derives from the fruits of expended experience. In the pre-Transition, "ripe" adulthood is still bound to toil and labor, and its character marks those who work from their late thirties until their rest, usually in their sixties. (The sixties, in fact, have been a traditional time for many to begin to put away their tools, if only for weakened health. The years of a "working adulthood" have, oddly enough, not elongated much since before the Great Transition, even while the possibilities for the "age of labor" have expanded, and, in many cases, economic demands have been enforcing its lengthening.) It is important to grasp the relationship between maturity and younger adulthood here, especially in an age like our own where roles have been reversed, and the counselors are often young researchers, and the power brokers are older. In the traditional generational landscape of creatureliness, active counsel devolves more naturally to those in their forties and fifties, as does the responsibility for engaging those who are younger at every stage. Counsel is the actual *work* of maturity, and its fulfillment marks in large part the probative criterion of aging in this movement of time. Young adulthood leads to older counsel. We survive the battering risks of our twenties and thirties for one purpose only: the sake of our children. This stands in stark contrast to a contemporary culture where adulthood today sees as its purpose not the corporate future but a *personal* material future, given economically in terms of "saving" and "retirement" and also in terms of the politics that determine the value of such economic goals.

More than anything the segregation of generations in post-Transition society is an assault on these most particular interactions, through which aging itself maintains its fruitful purpose. "Fending for oneself," along with "making one's own choices," as generational principles—incarnated in the consumer culture of age specificity and mirrored in the Christian church by the deformity of generationally detached mission, worship, and learning—marks a profoundly destructive dynamic. For it is just within the inextricability of the responsibilities among generations, expressed so clearly in the distinctive character of mutuality within adulthood's passing stages, that life for both young and old is given its direction as a creaturely gift. Instead, generational passage has become for many a fading movement into increased isolation and life's unravelling textures, whose threads finally separate and blow away with the descending wind of death.

The sixth age shifts
Into the lean and slipper'd pantaloon
With spectacles on nose and pouch on side,
His youthful hose, well saved, a world too wide
For his shrunk shank; and his big manly voice,
Turning again toward childish treble, pipes
And whistles in his sound.

"Pantaloon," in the comic plays of the European sixteenth and seventeenth centuries, was a figure of conniving and grasping, found among the older men of long-habituated avarice. For Shakespeare's era, "Pantaloon" or *pantaleone*, represented the reemergence of bad habits among the old—their "real" personality coming out at last, as the weaker controls of the flesh finally gave way to the inexorable shape of human character as it has long fashioned itself. If you want to know what a person is like "deep down," observe them in their still-functioning old age, where they finally express everything they have held back for so long, often in terms of bitterness and resentment. Or sometimes it may be even the display of generosity and joy. One of the truths emphasized by the "ages of life" tradition is that each stage is related to another. How we have navigated and been formed by one stage orders the next. And, conversely, our older selves will shape our younger brethren as well as illumine our own pasts. In a sense, then, old age—*senectus*—is the time when we are shown for who we are, in terms of our responsible selves, as we prepare to stand before God. The old teach the young; but they teach the young only in a way that exposes their own form. The old are thereby judged.

Augustine himself does not list this stage separately, but instead he lumps agedness and dying together in *senectus*. But old age comes upon us inexorably if we live this long. Because of its implication within our younger selves, old age unfolds in the diverse ways that we have earlier set our times to follow. That is, our old age is always an opening, not a closing. It opens us to praise or fear, as the outcome to our passage. How we are old is an outcome turned to the past in its origination; but more deeply, it is an outcome that rises up in the face of that which we cannot trace, our deaths. In this way, our old age is the form of our receipt, in its sheer form. "Reminiscence," often of family ties, becomes old age's conceptual form, for better or worse.[31]

This is not to say that our senility is the final form of our passive existence. Rather, it is the given form of our existence as it has been trained, followed through over time, within the ordering of our interactions. We approach our deaths in the posture of the those engagements with the world that we have learned. Indeed, this is what all our learning adds up to; and it is this summary that marks our learning—the wisdom that has emerged from interplay of receiving, giving, adjusting, remaking.

Old age, then, does not unfold our final quiescence before the truth of God. It is not by accident that one of the key words in the Christian vocabulary of creaturely life—what we call "morals," or the shape of our interactions—is "patience."[32] The word "passion," as in the passion of Jesus, is related to patience. So patience has to do with suffering, and ultimately sacrifice. But patience is also simply about time: living it, letting it be, letting ourselves be shaped by it, and engaging it. To learn as a creature is to be patient. Here the Ages of Life, however they are defined, come up against the *im*patience of a world like our own, which has forgotten creaturehood. One reason that adults cannot stick with things—marriages, their children, their jobs, the generations of their flesh and community, their ecclesial commitments—is because we have failed to learn the patience that comes with recognizing our lives as given, in an order, in time, in their places, such that we understand that our endings enclose and display the range of our wanderings. Adam to Adam is not a blank slate or an aimless track, though we often treat it as such: it is the form of a life that moves according to the figures of God's mercy and judgment both, given in the life of Israel. Our lives form a complex line of filiated strains, yet bound together in a certain way. Thus, every aged person in Scripture reveals the landscape of an entire people's passage, in the sense that it "proves" her or him within the context of their historical relationships, thus manifesting the probative dynamic of created life itself: Moses on Nebo; Eli with a boy who will replace his own sons; Naomi alone with widowed daughter-in-law; David numbed amid his blankets and women, shivering; all the way to Anna and Simeon slipping away in a doomed temple; or perhaps John, gazing into a pregnant mist, on his island. These are variously visions of uncertainty or hope that press forward. But the visions speak of the lives who now gaze into God's mysterious gifts.

> Last scene of all,
> That ends this strange eventful history,
> Is second childishness and mere oblivion,
> Sans teeth, sans eyes, sans taste, sans everything.

For Shakespeare, we simply return to where we began. There is some truth to this: as we end our lives, at least in extended years, we do so by confronting the reality with which we began them, grace and dependence. Our life is not ours, we are here by divine grace and, with our deaths, now approach the threshold of its limit, even its consummation. In our dying we experience a reduction of existence but also a question now posed that was never there before, the question of opening or closure. In Augustine's view, this "sixth" age is the day of human creation in two ways: first, that of the "old Adam" within the seven-day scheme of Genesis 1, but, secondly, that of the "New Adam," Christ, who comes upon the scene at the end of human history. So the term "threshold" is appropriate to dying since it points to the *limen* of redemption, in which now we can look back and forward at the same time. If we but allow it, now the form of our ordered (or disordered) life can be taken up by God anew for his own remaking. Whether it is in repentance, fear, hope, or gratitude, everything that comes before our deaths now shapes this moment, informs it, and is taken up by it.

Death, the Catholic theologian Karl Rahner insisted, is a *theological* claim.[33] He was thinking of the theoretical possibility that human beings might one day so advance their technologically driven extensions of the life span that "dying" would simply recede as a necessary part of human existence. To say that our deaths are "simply" or "purely" or "essentially" part of who we are is thus to claim something that goes beyond theoretical reason and actually engages our faith. (This is an important claim, since it points to the way that contemporary discussions about technological interventions in human life are in fact religious ones, not simply utilitarian in nature.) There is something important here to grasp: part of our Christian vocation is to proclaim the reality of death itself. Nothing could be more revelatory of contemporary forgetfulness—or faithfulness—than the disappearance of this proclamation from Christian teachers and preachers as a central part of the gospel they announce. The tradition of *memento mori*—"remember that you must die"—was not merely a medieval invention. It stands as a central scriptural focus (e.g., Ps 39:6; Luke 12:20). For to proclaim death, at least in its central aspect of our existence, is to return always to the form of our being as creatures. To announce our creaturehood is to proclaim God.

Rahner is surely right in his insistence upon the basic connection between our deaths and our faith. But the connection is not simply chosen according to our religious convictions. For every person will not only

confront this baseline of their being but has already done so in a fundamental sense. Repentance and conversion are always possible elements
of any life, and nothing is fated. Yet time is not merely a succession of
unconnected moments whose constellation is an ongoing work of a hidden God. Human time is ultimately a life, in its coherence and in its
framed relationships with other lives and with the objects of the world in
which it has moved and moves forward. Even if we confess such coherence as God's own handiwork in its final form, the apprehension of this
shape—our grasping of it, literally, as we engage its emergence—is a
responsibility we assume. We assume it through our willing and unwill-
ing encounters with our very being-from-and-with-God in the course of
our extended lives. That is, all of us have seen our deaths long before we
die. We have seen them in others; we have seen them in our own selves
and their fallings away, and in the world's immovable fragilities. And
as we have seen them with God or turned away from God, marked by
the texture of our common lives, we are readied for the posture of our
threshold walk. In this sense, Rahner is right when he speaks of death
being the "consummation" of our "whole existence," for it enacts that
existence in every step we take.

Of course, we do not know where we are going when we die. Here
Shakespeare's cynicism properly grates at all simplistic pieties: to our
deaths belong "oblivion," "sans everything." That is part of what death
*is*. For all the Christian exhortations regarding heaven and hell, and the
carefully wrought images of their reality that the church has fabricated,
this threshold opens up to something that must stay hidden from us
now and before which we must remain silent. Our sins, our distractions,
and the very nature of being alive as a creature mean that we cannot get
beyond our coming and going, our births and deaths, to see them from
the "outside in." If there is a "something" that death gives rise to, it is not
a something that is ours to take hold of, to turn in our hands, to plug
into this or that hole in our questions and missed opportunities. If our
lives are free, then we freely abandon ourselves into the incomprehensible
meaning of God's "hands," of a making that no metaphor will deliver; or
we freely withhold ourselves from that which will take us anyway. At this
point, our choices give way to "passion" in its finality.

The clock, by contrast, shows us what is *not* hidden, what we know
of our lives, and that which orders them. It cannot unveil to us the mystery of God. That is only God's to reveal, in a place that creatures enter
according to his will. Still, it is a will of which we know something. The

last and Seventh Age, for Augustine, is thus the Sabbath, the new creation in its fullness. Here, God steps across the limit of our created lives, from his own direction; and having moved toward us in our nothingness, God shares with us the bridge into his own fullness. Our generation is unveiled as God's own; our genealogy is uncovered as God's own line cast out to us; our testing has now given way to the final molding. During our Christian lives we are shaped to trust in this act of God, but only imperfectly: now perfectly. The promise of this "Seventh Age" is that it is in fact "out of time" altogether; it is not an "age" at all but the gift of something new that we grasp at and touch in our temporal lives, but that does not wholly belong to them. It is the clockless tick, whose singularity creates all distinction.

The final chapter of this book will speak to this Seventh Age and its relation to Christ Jesus. For now we can note how, in this perspective, "unfinished" lives and ruptures to the serial order of the six ages of worldly life need not impede us from being taken up by the Sabbath of Christ. Such ruptures, after all, can occur for a child, a foolish elderly man, or a young woman. Those "taken before their time," however, are not in fact stunted human creatures. For how each of us responds to such cutting short *is* in fact proportioned to our place in life; we are touched as we have been shaped. Death is the one event that most clearly divulges the creaturely miracle of our making. But unlike suicide, which nonetheless indicates the truth of life's giftedness negatively, the death of any person, when taken as an aspect of that person's whole living, extends the range of this giftedness infinitely. Every death, at any time, is revelatory of all that "is" in the created order as it stands with God. It closes the arc of our being as its exact representation.

There is more to say about individuals, in their specific places and conditions: those who die young, the childless, the single. What the arc of the life span demonstrates, even in the case of these specific persons, is that the meaning of this or that individual life is not bound up exhaustively or even primarily with its individual form, taken as a discrete figure. Every creaturely life is given in and by the whole in its interactions. What makes a creature a specific creature is the ordering of a life with other lives, never its individual being alone. A child not *only* is a child but is a child *for* the adult who cares for her; a young man not *only* is a young man in himself but is one for the sake of the older man who teaches him; an old woman not only is an old woman but is so in respect to the young she embraces and guides. The texture of generation, genealogy, and probation that marks human creatureliness is itself given as a comprehensive set of relationships whose shape can be determined only across time. The point is not that human creaturehood is species driven, with each individual serving the survival of the race. Rather, creaturehood is constellation driven: it is all about the landscape and its multiple objects as they exist together, encounter, engage, and crumble within the context of a divinely figured order. The famous words from Thérèse of Lisieux's opening chapter to her autobiography point to this:

> In reading the lives of the Saints I was surprised to see that there were certain privileged souls, whom Our Lord favoured from the cradle to the grave, allowing no obstacle in their path which might keep them from mounting towards Him, permitting no sin to soil the spotless brightness of their baptismal robe. And again it puzzled me why so many poor savages should die without having even heard the name of God. Our Lord has deigned to explain this mystery to me. He showed me the book of nature, and I understood that every flower created by Him is beautiful, that the brilliance of the rose and the whiteness of the lily do not lessen the perfume of the violet or the sweet simplicity of the daisy. I understood that if all the lowly flowers wished to be roses, nature would lose its springtide beauty, and the fields would no longer be enamelled with lovely hues. And so it is in the world of souls.[34]

This constellated "world of souls" given in the filiated breadth of created human life is precisely the kind of "context" that has been missing from our scriptural and social debates over human life in the era of the Great Transition.

A constellation, however, is not a straightforward or directed movement. If there is wisdom that is gained from the course of a life, it cannot simply be cumulative. The book of Job has traditionally been read as offering a defining vision of how wisdom is related to the life span. We could call Job "The Book of the Creature" in this regard. If nothing else, the book sketches, in a rather disproportioned way, the arc of life. It also attempts to delineate the nature of what Job learns by journeying across this arc. In doing so, however, the book demonstrates how the arc itself is experientially complex.

People have noted the asymmetry involved in the book of Job's narrative. The complete sum of the first two chapters is that Job has a wonderful and productive life, only to experience it as something that is all taken away. But the next forty chapters are a long give and take with his friends, in which there is no clear progression in thought, only a constant going back and forth of questions: Is God just? What have I done to deserve this? How mysterious is the world! How beautiful but also how frightening! God will vindicate me. One just has to wait. Is God just? What have I done to deserve it? . . . The book starts repeating itself, agonizingly so, with Job constantly circling back in a ruminating obsession.

One of the things all this shows us is that the movement of *coming* to wisdom actually defines the substance of wisdom. Godly wisdom is the form of one who is *driven* to such a context and landscape of listening and who perseveres in inhabiting it and moving through it until such light as God would give is indeed given and received. We have to stick with the life that is ours, with its limits, edges, bumps, and filling. By passing through it steadfastly, we learn deeply and we gain wisdom. The arc of life is never a smooth curve, and any suggestion otherwise is not only misleading; it is manifestly contradicted by experience.

All the early Christian writers on skinfulness, the *tunica pellicea*, have stressed the fact that the skins themselves tie us to the earth somehow. Marks of God's compassion, they are nonetheless indicative of our *need* for such compassion, of the fact that we have a landscape to cross whose texture is bound up with our own dirt-based constitution, "formed from the dust." The skins are also signs of that "humility" that finally God himself assumed in the flesh of Jesus, on his own "adventure," as Péguy puts it. This adventure or movement of *humilitas* is one where there is indeed a growth in knowledge, understood in terms of the Christian's own transformation in the hands of God's providential gifts. But it requires perseverance in that this growth is not a simple linear progression but one that must be able to circle back on itself, apprehending God's gifts in the form of one's own body and life, subjecting the self to God's time. The body's aging is an essential aspect of this trajectory, and the skin discloses this entire journey.

Over time, the "skin" most especially withers, dries out, thins and weakens to the point of translucence, as it covers the ebbing fluids within. While Scripture's prohibition of self-mutilation (Lev 19:28; Deut 14:1) has a range of meanings, the increasingly common usage of tattoos has its own incoherence in this context: so often signals of skinful strength, they end up becoming an undesired *memento mori* of a perverse kind. Job, by contrast, is the man whose skin is eaten away by life and whose travel across his own arc of existence suddenly meets an impassable barrier. Now we ask if his humility, in some manner celebrated by God before Satan, gives rise to anything. Wisdom is truly hidden, Job announces in chapter 28's almost terrifying image of the dangerous and futile work of mining in the tunnels of the earth. Wisdom is hidden even from the wise, even from those who seek God with all their heart and soul. Here at the border of human capacity, Job finally articulates a word from God in 28:28: "And he said to man, 'Behold, the fear of the Lord, that is wisdom; and to depart from evil is understanding.'" Job has reached the summit of human faith, which nonetheless looks down into and across an abyss. It is a central claim of the entire Bible, as we know (cf. Ps 111:10; Prov 1:7; 2:5; 9:10; Eccl 12:13; Isa 11:3; Jer 32:40; John 1:16; and over and over again in various formulations). "Fear" of God, in its root Hebrew meaning of terror and reverence both, is made the universal standard of theological truth, both in its content and in the posture of the knower: to "fear God" is to know who God is; and such knowledge is articulated in the form of reverence.

Yet Job had begun the book as a God-fearing man (1:1)! If anything has changed for Job in this respect in the course of the book, it is only the *character* of Job's fear. Now Job fears as he has never feared before. If we turn to the Gospels, we see this same movement over time from fear to a better and wiser fear. From shepherds before the angel's announcement (Luke 2:10), to crowds before the works of Jesus (Luke 5:26), to disciples before his power over the natural world (Matt 14:26), to thieves on a cross shared with God (Luke 23:40), to a centurion, to women disciples before an empty tomb (Matt 28:8), to the church's own mission in the world (Phil 2:12), there is a drilling down of fear. While "perfect love casts out fear" (1 John 4:18)—the fear of those who stand without hope before God's judgment—the "fear of the Lord" marks the new disciples of Jesus the Christ (Acts 9:31) precisely because now it is grounded in hope, and such a fearful hope as will continue to mark their life in the world as a life that is true to God's own life given in his Son.

The difference between the Job of the book's beginning and the Job of the book's end is tied to this final fear that stands as the Christian's hope in death itself: over time, through fearing God, Job has been opened to receive everything and anything as a gift, even and especially God himself. All is gift; all is a filiated adventure. Though Job finally asks (31:35) what he has asked before, that *God* listen to him, the difference at the end of the book is that Job himself is now ready to listen directly to God. Here, he falls silent. His posture no longer reflects a demand or a need but is the mark of having opened all things of his own being to God. Job can listen, because Job has nothing left to see: his words are "ended" (v. 40). God can "hear" Job's silence, a sign finally of his readiness. Now Job too "reminds God of his Son"—not as an innocent child, but as a broken old man. Finally, with the book's close, we are told that, from this broken and opened man, there somehow sprang yet more life. Job 42:12-17, which has often been read as a kind of unhelpful tidying up of the moral disaster that the book as a whole presents, should rather point us to the fruit of the cross.

This is the movement of the creature's life: to begin in crying and to end in the silence of worship and praise. All the struggles, the orderings, the limits, the wresting and resting, the overcoming—this is how wisdom comes to be, and the gift that is our creation is finally received as an eternal gift.

# V

# The Vocation of Singleness

## The Modern Question of Diversity and Inclusion

One of the great intellectual and social shifts in the modern West is its embrace of "diversity" as a deep human value. This chapter will examine the character of diversity within the human community as it is disclosed in the normed relationships between single and married creatures. However novel the modern celebration of human diversity may seem, valuing its revelatory nature has in fact been central to much of the Christian scriptural tradition. What is distinctive in this tradition, however, is the way diversity serves the grace of mortal limitation.

Long before modernity, Western literature had reveled in the descriptive multiplicity of human persons. Homer has Odysseus, as he wanders about the world, engage the "multiplicity of human being" (*polloi anthropoi*) and their outlooks; Herodotus delights in the diverse customs he learns of through his own wide travels; the very character of "history," "geography," and even the early medical studies of Hippocrates is founded on gathering data about dispersed cultures and attitudes. The notion of a "catalogue," itself a part of classical and then medieval rhetoric, is a profound and liberating insistence on the value of that which is various. This was already true in the Middle Ages, and the proliferation of Renaissance treatises on the "variety" of nature—trees, animals,

plants, bodies, and, bit by bit, parts of the world—was continuous with
the classical sources that, from one perspective, fed them.[1]

Still, the modern world is driven by a new sense of what diversity
signifies. The widely influential sixteenth-century essayist Montaigne
wondered about the variety of customs and peoples around the globe,
descriptions of whose existence were now flooding the literary world of
his circle through accounts by people like Francisco López de Gómara,
André Thevet, and Jean de Léry. This "new world" truly did change
how Europeans understood aspects of their place in the universe, even
if it did not do so in a straightforward and objective fashion. Aristotle
himself never traveled far. He could write about women and slaves, free
persons and barbarians, in part because he had inherited limited and set
ways of construing the relational lives of these persons. The great church
leader Bartolomé de Las Casas by contrast, in the sixteenth century,
had traveled from Europe to the Caribbean and Mexico and back several times. The human beings he wrote about were ones he had actually
encountered in a dizzying variety and immediacy. The literary genre of
"captivity narrative" that arose already in the sixteenth century, written
by escaped or returned European prisoners from among indigenous peoples, had a two-edged consequence: while these accounts often depicted
native peoples as dangerous, overall their effect was to demand difficult
reorientations in understanding "humanity" and to inform a new conscience about it. In some ways, diversity was not so much discovered in
the sixteenth century and beyond, as finally located: decidedly within
the creature, the what-it-means-to-be-a-human-being. Lynn Hunt's controversial thesis that the modern development of the notion of human
rights depended on a growing imaginative empathy, nurtured by novelis-
tic literature, is hard simply to dismiss, in the light of encounter, description, and finally presentation of difference. There were, of course, the
foreigners in strange clothes, as popular books catalogued them; there
were also the poor, the farmer, the schoolchild, the housemaid, and the
criminal, as sermons, paintings, poetry, and then novels displayed them.
These writings were widely published and read, engendering a new sense
of connection across the lines of difference. Diversity carried with it a
common calling.[2]

Some of the political consequences of this growing apprehension of
human variety have proven ironic. So, for instance, diversity becomes a
sphere that requires civil protection, precisely because all the details of
difference are increasingly seen as being more and more epiphenomenal

to a deeper unity among things. This enlarged sense of human commonality proved a moral gain. "Am I Not A Man And A Brother?" went the
epigram of the famous 1787 medallion of Josiah Wedgwood, designed
to further the abolitionist movement. The sphere of "the human" has
enlarged, then, but only by taking with it, and thus muting, specifics of
one kind or another. Over the past forty years especially, we have seen
yet a further shift in the notion of human diversity, now construed in
terms of the way many understand "the human" as a sphere of cohesive
responsibility. No longer is something called "common humanity" the
value; rather, it is difference itself. What had been the hard-won value of
"multiplicity in humanness" has now turned into humanness in multiplicity. Where once "inclusion" and "exclusion" referred to the sphere of
common human life—schooling and disabilities, poverty and decision
making—now human life is, politically, increasingly viewed as but the
agglomeration of disparate forms, whose only relation one to another
is the moral demand for political confirmation. The development over
the past few decades, for instance, of a notion of "deaf" culture, to be
guarded and treasured rather than to be dissolved by new hearing technologies, is a mark of the way that "marginalization" has gained its own
intrinsic values, at least insofar as it designates particularity itself. "Inclusion" and "exclusion" are now defined in terms of this protected dispar-
ity, which has had the effect of making commonality itself a kind of
enemy. "Mainstreaming" once meant bringing the "marginalized" into
the sphere of normality. Now "normality" is itself suspect as a usefully
defining concept; often, it is but a conceptual tool for oppression.[3]

These have become deeply fraught political questions. Sometimes at
great cost, we are being forced to decide who gets to define the parameters of "working" inclusion, or whether people can choose "exclusive"
forms of life as parts of their "diversely enculturated" communities or
individualities. At stake is the very nature of a "social community" and
the ways that diversities undermine such "community" or build it up.
The migration of "inclusion" to specifically sexual and gendered politics
demonstrates some of the issues in play. Obviously, gay marriage and
adoptive or surrogate-conceived families are a point of contention, even
within diverse sexual communities. Some of these elements are contested
within feminist debates, where "sexual difference" is sometimes granted
and sometimes denied specific "rights" and duties.[4] These debates have
had enormous implications especially for the Christian church's understanding of what constitutes "inclusion" in a responsible and evangelical

way. More public discussions about these knotted questions will usually appeal to still common notions of "human dignity," but it turns out that the notion is not so commonly understood as we thought: abortion is not clearly a "human right"; no one is agreed on how the "rights of women" should be bound up with certain sexual freedoms that affect procreation or family organization; there is little consensus on where the "rights of children" intersect with other rights, such that human dignity is both respected and furthered. Given these confusions, it is not surprising that the church herself struggles to articulate how heterosexual and procreative "marriage," understood in a certain way, may be essential to human dignity. Not only have the categories of "inclusion" and "exclusion" become moral wax noses; they cannot help but be so in a context where creaturehood has been socially occluded.

What one finds, in current debate within the churches, is an often tendentious approach to scriptural interpretation on these matters, in a way that reflects rather narrowly the political debate in the present. In particular, the treatment of, for example, Leviticus and the Old Testament Law often veers toward an almost Marcionite reading of the biblical text, as if the Old Testament Law were the product of culturally self-centered and self-righteous Hebrew nationalism, literally "pharisaic" in its caricatured meaning, "exclusivistic" in more contemporary terms. It is not insignificant that Judaism itself is often described today in terms of its "exclusionary" attitudes, since, in this case at least, it indicates that the vocabulary of inclusion and exclusion is at least sometimes but a contemporary version of long-standing social prejudices rather than a reflection of emancipatory progress. In the context of this contemporary social Marcionism, Jesus is then depicted as having arrived on the scene to overturn exclusivism and throw the doors open to a more loving God's true purpose, only hinted at, yet misunderstood, within the Old Testament. Much of the popular Christian literature on same-sex affirmation sounds like a modern version of the second-century *Epistle of Barnabas* in its worst aspects.

But none of this makes any sense. As it turns out, the category of "inclusion" is not one that is mentioned in either Testament in a direct way. Modern authors, to be sure, have spoken of the "inclusion of the Gentiles." That is a contemporary term, however, not Paul's. In Romans 11:12, Paul instead uses the Greek term *pleroma*, which has a very different connotation, pointed more towards "fullness" ("Now if the fall of them [i.e., Israel] *be* the riches of the world, and the diminishing of them the riches of the Gentiles; how much more their fullness?" [the RSV and NIV, before the politicization of the word, do indeed translate this as "inclusion"]). Paul will also use words like "reception"—"receiving" the Gentiles—where the issue is one of calling and grace, on God's part, given to Israel and then to others in the sacrifice of Christ. Even this is conditional upon obedience of some sort.

Jesus' own central ministry of calling to repentance, baptism, and the demands of discipleship is too easily glossed over in this context. He comes to call and bring in the "outcast," something we understand well enough. Yet the word itself is a modern one that has no place in Scripture, at least as a broad social category. In the Old Testament, what we translate as "outcast" speaks to formal understandings of banishment (cf. 2 Sam 14:14), which color its figurative use (cf. Ps 5:10, where God is asked to "cast out" the unrighteous). The New Testament, on the other hand, speaks of calling "sinners," "the sick," or "the lost" (Mark 2:17; Matt 5:30; 18:11; Luke 7:22). Some modern interpreters, like the *Catholic Catechism* (par. 1033), have spoken of the obvious way that Jesus' words differentiate destinies (e.g., Matt 22:13 on being cast into "outer darkness"), and they describe this in terms of "auto-exclusion" or "self-exclusion," which is certainly one possible way of conceiving the matter. But there are also responsibilities alluded to in these "exclusionary" texts that imply the disciplines of formation and self-ordering: for example, the need to cut off hands and tear out eyes in Matthew 18:6-9, and the warnings regarding "scandal."

Although scriptural usage cannot sustain contemporary categories of "inclusion" and "exclusion," nonetheless the notion of Jesus' ministry as paradigmatically one of "inclusion" has become a cultural commonplace and touchstone. Any positive defense of traditional creaturely ordering, such as this one, must therefore strike a contemporary Westerner as built upon a retrogressive scriptural sociology of exclusion. Any substantive theology of creaturehood must answer the cultural challenge of whether it is calling for a straitjacket to be placed upon the intrinsic diversity, multiplicity, and finally *beauty* of the world. Such a theology must be able to embrace the reality of the single person, the homosexual or asexual, the disabled, the sterile, and the transsexual. For "creaturehood" cannot simply be a cipher for an imposing and deforming "normalcy" whose attractiveness is driven by the specific interests of this or that group or sex. What follows in this chapter is an attempt to think this through, with respect especially to singleness in relation to married life within the larger context of creaturely context existence.

## Norm and Creaturely Diversity

The English term "norm," and hence "normal," refers to some kind of standard rule; it derives from the carpenter's right angle, used to aid in cutting and building. But the word "norm" is also one of only recent common usage (mid-nineteenth century at best). It connotes what are properly "moral" realities rather than rigid natural determinations. That which is "moral" is that which manifests a "way of life," what used to be called "manners" in the deeper sense of how relationships are carried out in this or that context. Gaining wisdom, as our last chapter indicated, is given in the more basic dynamic of creaturely growth, which involves learning in itself: the project of relating, responding, and learning language. All this must fundamentally define life as a creaturely reality. The "moral life" of the child and adult varies across individuals and groups and cultures. But that there *is* such a life—emerging from the *mores*, or engaged context, of some set of interactions—is inescapable for all persons.

Just such relationships are meant to found, in the sense of preserving and opening up, the diversity of the world. Among the most perceptive writers on this matter was the (Christian) anthropologist Mary Douglas. Douglas' early work on "taboo" behavior, *Purity and Danger*,[5] in fact included Leviticus in its examination; and to some degree, her reading of the book in the context of discussing taboos proved an influential element in solidifying the popular view of the book as quintessentially "exclusivist." Yet Douglas continued to be fascinated by Leviticus, and thirty years later she returned to the book on more than one occasion, offering a refreshingly provocative, even revolutionary, look that revised her earlier rather narrow judgments. In *Leviticus as Literature*,[6] Douglas convincingly showed how the difficult categorizations of clean and unclean within the Mosaic law in fact function as a profoundly *opening*, as well as an ethically sophisticated, approach to God's creation. As presented in Leviticus, these distinctions map out a world that is both diverse and complicated, but also God's—where life's form, in its multiple forms, is a matter of both responsibility (the clean) and human self-restraint (the unclean, directly under God's sovereign claim), before the mysterious demands of survival that cannot simply be brushed aside. The law of "difference" here, Douglas now argued, was not exclusionary at all but rather preservative of God's own creation in its complexity and of God's exhaustive sovereignty over it.

The building of the Tower of Babel, with its story of hubris met by the sudden differentiation of languages, logically imposes itself on this vision. Difference among creatures and difference among human beings specifically must somehow be coordinated theologically:

> And the LORD came down to see the city and the tower, which the children of men builded. And the LORD said, Behold, the people [is] one, and they have all one language; and this they begin to do: and now nothing will be restrained from them, which they have imagined to do. Go to, let us go down, and there confound their language, that they may not understand one another's speech. So the LORD scattered them abroad from thence upon the face of all the earth: and they left off to build the city. Therefore is the name of it called Babel; because the LORD did there confound the language of all the earth: and from thence did the LORD scatter them abroad upon the face of all the earth. (Gen 11:5-9)

The traditional Christian reading of this story sees human disorder here given as a punishment for sin. Opposed to this is the hope for some kind of "unity" read back into the original creation of the garden and then read forward into the consummated age of redemption, when Babel will be "reversed." Without doubt, this reading placed a high value on "order" and on the social means of achieving or even enforcing such order. "One language," though the base from which divided nations arose, became nonetheless the nostalgic image of the healing of the nations as well. By the seventeenth century, when the terrors as well as moral challenges of division and diversity had been well etched in the European psyche, the search for an "original" or "universal" language became a holy grail of sorts, involving figures still well known, like the philosopher Leibniz or the originator of the decimal system, John Wilkins.

More recently, however, Babel has been reinterpreted in a way almost antithetical to this Christian tradition. To take the example of the French philosopher Michel Serres, we see the "sin" of Babel's builders was not their pride, per se, as much as their *mis*valuing of unity itself. Hence, the fall into linguistic cacophony was not a "fall" at all but a realization of the truth of the world: multiplicity itself.[7] Serres is alluringly exemplary of a common postmodern worldview, informed by the newer mathematics of "chaos" and topology, although ultimately and explicitly going beyond them in his antirationalism. The world is too complex, dynamic, evolving, and paradoxical, he insists, to permit "conceptual" and "classifying" logics to be imposed upon it. Learning is

about "mixing" and "inventing" through novelty and difference. Hence,
"order" itself will always necessarily move against the truth of the "way
things [plural] are." Babel was a blessing and the first eye-opener to the
wonder of the world.

But variety itself is not the issue in the case of Babel. The generations of Noah's sons, outlined as a whole in Genesis 10, emphasize the
establishment of diversity in geography and language even as a natural
part of generation—"scattering" and "dividing" in their specific termi-
nology. Already before Babel, we are told, the "nations are divided" into
their distinctions (cf. finally Gen 10:5, 32). Linguistic difference "scat-
ters" as part of the movement of grace out from the flood, repopulating
the earth. It creates "distance" in some fashion, which is relational, not
simply based on nonidentity; but it denotes nothing more than that.
The word used in Genesis 10 for language, "tongue," is, like the English
word, used for both the part of the body and, by metonymy, speaking.
In Genesis 11, however, as the Babel story unfolds, a new word is introduced for language, one that indicates not the tongue but the "lips."
One set of lips becomes many sets, and they are "confused" (11:7), in
the sense of being mixed up. What is the difference here, except that one
can no longer distinguish a common meaning within the many tongues?
Hence, we are talking now about *understanding*, not the character of
sound; we are talking about common purpose, not variety of being as
such. Babel is not so much about the disorder that comes from diversity;
but nor is it about the revelation of diversity either. It is about diversity
as it works together, or fails to.

Thus, when, before the throne of the Lamb, innumerable peoples
sing in their innumerable voices before God, they do so in innumerable languages as well. This variety is good. But in this consummated
moment, these many sounds speak the same *meaning*: "Salvation to our
God which sitteth upon the throne, and unto the Lamb" (Rev 7:9-10).
It is the fulfillment, cosmically, of the beginning made in the apostolic
Pentecost, of Acts 2:4-11. Such variegated unity in a common praise of
God is one that can be understood because it is speaking of the same
thing in a way ordered to the same person. But "variegated unity" is a
reality troubling to *both* interpretations of Babel I mentioned earlier—
the sin of disorder or the blessing of disorder. As with human flesh itself,
God "assumes" in Revelation the diversity of languages, by granting
them a common voice of praise. Such an assumption is one of the odd
elements of redemption: the distinct, the different, the *solitary* is joined

as such to the choir. This is a divine act, and it is ultimately one with the genealogical significance of fruitfulness (cf. Ps 68:6: "God setteth the solitary in families: he bringeth out those which are bound with chains: but the rebellious dwell in a dry [land]").

To speak of "chaos" in the context of Babel, as a kind of descriptor of humanly unorderable diversity, is thus probably unhelpful. Chaos, as a term, is used to all kinds of ideological ends in our day, good and bad. Yet we cannot link chaos with God's act of creation, either as its substratum or as its consequence: God creates out of what is, to us, a complete mystery in its nothingness. And it is a mystery wrapped up with our own nonbeing, our deaths. Hence, the fearfulness of "formless void"—spoken of in Genesis 1:2, or its extension in Jeremiah 4:23—is quite specific. If we wish to translate this as "chaos," then we are choosing to cast chaos in a profoundly negative way, just as the "chaos" of war is rightly fled as the embodiment of death itself (Jer 4:29-31). Contemporary notions of "turbulence" as creative (as someone like Serres insists) can certainly stand. But to make them the basis of an entire hermeneutic is scripturally absurd.

The link between Genesis 10 and Genesis 11, by contrast, is parallel to the provision by God for Adam and Eve's ejection from the garden. In the former case, the incoherence of many languages can at least provide the basis for distinctiveness' preservation through fallen time. We remember, after all, that creation itself is about the separation of that which is not-God into the distinctions of creatures. Now, out of Babel arises the means for particularity again, in its survival, its skinfulness. This must include the world itself, in its fullness and variety, hinted at in Genesis 1 (e.g., v. 22), given voice in its "naming" by Adam in 2:19-20, and finally established again after the flood in Genesis 9. With Babel's "confusion of tongues," this multiplicity is now opened up to human history. Genealogy is nationalized, spoken of in many ways, "named" in fashions that are no longer easily understood by all, yet nonetheless given its apprehended specificity. This is a kind of fallen, yet preservative, mirror in human life, to the multiplicity of the world. The Psalms, especially, will insist on the ongoing integrity of this multiplicity from and oriented to God (e.g., Ps 148), and it is this that is finally intertwined with human praise in Revelation before the divine throne. Babel's multiplied speech is not chaos at all, for here the "folds" in genealogy are given their place in this grand movement wherein time is twisted and knotted and bent back against itself, in a redemptive key such that creation can "appear" in its glory before the eyes of fallen men and women. The vision remains continuous, in fact, from antiquity through early modernity (and even now, for those with eyes to see and ears to hear).

The *individual*, then, is a gift given in the wilderness, not only in the garden. Indeed, this gift is granted a kind of new specificity—through *many* distinct names—in the wilderness. Adam and Eve, although named in the garden, have no named children there. Genesis 4:1-2 becomes crucial here: "And Adam knew Eve his wife; and she conceived, and bare Cain, and said, I have gotten a man from the LORD. And she again bare his brother Abel. And Abel was a keeper of sheep, but Cain was a tiller of the ground." Generation and genealogy (and very quickly, in what follows, the probative nature of each) are presented here for the first time in their concreteness. That is the point of the Genesis account: by becoming concrete, individuals are named. Having conceived a child with Eve, Adam "said," "I have gotten a man from the LORD" (4:1), now named Cain, and then another, named Abel. This "man" (*ish*) is, for the first time, the actual embodiment of the promise that Eve should be the "mother of all living" (3:20). Hence, only outside the garden do the names of Adam and Eve represent two *individual* human beings rather than "the first Adam," or "Eve" as the first "mother," the two being "our first parents" (in a common patristic phrase). It is not so much that, in the garden, Adam and Eve are but "symbols." Rather, only there do they exist in their inclusive (and I use the term here deliberately) being, as containing all persons of history, in analogy to the Second Adam's inclusive humanity. But having stepped out of the garden, their creaturehood becomes distinct in its individuality: they are historical beings, caught in the flow of time, whatever that may be, clothed in skins, living the one life that we ourselves follow within, each in our particular way.

This filiated individualism needs to be emphasized even as it must also be understood within the context of communal relation. The truth of human creaturehood is not something to assert simply against the cultural sins of modern atomism. It is true that "individualism" *is* a moral challenge in our culture and that individuals *cannot* be stand-alones within the world, if only from a biological point of view. There is *no such person as an individual person*. Nonetheless, it was a common view among Christians, at a time when theologians worried about such things, that angels were made by God all at once, in their full complement, simultaneously—but that human beings were created, in God's providence, via temporal generation, one after another, in the form of Genesis 4.[8] "Men" are what God makes (and here the *non*inclusive term is helpful, if culturally confusing), creatures in their individuality, not widgets from divine machine dies. The rise of individualism,[9] furthermore, however we date it, had a redemptive function, in the sense of being an act of compassion, a divine covering. It marked an increasing ability to see the world's goodness in its specific contours in a new and necessary way, which followed some of the deeply existential concerns listed at the beginning of the chapter—the dignity and beauty lodged in human diversity. Individualism, in this sense, helped to keep time from simply wearing down the race through the grinding down of human creatures by (the quite individual) forces of sin. Whether modern individualist thinking and political ordering actually serve to *open* human creaturehood up to its divine context is another question. Individual particularity finds its place *within* the filiative genealogy of human creaturehood; and it does so in a probative fashion. One of the inferences from this is not that particularity disappears but that it actually manifests itself only as the form of genealogical traversal, only as human beings are born to mothers and fathers and exist within the stream of this generative existence. We are "special" and unique, as our culture likes to call us, only within the context of the landscape of skinful and filiative pilgrimage.

## Singleness as an Open Window onto the World of Creatures

Singleness offers a specific paradigm of this particularity-in-filiation, given its seeming detachment from, and perhaps even opposition to, the genealogical tree that has been part of our focus until now. There are other possible paradigms to examine as well: married couples without children, or older persons who have married late in life. These human couplings do not fit clearly within a framework of existence founded in generative ordering. But to some extent, their fruitful meaning is analogous to that of the single person.[10]

It is a common complaint, and a well-founded one, that traditionalist Christian emphases on "family," especially as they have adopted conflictive edges within the polarized cultural battles of the present, leave single persons adrift. Churches are often the last place single people like to spend time, certainly not in terms of congregational activities. Those churches with sufficient size and resources can provide "singles groups," but these often end up being places whose existence is governed by a hidden ideology of stigmatization.[11] Thus, Internet dating, for conservative Christians, has become a safer realm of interaction. One could—and should—add to these dynamics the complicated demise of celibate religious vocations, even within the Catholic Church, which, following an inbred Protestant cultural ethos, has unwillingly and unconsciously come to denigrate this form of life as well. Finally, the culture of confusion over what constitutes "sexual identity," coupled with the breakdown of ordered adolescent socialization as an integral part of the creaturely life span, has left many individuals dangling and agonizing over what it means to be a sexual being altogether. They are left uncertain of their singleness from the start.

The proportion of single adults within Western populations has been growing steadily over the past few decades. It is one of the many indirect fallouts of the Great Transition. That need not make singleness "good" or "bad." What is obvious is that, as with many of the changes in our era, there is little sense of clarity about how a person might understand their creaturely being within this trend's confused dynamics. As Eric Klinenberg has said, synthesizing a wealth of data, the trend toward increased singleness and the experience of confusion over its meaning is a movement contrary to everything we know about human history and diverse human communities. Virtually all social entities we know that have survived (even the Shakers) have all and "always" been based on integrated forms of living arrangements, where individuals seek and are given ways to exist *with* others, not apart from them:

> Numbers never tell the whole story, but in this case the statistics are startling. In 1950, 22 percent of American adults were single. Four million lived alone, and they accounted for 9 percent of all households. In those days, living alone was by far most common in the open, sprawling Western states—Alaska, Montana, and Nevada—that attracted migrant workingmen, and it was usually a short-lived stage on the road to a more conventional domestic life. Today, more than 50 percent of American adults are single, and 31 million—roughly one out of every seven adults—live alone. (This figure excludes the 8 million Americans who live in voluntary and non-voluntary group quarters, such as assisted living facilities, nursing homes, and prisons.) People who live alone make up 28 percent of all U.S. households, which means that they are now tied with childless couples as the most prominent residential type—more common than the nuclear family, the multigenerational family, and the roommate or group home.[12]

Many people *want* to get married but cannot for a range of mostly socially imposed reasons—economics, customs of expectation and inter-action, and, in the case of some single parents, the brokenness and sin of partners and the consequences that follow. Some of these reasons as they are internalized, furthermore, are bound up with deep misunderstand-ings and sometimes resentments about marriage itself and its rooted-ness at the center of creaturely life. Some social critics have wondered if marriage is intrinsically oppressive to the personhood of its partners (women especially) or if it fosters "intimate partner violence." (Actu-ally, marriage seems to correlate with far less of such violence than does singleness, but the reasons are not clear.) Other critics have argued that marriage undergirds systems of economic and social purpose that mar-ginalize whole groups outside of its sphere. In the face of these acute challenges, the argument regarding mortal creaturehood cannot be used to commend marriage or singleness for this or that person so much as to try to trace the relationship between these two conditions within a faith-ful life span. Such a sketch must necessarily place the married life at the center and place the single life in a proportionalized noncentral location; but it is the *relationship* of the two that is "normalized," not one "over" the other. Furthermore, the argument for this relationship is relatively simple: individuality does not disappear within the genealogical tree; rather, individuality is *given* within the growth of this tree. Singleness, that is, emerges out of the genealogical movement, as a part of its being. It is a part of it, just as the long line of ramified languages and cultures arises out of the tide of Noah's generative heritage. The very English word "single" was used almost from the start to designate an unmarried person by contrast to a married one—but always in a kind of symbiotic correlation. The single person is a kind of mirror to the individuality of generated creatures, the detailing of their form. Particularity, as it in fact fashions the elements of the great traversal, opens up to view in the single person, and in a variety of ways.

One can begin to see how this is so even in the (in)famous Pau-line text on marriage and singleness in 1 Corinthians 7. Paul has been addressing, with some practical complexity, questions of marital rela-tions within a context of diverse Christian commitments—believing and unbelieving partners, their children, pressures to marry or not, and concerns about vocational faithfulness. These are major issues for the young congregation he is writing to. There is a good deal of debate by scholars over Paul's exact meaning in his responses, and here the focus is on only one portion of this dense passage, where he seems to be explicitly *contrasting* the single and the married life, to the advantage of the former.

In verses 32 to 34, Paul sums up the thrust of his argument by saying that his goal or hope is to have his Christian charges be free of "care" or "anxiety." As he explains, being married necessarily brings with it a "concern" for the spouse. The single person, he notes, has "concern" only for "the things of God." Finally, in verse 35, he says his hope is that all believers might be attentive to the Lord in a way that is "undivided."

One wonders here what Paul means by concern for "the things of the Lord" (v. 32) or by "undivided" attention (v. 35). Both of these, he seems to suggest, are more readily experienced by the unmarried person. If we understand "the things of the Lord" as those things that God "wants," then Paul is saying that the unmarried are simply better able to fulfill them. The "things of the Lord," in Leviticus and Deuteronomy (as given in the Greek version of Paul's day), seem to refer to matters of the Law (e.g., Deut 29:29), which are there to be obeyed. Hence, the point would be that married life is distracting from obedience to God. Scholars often quote from Paul's near-contemporary, the Cynic philosopher Epictetus, on this one.[13] Epictetus is describing the Cynic's need to maintain a freedom from distraction, for the sake of following the good:

> But in the present state of things which is like that of an army placed in battle order, is it not fit that the Cynic should without any distraction be employed only on the ministration of God, able to go about among men, not tied down to the common duties of mankind, nor entangled in the ordinary relations of life, which if he neglects, he will not maintain the character of an honourable and good man? and if he observes them he will lose the character of the messenger, and spy and herald of God. For consider that it is his duty to do something towards his father in law, something to the other kinsfolks of his wife, something to his wife also (if he has one). He is also excluded by being a Cynic from looking after the sickness of his own family, and from providing for their support. And to say nothing of the rest, he must have a vessel for heating water for the child that he may wash it in the bath; wool for his wife when she is delivered of a child, oil, a bed, a cup: so the furniture of the house is increased. I say nothing of his other occupations, and of his distraction. . . . [I]s it not his duty to supply clothing to his children, and to send them to the school-master with writing tablets, and styles (for writing). Besides must he not supply them with beds? for they cannot be genuine Cynics as soon as they are born. If he does not do this, it would be better to expose the children as soon as they are born than to kill them in this way.[14]

For Epictetus, the demands of obedience stand in contrast to the "duties" of genealogy altogether. Better the former than the latter (although the latter's descriptive edges are sharp enough to indicate that the single Epictetus knows well the contours of the normal world; he was, after all, someone's slave for a long time).

We should not take this parallel seriously, however. For whatever Epictetus may believe, Paul surely cannot think these very duties of genealogy are actually contrary to the demands of God (cf. Phil 2:20 etc.). There must be some other, if related, contrast that is at play in his mind between the married and the single. Paul's actual "intentions" here, furthermore, must be informed by the broader frame of the Scriptures in which his remarks are placed. From that broader perspective, in fact, "the things of the Lord" point to creative "fullness" rather than to a set of divine directives: "The earth is the LORD's and the fullness thereof, the world and those who dwell therein; for he has founded it upon the seas, and established it upon the rivers" (Ps 24:1-2 RSV). Obedience, rather than turning away from the world, turns out to be a way of opening up oneself to the "things of God" that now stand as God's creative fullness: "Now therefore, if you will obey my voice and keep my covenant, you shall be my own possession among all peoples; for all the earth is mine" (Exod 19:5 RSV). The foundation of obedience, as well as its thrust, lies in this "beholding": "Behold, to the LORD your God belong heaven and the heaven of heavens, the earth with all that is in it" (Deut 10:14 RSV). For Paul, this is in fact the basis upon which a person's duties to others become obedience to God (1 Cor 10:26—"for the earth is the Lord's, the fullness thereof"). This exhaustive creative possession of all things is, finally, the "answer" to the strange mystery of the life span itself: "Who has given to me, that I should repay him? Whatever is under the whole heaven is mine" (Job 41:11 RSV). "The things of God," then, have to do more broadly with that which God has of his own. They mark the Levitical aspect of God's direct domain: the world as God's creation in which God's will and purpose, in its mysterious breadth, is to be engaged.

An unmarried person, thus, can be concerned with "the things of God." And "all things" come into view, then, as the one life—any life that is this creaturely mortal life—that is seen for what it is before God. "Undividedness" or "attention" to God, in this perspective, is the special realm of the single person, in the sense that the "things of God" are not so parceled up into their bundled uses as they are for others:

their "wholeness" is visible in their discreteness. "Render unto God what is God's" (Matt 22:21), Jesus' response to his enemies' trick question, plays upon the "things of God" that are in fact "everything," without ever sorting it out with respect to social obligations. An "undivided" concern with "the things of God" must inevitably break any straitjacket of attention that such obligations might impose. God deserves "all one's heart and soul" (Deut 10:12), as Jesus emphasizes (e.g., Mark 12:3), which brings the individual human spirit into some kind of analogue to the completeness of God's creative range. If "everything" is God's, then Paul's list in 1 Corinthians 7:29-30 is less aimed at "letting go of" aspects of human life—spouses, affection, property (wives, weeping, rejoicing, buying), the full usefulness of existence—than at simply letting things be as they are. For it is in their createdness, in our enmeshment with this createdness, even in our "passing away" (7:31) with the world, that they and we are God's and point to God. The single person is "but a creature," and, in this, the single person is a mirror of such creaturely "butness" that underscores this coming-to-be and "passing away" of created "form" itself.

This conclusion is both eccentric and abstract, but it is compelling if we see how it worked itself out in practice. The early Fathers of the church, as we know, increasingly valued the condition of the "virgin," both male and female, finally embodied in the monk or nun. Much of their praise for this way of life was oriented, as with Paul, to the question of "attention" to God, now described more particularly in terms of "contemplation." Their own commentary—for example, that of Clement, Chrysostom, and others—on 1 Corinthians 7 witnesses to this growing focus on contemplative virginity, and they seem to assume that Paul was thinking of the monastic vocation already.[15] Augustine in his discussion, however, indicates some of what is at stake here, in a way that goes beyond social or ecclesial ordering: such disciplined attentiveness to God that the single person ought to embody both forms and reveal the "beauty" (*pulchritudo*) of the human "soul" before its Maker. That is the point: beauty itself is revealed in this specific attentiveness by the particular created person in her or his placement in the world, oriented outward "to the things of God."[16]

This way of reading Paul does not mean that the proper form of singleness is in fact exclusively that of the celibate monk or nun. Jesus speaks of "eunuchs for the kingdom of God" (Matt 19:12), but he does not concretize this servanthood vis-à-vis other kinds of service. It is not clear he is even thinking of married *versus* single here, since the issue he is speaking to is interior physical desire rather than social relations. But if we look at scriptural figures, of eunuchs and single persons known as such, various clarifications begin to emerge. Eunuchs themselves have a role in the Scriptures, largely by "presenting" particularities of the kingdom's life. They display to the world royalty in its arrival and departure in judgment (cf. with Jehu and Jezebel, in 2 Kgs 9:32); they guard and bring forth the comeliness of female companionship, including leadership (as in Esther); they preserve and give back the prophetic voice of God's word (cf. Jer 38:7-13); they gather and name the witnesses of God for the sake of the nations (Dan 1:7); they engage the differences of the nations as they are assumed by the geography of the gospel (Acts 8:27), so that yet more of these differentiated peoples can be drawn in (Isa 56:8). In short, the eunuchs of Scripture are gatherers of diversity in its beauty. Something similar could be said of the widows, from Naomi and her bringing in of Ruth, to the key roles played in the propagation of the gospel in Acts, where the movement from Jerusalem to Judea to Samaria to the "uttermost part of the earth" (Acts 1:8) is taken up in a specifically receptive and facilitative way by the Lydias of the apostolic church. There is the generational responsibility that widows play within the arc of life, in, for example, Titus 2; even more, the various greeting lists of Paul in his letters show that far more active roles in this world-ranging embrace are played by women who, most likely, are single.

One should not press the details in this scriptural context too far. There is no question, all the same, that singleness moves through the landscape of mortality as a diaconal complement to marriage's genealogical service, always pressing it outward, opening it up, to the distinctive realities of the gospel's expansive movement. The philosopher Bernard Stiegler, drawing on the work of Gilbert Simondon, has insisted on the need for this kind of complementary interplay, more generally: individuals are such as they *become* players within the collective identities that form them reciprocally. Each—the individual and collective identity of the community—is always in process. He calls this "individuation," on both a personal and a social level, which he contrasts with the kind of static imprisonment of modern "individualism" and the social desiccation that reflects it. Stiegler has gone on to propose reforming education *back* toward the collective history of cultural life rather than away from it, simply because young people become people of their own only in inhabiting this tradition. In this, he follows someone like the Roman philosopher Seneca, who saw the "past"—and especially the writings of the past—as the only real "time" that existed, free to roam in, question, engage, and learn from.[17]

Stiegler has movingly described this tradition-based process of individuation in terms of his own experience as a young man, when he served a five-year sentence for robbery. While incarcerated, he learned, through his reading of philosophy, "who" he was as an individual—indeed, *that* he was—by engaging in the formative life of the collective culture moving to him from Plato and others.[18] He would go on, after his release from prison, to study formally, to teach, to marry and raise a family, and to engage the larger civil society in a range of creative ways. But the five years of his incarceration—Stiegler self-consciously uses the vocabulary of Christian monastic asceticism (although he is not a Christian) to describe this—were the necessary ground of this larger network of relations. One *must* be an individual in order both to inform the social realities of which one is a part and to be so formed into an individual who can grow continually. This kind of healthy "individuation," which can intertwine persons in their fertile associations, requires the constant injection of *individuals* into the associative cultural process.

The philosophy behind this kind of outlook is in many ways incoherent with Christian understandings of God's creative priority, in that it ignores the divine ordering of the "process of individuation." But there is something important to learn from Stiegler and his colleagues for our purposes: singleness, in its life form of individual engagement, is a responsibility taken up and offered to the human collective, part of whose gift is, in return, the shaping of individual "beauty," to use Augustine's term. It is a "vocation," a form of life in which God calls out the particularity of his creation so that it can "color" the praise of the whole. As a result, the whole, in its ongoing life, can continually be pressed to *see* the fullness of created diversity, without succumbing to its tyrannical blinders and narcissism. In its own often obscure and obscuring ways, the church understood this complex relationship between singleness and generative collectivity by ordering celibate lives as a path parallel to married and "normal" human existence. The historical movement along each line, when taken together, represented the church's single journey toward the great Marriage Feast depicted in Revelation 19. Here, the gathering of peoples, from the breadth of their national and temporal particularities, is presented as a "virgin" and "pure" bride to the Lamb.

Each stream—generation and virginity—has somehow contributed to this final embodiment of Adam drawn into the New Adam.

In this figural movement, finally, we can see the more particularly sexual aspect given its shape for single people—that is, "the state of chastity" or giving over of erotic desire to some service other than individual gratification or generative responsibility. "Virginity" is, within the church's traditional life, a key element of singleness—the term was early applied, in English, to both women and men. Virginity marks the specifically diaconal character of sexual life, understood more broadly, for the single person in particular, whether permanently or for the period that might precede or follow married life. Virginity is not, to be sure, a denial of sexuality in itself. Rather, it marks the way that single persons consciously decouple the arousals of physical attraction from the other gifts of creaturely existence they engage.

Versions of this vision of figural movement were described in the early church by writers like Methodius,[19] though they often became troublingly disequilibriated as the monastic side of the movement took over. Nonetheless, the historically failed balance does not negate the necessary understanding of singleness' essential contribution to the human traversal of life's landscape. Singleness is often figured in the person of Mary, whose attentiveness to Jesus (Luke 10:41-42) became the sign of singular contemplation. But we can also orient the figure toward its deeper purpose: bringing to bear the textured breadth of creation—"the things of God"—on the probative concerns and responsibilities of others.

The single person and the single life do this in two particular ways: friendship and work. Neither are, in themselves, peculiar to single people. But that is just the point: as aspects of every person's life, single persons engage these elements with the attentiveness that permits creation's particularity to come into view within the mix of common life for all.

## Friendship and the Uncovering of Individuality and Particularity

Recovering the special task of singleness is important in our own day because of the way that creaturely diversity has been subverted though Western society's radical reordering of friendship itself. "The things of God" require friendship in order to be apprehended. It could be argued that the rise of monastic celibacy in the fourth century performed some kind of creatively reorienting role by almost savagely holding on to moral attentiveness in the midst of social disorder. This monastic gift was the religious side of the well-known claim, taken from Thomas Cahill's 1995 best-selling book *How the Irish Saved Civilization*. Today we could perhaps speak of "how single people saved delight in the world, through friendship," if only this task were readily assumed.

Friendships have, in fact, been starkly severed from their traditional place in the creaturely, and hence sexual, lives of persons, in the sense of being essential and ongoing aspects of human flourishing. In contemporary Western societies, friendships are often ranged over and *against* sexuality, the latter something that is acted out constantly, profligately, cheaply, and hungrily, tied to fleeting moments and the spilling of money; the former, hard, uncertain, precious, regretted. This is so because of the real worries people have over the lines of demarcation between friendship and what we might call simply "erotics," the physical arousals of sexual beings. We can, for the sake of ease in understanding, speak of "friendship" as affection and "erotics" as sexual pleasure. The two are, obviously, never so easily separated individually, although societies have provided ways by which they can be at least commonly identified and navigated. This is precisely what contemporary Western cultures have forgotten how to do.

We can see, for instance, how, in the West, and in North America particularly, male friendship has suffered a strange fate. Subjected to enormous pressures over homosexual "concerns"—"homophobia," properly used as a concept, in the sense that one fears male closeness might be taken as or even involve homosexual erotics—close male friendships are today often suspect or given over to intrusive deconstruction by observers. Physical affection is virtually never expressed except in a few places like the military or, to a lesser extent, sports (and increasingly these have become places injected with the homophobia that must inevitably follow militant "inclusionary" demands). By contrast, we see, through cultural narratives, an expressed need to restore friendship among males, now given in terms of a subcategory of erotics—for example, the "bromance"—where male friendship is underlined in "buddy" films but now presented with a knowing and almost dissembling self-confidence. The search for sexual partners always offers the *obbligato* to these stories, just as they do with female analogues (e.g., the TV series *Girls*).[20]

To be sure, there have been unavoidable social aspects—often "spatial" in character, and sometimes connected indirectly with the Great

Transition—that have contributed to this refashioning of friendship's possibility. Geographic mobility has crucially subverted friendship, repeatedly separating individuals at various points in generational growth; but so has the breakdown of long-term family cohabitation. The relation between the two is interesting but well-developed in human history: men and women's friendships have historically been linked to the networks of stable families and shared needs of children and work. Tied to all this, in addition, we have seen a consequent inflation of erotics as the central form of human sexual relations, both heterosexually and homosexually. Completely missing from social discussion and experience has been the active realm of celibate existence, wherein friendships of a certain kind have always been central and have provided a kind of nurturing spring.[21]

Historically, in the West, the person who singlehandedly ordered the categories in which we think of friendship was the ancient Greek philosopher Aristotle (*Ethics*, 8 and 9). Aristotle outlined three kinds of friendship (*philia*): liking someone because of their good character; or because of their utility; or, finally, because of the pleasure experienced with them. The first, friendship based on character, is clearly the best in Aristotle's eyes, and the best of this is when each friend has an *equally* good character. When characters—and for that matter, utilities and pleasure—are unequal between the partners, all kinds of problems can ensue, although with discipline they do not always have to. A perfect friendship that is equal is one in which each partner seeks the welfare of the other based on the same character and values. While Aristotle considered the relationship between household members (i.e., in families) as falling within "friendship," he was most interested in the friendship between fellow citizens—equals in a very precise way (and these were only men, in any case). For all the detail of his discussion, however, there is also a sense in which Aristotle founded friendship on a kind of abstracted "singleness." This was, and remains, important.

Aristotle's discussion of friendship was unprecedented, in part for the importance he placed on it as an essential aspect of human flourishing: it is through friendships that we either become virtuous or exercise virtue—justice, mercy, benevolence—and so in fact enact what human happiness is all about. A true friend is "another self," he said, a phrase that has been much debated but that seems to reflect his understanding that by growing and sharing in common virtue with another person, friends are indeed "equals" in the deepest sense. Obviously, friendships based on the good character of the other engage this flourishing equality more obviously and fully than any other kind of friendship; but in fact, utility and pleasure can be a part of this, if not a fundamental part. Friendships that are solely utilitarian or pleasure giving, by contrast, are ultimately perverted.

Aristotle left open many questions regarding friendship, and philosophers, theologians, and social critics have each argued about his meaning, pursued supposed inferences from his claims, or sought to dismantle some of his prejudices. Most, however, have followed in his wake, including Cicero, most influentially, who wrote a treatise on friendship that became central to Christian discussion for centuries, including within monastic circles. Ambrose, Cassian, Gregory the Great, and Aelred of Rievaulx all wrote works on friendship. Each took up these Aristotelian notions of the "friendship of virtue" and then restated it in terms of various frameworks of specifically Christian virtue. These writings deserve consideration in their own right. They also raise together general issues that inform the larger argument here regarding singleness and friendship, revolving around the "self" and the "other"; attraction and responsibility; the personal and the impersonal (or particular and general); immediacy and time; and the question of "equality," which was so important to Aristotle.[22] In other words, the Christian tradition of reflection on friendship has left us with a host of questions, most of them unresolved even as the social dislocations of the Transition overtook their discussion. In particular, the question of whether friends are given (by God) or constructed gradually over time from any possible range of persons has proven challenging. Likewise the question of the purpose of friendship (Is it "for itself," or does it serve some further good?) has loomed large.

In general, those who have thought about friendship have come down on the "personal" side of things: friends have to do with *just these* two people—although not necessarily "only" these two; it *might have been* another person (that is debated), but, once engaged in a friendship, that relationship is "irreplaceable" (nonfungible). It was Montaigne who said, about his friendship with La Boétie, "If a man urge me to tell wherefore I loved him, I feele it cannot be expressed, but by answering; Because it was he, because it was myself" ("Si on me presse de dire pourquoy je l'aymoys, je sens que cela ne se peut exprimer, qu'en respondant: Par ce que c'estoit luy, par ce que c'estoit moy").[23] Hence, most critics believe that the fact of friendship indicates some kind of historical particularity: who friends are and, more importantly, what friends have lived together, what they have shared and how they have engaged over time. This is also Montaigne's claim when he speaks of the thousands of individual "threads" of experience that make up a friendship but that, in the end, simply cannot be unwound and identified. Time is thus deeply implicated in friendship, along with place. Friendships "denote" rather than "connote": they point to the "just this" of people, times, and places, and not to some reality "beyond" them. Friendships are "things in themselves" rather than signs of something else.

Historical and sociological studies of friendship, not surprisingly, have uncovered the often complex as well as sometimes rigid elements both time and place have provided friendships, and in ways quite independent of any affective aspect. But even in our era, when friendship tends to be understood mainly through an affective lens, one cannot escape the basic conditions that physical proximity and temporal extension place upon friendships, even those now begun through the Internet. This may be of particular importance in contemporary challenges, where precisely temporal stability with given physical connections in relations is difficult to achieve, let alone maintain. On the other hand, the emphasis—still generally shared—on the "equality" of friendship is deeply problematic and probably undercuts some of the other elements just noted: that is, the particularities involved, the responsibilities engaged, and the very character of extended temporal engagement. For just these particularities must, in the end, overturn all equalities, except the larger shape of our creaturely passage. The Christian society of the West, in fact, began to rethink this element quite concretely during the Middle Ages, and its developing reorientation over the centuries had great political consequences, as "friendship" between classes and vocations became an ideal—if rarely a common occurrence.

Scripture's figures of friendship are complex and do not easily settle into the categories of vocabulary that are often used to parse the topic. Hence, something like the strict categorization between "kinds of love" that C. S. Lewis and many others have claimed probably does not cohere well with the Bible itself.[24] In the Old Testament, a common term translated as "friend"—*rea*—is used of a sexual partner (Song of Songs 5:16; Jer 3:1, 20; Hos 3:1); of a friend of the same sex ("companion"); or of a "neighbor" (Exod 20:16; Lev 19:18). It is even used of God (Exod 33:11). Similarly, the term *ahav*—which has more the sense of "desire" in its association with "breathing" or panting—is used in various forms, within the family (cf. Gen 22:2, where Isaac is the son Abraham "loves";

as Isaac in turn does his wife, in Gen 24:26), and for neighborly love, in the famous text from Leviticus 19:18, in its verbal form (something the Greek version of the LXX translates as *agape*). But the word can also refer to a "lover," as in Ezekiel 16:33ff., or the "love" of the Song of Songs 8:6 that is "strong as death." Yet this panting love is, like *rea*, also applied to the affection offered to and received as love from God (cf. Jer 31:3). There are other words besides these that move across the boundaries of reference with respect to affection.

Moving to the New Testament does little to provide strict theological clarifications for this fluid and rich description. Thus, efforts to parse *philia*, *eros*, and *agape* (along with other terms like *storge* and *splagchnon* [affection] or *philadelphia* [brotherhood]) in carefully delineated ethical terms is probably not sustainable or helpful. It is better to look simply at the figures themselves. So, for instance, Jesus speaks about friendship rather concretely in John 15:13-15: "greater love" has no one than this, that one "lay down his life for his friends; and ye are my friends." Here the term is *philoi*, and it is joined directly to *agape*, the love of laying down one's life. This is contrasted with being a "slave," on the basis of "knowledge" that is shared: slaves do not "know" what their master is doing or intending; only friends do. In this case, though, the friend's knowledge is peculiar: it is the knowledge of what *this person in particular*, Jesus, is *doing*. What Jesus does, shockingly, is what a *slave* does (Luke 22:26-27; John 13:5; cf. Phil 2:7). Furthermore it is this doing of the slave, assumed by his followers (Mark 10:44), that makes them his "friends"—that is, as they "obey" his "commandments" (John 15:14). All these "friends" and "brethren" (*agapetoi*, *adelphoi*) are simply members of the local church (3 John 5)—hence, friendship, slavery, obedience, and love all coalesce in this common life of the "body of Christ."

Paul, however, is clear that God's love (*agape*) is not for friends only but for "sinners" (Rom 5:8). He uses the vocabulary of such love in Ephesians 5 to indicate the relationship between husband and wife. Hence, love—which is bound to the affection of friendship—is given over to married life in a way that is seemingly meant to model *all* relationships of divine affection. This is a great challenge for Christian theology, because it both renders affection something universal, from a divine perspective—it applies to neighbors, enemies, spouses, companions, the good, and the bad—and is given as a sign (a "mysterion" [Eph 5:32]) in the spousal relationship of husband and wife in some kind of special way. To this extent, married life *deepens* friendship by elevating it into the realm of divine love. But thereby the fact of this deepening also allows friendship a kind of independent social status: friends, who are not married to one another, can live the life of the married couple *at least insofar as affection* or love is concerned. Furthermore, the reality of friendship is one that provides a ground for other relations; it is not only a parallel or alternative to these relations.

Thus, the affective aspect of friendship—love—is divinely significant in its own right. Although its expression, and probably personal experience, has varied in times and cultures, friendship has always involved, according to those who have described it in these various settings, some "virtue," in the sense of internal and effective power, whether it is "kindness," "respect," or "benevolence." This affective strain is bound up with all the most important aspects of human relations. "Friendship" is, thus, that aspect of our lives, including our sexual lives, where affection is most singularly and purely located (vs. erotics and generative genealogy). Therefore friendship's cultivation is indeed a "responsibility" to be taken up, pursued, ordered, and cultivated. From the pastoral side of things, we can assuredly say that the church must teach people *how to be friends*, because it is a significant aspect of every relationship. Second, in doing so, the church will surely be clarifying particular relationships of love with respect to the genealogical aspects of procreation and erotics in particular. We must also say that the failure of the church—along with our larger society—to engage in a deep articulation and formation with respect to friendship is bound up to many of the key confusions over sexuality in our own era.

Many of the details with respect to what a friend is, and how the church can teach about this, are too localized culturally to generalize from in the context of a broad discussion of human creaturehood. They have also been so ignored by the church as to demand deep and constructive study and treatment. It is major work that still awaits engagement. One central area where the truth of friendship, divinely revealed, demands renewed attention, especially, is precisely that of *inequality*, the place where contemporary discussion of inclusion and exclusion seem to focus. God's "love" is intrinsically bound to inequality, of an infinite and incomprehensible sort. Life itself, we have seen, is bound to this chasm of inequality, the immeasurably asymmetrical aspect of our creaturely existence that is utterly outside our control. Life is nonquantifiable in a human sense, and thus all utilitarian calculus is empty and probably even perverse: one life is not "worth" another's, let alone "two" or three. It is not possible to determine that this or that life has "lost" its value, as compared with other known values. The category of "equality" does not apply to human life, or any life. Nothing, among all created things, is equivalent with anything else. Friendship—that is to say, the love of another—is thus given here, tottering on the edge of an abyss of created being. I love, and *can* love, another person, not because they are "like me," or because they deserve my love, but only because they are *not* me, because they are utterly unlike me, unconnected, separated, discrete, and particular. I can love them because they are a creature, which simply means because they are *God's* creature. They exist alongside and with. But they are *not* me. Everything about life is learned in this form of friendship, because it is here that the edges of creaturely existence come into view.

Single people, just because of this, have something essential to contribute to this inescapable aspect of being a human person. The "just this person," the "just this place and set of circumstances," the "just this" that friendship, in various ways, engages, is something that is always a prod for the affective lives of all people. There is, of course, always the inevitable pull of Aristotle's "similarity" factor or "homophily," as it is called in modern sociological theory: people are drawn to others who are somehow "like them," from similar backgrounds, with shared interests and experiences. This was a part of social context behind the same-sex sworn brotherhood that someone like Alan Bray has traced in medieval and early modern times. But as a basis for affection, the homophilic similarity factor is to be resisted as fundamental, and, in all friendships of depth, there is always the realization of the glorious victory of difference over likeness, as studies like William Rawlins' have argued. As we deepen friendships, differences emerge that are both difficult but finally delightful and, hence, "beautiful." Their extended apprehension by a single person is partly what renders his or her individuation into the practices of generative existence—always a grating but also a formative process.

Friendships constantly press against these edges of distinctions, and the resistance all of us experience in this is often the hardest to bear within the communal dynamics of genealogy—families, cooperatives, polities. The sexually partnered existence that constitutes marriage and moves into family quickly subsumes, and often avoids, this grating character, except when the challenges of mortality slink in through the cracks. The single person here is the sound of every person's movement across the ground and needs to be heard and in any case eventually will be. It is hard to remember one's spouse's individuality. But we must, but this is the impulse of our affection. Yet creaturely existence often involves the juggling, lost balance, and dropping of affection necessarily linked to generation, so that friendship itself loses its way within the community of generative existence—but for its constant kindling and challenge by single persons through the press of their friendships within the unconscious flow and forgetfulness of ordered community.

Friendships are cultivated with all the care and dangerous fragility of any sustenance agriculture. There is the careful time of discerning and planting—and here wisdom and experience can bring only success—and not a little luck. There is the giving over of oneself in loyalty, the breaking up by betrayal, the hard and welcome corrections and growth, the difficult learning and respecting of limits as in all things, and long-standing reaping and replenishing. Friendship is a life's work. It can, furthermore, be deformed, as with the many friendships we know that become privatized and possessive, tyrannical and oppressive. So too, of course, can the "collective" demands of survival itself. The friendship, however, that is marked by whatever confluence of location, shared acts, doing, and attention will ever uncover more and more "just this person" in "just this time and place." Such an uncovering is to say in the psalmist's voice that *this* person, and through them my own self, is "fearfully and wonderfully made," each "member" "written" "in thy book," each "fashioned" over time by one who tended to just this task (Ps 139:14, 16); it is to say, just this and here is God "numbering" and "naming," as with every distant star (Ps 147:4). It is to say, "God has made me, praise be to God," because in so naming "just this person" and "just this place" and "just these words and actions," in the context of a moral life, a person is gently turned, sometimes wrenched, toward the overwhelming beauty of God.

Friendships are for the sake of others, however. Thus, the friendships of single people are to be cultivated, protected, honored, and then brought into the whole, the ordered life of families, wherein others may learn from them. The notion that married people are not lonely is a falsehood. They are not physically isolated, to be sure. But, as Epictetus wrote, the character of their selves, and their relationship to the selves of others, is often lost amid the pressing demands of generative existence. True friendship is a treasure, often most deeply discovered by single persons, cherished, burnished, garnished, but then offered to others. This happens through the means by which all gifts are shared: the common labor and the common meal, to be discussed in the next chapter. Generally speaking, this sharing, however unequally borne by those who can attend to it, is something that is the responsibility of married and single together. Just as the generational arc is oriented toward, and calls out for, the integration of ages in specific ways, the place of friendship among single and married persons is also oriented toward their integration. To the degree that single persons have as their close friends only single persons, persons like themselves, their friendships are stunted; and the same goes for married persons. Each is driven to engage the friendships of single and married both. This very openness is fundamental to the ongoing energies of the movement through life and to the becoming that is the learning of wisdom. This should be obvious, but its forgetting has informed a central aspect of ecclesial and social disintegration.

## The Vocation of Singleness

"I am born; I grow; perhaps I am confused in my adolescence about my desires; I learn this and that; the notion of marriage simply does not arise clearly—no individuals, no deep attractions, obvious impulses of relationship or location." Each of us asks, in the wake of this common set of experiences, who we are.

The central element of our calling as creatures is to engage in the growth of affection: to love God and neighbor. We know, in some kind of general practical way, that this is where it all comes down to, and we have the immovable ensign of the Great Commandment to confirm this (Matt 22:37-40). Friendship is rightly seen as the most crystallized form of affection, such that "friendship with God" itself became a vision of redemption in writers like Irenaeus and long after. It has become commonplace to describe modern marriage as a relationship only recently defined in terms of "love" and affection—the "romantic" ideal of the "companionate" existence.[25] There is some truth to the fact that, in the Christian tradition, the "goods of marriage" did not place mutual affection at the top of any hierarchy of value until only the modern era. Yet it would also be wrong to imply, by this history, that affection was ever viewed as ancillary to marriage's own generative character. Certainly, within the scriptural narrative, the "loving" of husband and wife, and through them of children—and sometimes, the injurious parceling out and withholding of love—was absolutely central to the figural traversal of life's landscape. The "desire" of Eve for her husband (Gen 3:16; cf.

Song of Songs 7:10, for its reciprocal sense), and Adam's own sense of utter intimacy with Eve, translates, as the generations pass, into quite explicit affective descriptions of Abraham and Sarah, Jacob and Rachel, and of their parental love for their children. Onward it moves, such that Paul's final picture of the marital relationship of husband and wife is one of a "mysterious" enactment of God's love in Christ. There is no way to pull friendship out from marriage's central meaning. Even if, as Stanley Hauerwas has said, in marriage "you always marry the wrong person," the point is that marriage becomes the place where one learns to love just this person, in some shadowing analogy to God's love for sinners.[26]

Thus, the friendships we establish are bound up with the same dynamic as married affection and its trajectory. Single persons, in the end, are not outliers to the genealogical movement of creatureliness. They are, as defined selves, "passable" characters within this movement, to use Timothy Reiss' characterization, themselves shaped as selves by their entwinement within it. Part of this engagement, however, is as friendship cultivators. This is properly speaking the ground of their own particular being as individuals, and thus the fashion by which their beings, at whatever point in the arc of their life span, display the shape of human existence as we are made. Who am I? the single person asks: I am one who discovers friends and who is a friend and who shares my friendships. There is no more to be said, in a sense, than this. Because with this, the contours of the created world are given voice within the great traversal for all people.

Creatures are mortal lives, made by God, and, in their being, places where God's love—God as love—is displayed in its glory. Generation, genealogy, and probation constitute only ways of talking about creatureliness. They are not principles or divine forms in their own right. But in talking about creatureliness in some truthful measure, they indicate elements in this life—one that displays God's glory—that are in fact actually bound up with the display and that are actually glorious in that they are the elements of such a life as God has made. It is not enough to say that human beings are diverse, or that human beings have always reproduced, or that sexual life can look like this or that, and, thus, that our social goals aim simply at expressing this and that in ways that do not foment violence, or that are relatively agreeable to this and that person. To speak this way is to speak in terms of a desiccated individualism. Life actually *is* something, given in actual creaturely artifacts that move through time in such and such a way, so that such and such objects can in fact be what they are within this movement. From the point of view of current debates over sexuality, the three elements of procreation, affection, and erotic attraction or pleasure combine in different ways: marriage may have all three, but it may not. Same-sex partnerships may have two of the three, but maybe not that many. Friendships have only one. Value is not, however, assigned to relationships based on the sum of these elements in any given case. Indeed, "value" is not the issue at all, but rather the shape in which these elements move together in the display of mortal life as God's gift.

Taken together, however, the arc of the life span represents a common shape, whose skinful bearing is the gift itself. Within it are held innumerable elements that vary by culture and time, and whose exact form is contestable according to various ethical and political views. It was one of Montaigne's great virtues that he was honest about what most people only silently suspected on this score. By the same token, work— which is the topic of the next chapter, with its various modes of organization, selection, and practice—has also varied, and in contestable ways. It is nonetheless appropriate to gauge both the arc and its toil in terms of steady forms as well, those that carry on the movement of generative genealogy, in its accountable integration of particularity.

The scriptural figures of the patriarchs and of those leading up and into the Pauline communities are likewise varied, but they are also bound together in many common ways, whose shape continues, for all the masks we have put on it, to mark our mortal life spans. One of the great failures of modern scriptural reading, which relishes diversity and contradiction, lies in forgetting just this obvious point. Within this common shape, at the turn of the Testaments, we encounter the critical engagement of singularity on its cusp in John the Baptist and Jesus, given in the form of judgment and mercy. The skins of John and the flesh of Jesus are both lifted up, in their particular way, for view. We properly focus on this cusp. We note its distinctiveness, as well as the way each speaks to all, even as they are welcomed most by the "tax-collectors" and "prostitutes" (Matt 21:31-32). The "normal" seems upended by the "abnormal," and this fact has become a common homiletical message. What is important to stress, even in this focus, is the way that neither skin nor flesh is thrown away by this welcome that is offered them by the socially marginalized of their time; nothing has changed in the larger shape of life within the complete passage of both Testaments. Here, the critics of Christianity know better: life is "just the same" as before (cf.

2 Pet 3:4). Where the critics go wrong is in thinking this fact of continuity in experience is a problem. People are born, they grow, they reproduce (or not), and they die, leaving their offspring and friends to mourn them, to question, to forget, to hope. The meaning of this movement is neither transcended nor discarded in the "cusp" of John and Jesus. It is transfigured. It is significant that the form of this transfiguration is given in "friendship" among the followers of Christ, not in any new arrangement of the life span. Friendship, even in this case, is embedded in this life span, not imagined in some isolated realm. Like John the Baptist and the man Jesus, single persons, as they make their way through time, point to this fact most clearly. And, like all persons, they too are held accountable, in judgment and mercy both, for the ways they trace this passage, as they work together with others in the passable realm of common existence.

# VI

# Working and Eating

The integrating thrust of friendship into the filiated realm of creaturehood has as its purpose the unveiling of creaturely particularity in its individual clarity. Thus, friendship's deeper impulse and movement is the discovery of delight. The single person's gift, as single rather than married, is epitomized in bringing friendship into the midst of the generative community. This happens in two key areas: the workshop and the table.

## Singling Out the World's Artifacts for the Common Good

In the integration of singleness and married life, persons of each condition now share creaturely existence in a specific way: the single person brings forward the particularity of the world; the married person distributes it. Both "suffer" its reality in its life-giving limitations. Through this interplay, creation itself is, in its halting way, made a shadow of its full glory.

The single person's life, even in the tasks of his or her friendships, is bound to this gathering through the cultivated smallness of life's coming and going, its labor and deficiencies. In 1904 Vernon Lee (the pen name of Violet Paget, a remarkable author of stories and essays) published a short book called *Hortus Vitae*, a Latin phrase to be translated as "the

191

garden of life."[1] It was a collection of short essays on various aspects of what, Lee said, could contribute to a person's "happiness," even if happiness is *not*, as she was certain it was not, the "aim of life." She begins with a quote from Voltaire's *Candide* and then explains her purpose:

> "Cela est bien dit," répondit Candide;
> "mais il faut cultiver notre jardin."
> —Romans de Voltaire

This by no means implies that the whole of life is a garden or could be made one. I am not sure even that we ought to try. Indeed, on second thoughts, I feel pretty certain that we ought not. Only such portion of life is our garden as lies, so to speak, close to our innermost individual dwelling, looked into by our soul's own windows, and surrounded by its walls—a portion of life that is ours exclusively, although we do occasionally lend its key to a few intimates; ours to cultivate just as we please, growing therein either pistachios and dwarf lemons for preserving, like Voltaire's immortal hero, or more spiritual flowers, "sweet basil and mignonette," such as the Lady of Epipsychidion sent to Shelley (pp. 1–3).

The kinds of things Lee wrote about in *Hortus Vitae* included reading, sitting quietly, giving gifts, having a bicycle, and so forth. She was, however, wrong, I think, in believing that these elements were both almost secret aspects of life and unconnected pleasures inevitably lost in life's otherwise difficult stream. They are, in fact, just the things necessarily brought to bear within a life. For a person's life is made up of just such things, even if too often they are unaware of "just such" as these things are, bound to the beauty of the world's transience. In an almost exemplary way, Lee fulfilled an aspect of her vocation as a single person in not only engaging but publicly writing about these elements. All of this was her "work."

Work involves making, in some fashion or another: growing things to eat and, in that sense, "making food" with all that is involved in such confection, making meals, making the ordering elements that permit eating, nurturing, sharing, teaching, relating, healing, dying. Yet this "making"—the results of which we often call "artifacts"—is not just about objects that are in some sense bound to human tools. These tools themselves are used, as it were, to dig out to view the artifacts of God's own work. An "artifact" is anything that is created. And in that sense, and in the perspective of God's own work, an artifact is *any* created being, living as well as humanly constructed. A key element of work is to unveil the work of God.

Hence, the dichotomy between the "natural" and the human world is a false one. This false dichotomy has been used both to justify human destruction of that which is nonhuman and to attack human hubris in its technological creativity. Contemporary philosophers like Bruno Latour have, in contrast, wanted to include "the human" within the "natural."[2] The dichotomy is overcome, however, and the kind of claim Latour makes is only true if we see nature as a whole as the set of divine artifacts—that is, as God's. Far from the Christian faith having encouraged ecological devastation, as one modern myth insists, it is forgetfulness of God's creative priority over all things that is at the root of the dichotomy's vying sides.[3] Framing an opposition of "technology versus the natural world" has misled us deeply, both in its positive and in its negative connotations—domineering and ruining. Artifacts—from tools and clothing, to domestic accoutrements, to playful instruments and their sounds, to religious objects and social monuments, to machines and computers (clocks included)—all these stand alongside the coney and the mustard tree in the psalmic catalogue. They do so purely in their singularity, first of all, and, second, in the web of their usefulness as it encompasses the skinful ordering of life. We must first appreciate the singularity of artifacts, however, so that their useful application does not drag us down into the death of mortal despair given in wastage, disrespect, and wanton destruction. Artifactual cultivation is an essential aspect of stewardship but, more importantly, of creaturely self-understanding. Just there, in the artifact, is the creature on view.

This revelatory aspect of the artifact can be noted in the strange relationship between what the Christian tradition has called "vanity" and the created forms of the world. This relationship was originally epitomized in the discussion of the book of Ecclesiastes, where in chapter 2, for instance, vineyards, fruit trees, fields, watercourses, houses, and then a range of cultural artifacts are listed as ultimately useless and "vain" (2:11). All created forms, human beings and the beasts, seem to end in the same emptiness of death (3:19), as if mortality itself eviscerates the meaning of "things" and of creatures themselves. Christians reflected and elaborated upon some of these themes and, by the sixteenth and seventeenth centuries especially, had developed complex symbolisms for expressing them. Among the most compelling were those given in pictorial form, the so-called *vanitas* paintings, to be hung in the home. These were generally in the form of "still lifes": a table, often cluttered, or simply laid out, with a range of objects, each of which represented aspects of human creaturely existence—perhaps just the slightly rotting fruit in a bowl, or, more complexly, a range of fabricated articles (a musical instrument, a book, a glass or watch, a mirror, a beautiful portrait in a locket), and, of course, a small skull in a corner, pointing to the end of all things in death.[4]

These representations of the *vanitas* tradition, however, are often misunderstood, as if they were depicting objects—artifacts, creatures—that were "vain" in the sense simply of being "empty" of significance. That is not the case at all. Their "emptiness" lies in our holding on to them, rather than acknowledging their being for what they are: gifts, and hence mortal in their givenness from God. Indeed, the technique of the *vanitas* painting gave rise to what are among the most luminescent representations of objects in human history, distilled in the genius of painters like Vermeer or Chardin. The artifacts of the creaturely world are *beautiful*, in themselves. Non-Christian intuitions about the objects of the world are telling here: writers who dwell on the beauty of "what is" often understand deeply the gracious character of "things" far better than do modern Christians. This is true for a writer like Élisabeth Barillé, whose slender volume of essays entitled *A Small Commendation of What Can Be Touched* (*Petit éloge du sensible*—a title that is really impossible to translate into English) contains a number of essays that, like Vernon Lee's, explore and glory in the often unnoticed elements of our lives that touch "sensibility": onions, bodies, cats, the light in a room. In one essay, she reflects on the early twentieth-century Japanese writer Natsume Sōseki, who, at the point of death from a stomach ulcer, remembers the wonder of a bowl of rice broth he was given. He drinks it up, and it "pours on his insides droplets of springtime," as he writes about it later. It is an "ecstatic" moment. Notice these things! Barillé urges.[5] She is, of course, talking about grace. But in her telling, luminous though it is, it is a grace without a giver, and so all things simply dangle, beautiful but alone and immobile. This itself unveils a deeper vanity.

On the other hand, "sensibility" has its rootedness in the gift of life itself: things are "sensible," touchable, feelable, simply because existence in its individuality has come into being for this and that and in this and that place. Such "thisness" is a definition of God creating, in the very way we spoke of the character of life in an earlier chapter. It is important to see that, however much the *particular* life that is a human person's is unique, creaturely existence in all of its forms is bound up with the life-giving act of God. Hence, all things can praise their Lord. At the same time, therefore, all things participate within the generative order of creaturely mortality, each with its own span and of its own kind. Only because their mortality is given substance in their relational passability is their origin as gift revealed.

The early nineteenth-century French politician Brillat-Savarin, who made an important journey to the young United States during an earlier time of exile, was among the first to engage in a philosophy of food. His *Physiology of Taste* (1825) remains in print, in French and in English. Working his way through the various physical senses, Brillat-Savarin orders them in a certain set of relationships, with "taste" exercising a gathering capacity that offers the variety of the world to be, literally, "savored."[6] Given this framework, the importance of food's care, enjoyment, and social role becomes obvious. At the same time, however, Brillat-Savarin also posits a "sixth sense," which he calls the "genesic" sense. If taste gathers variety, the genesic sense takes hold of this variety and wonder and lifts it all in a transcendent act of procreative fruitfulness. "Genesic," in Brillat-Savarin's neologism, refers to the generative sensibility that includes sexual and affective movement ordered to a certain kind of generative and reflective offering to God: the "things of God" are both lifted up and reenacted in a celebrative fashion. It is an idiosyncratic philosophical system, to be sure. Indeed, it is hardly a "system" at all, and Brillat-Savarin's literary approach to his topic is maddeningly digressive and anecdotal. But this actually reflects his vision: the character of "taste," as given form in food and its ingestion, is actually part of a larger social fabric of families, friends, journeys, conversations, affections, losses, and time. If nothing else, Brillat-Savarin uniquely articulated a truthful intuition into the way that sensible particulars are actually necessary elements within the generative cast of creaturely traversal.

The celibate gatherer is the servant of such "sensibility" and is rightly disciplined in the works of sensibility. Some have argued that single persons are more likely or at least freer—in St. Paul's sense—to engage in the creative distillation of particular delights within the larger realm of divine artifacts; they are, perhaps, more "artistic." One could debate whether it is usable time itself or a certain engagement of gifts—vocation—that allows them to take up these aspects of cultivating, of making and gathering. Klinenberg, in his study of the recent increase of people living single lives, raises the question. Whatever the case, the service of sensibility is a necessary vocation. It does not demand a specific profession, however. It is rather a matter of orientation to one's work—in care, in space, in attentiveness to detail and implication. The world of "artifacts" is in fact the "stuff" of the world, not an addendum. The whole creation appears to us as "noise," in Serres' provocative reading of Genesis;[7] or, in a more measured perspective, it is a kind of enveloping realm of "experience," in Isaiah Berlin's expression.[8] But in either formulation, creation comes to us as a usually undifferentiated substratum *out of which* particular "phenomena" arise, as "figures" and information. Everything "else" than us is the stuff of being because this is what being is. From a Christian perspective, however, we want to emphasize not the undifferentiated and chaotic aspect of creation, as we have said earlier, but rather its always intrinsic particularity, however difficult it is to identify. Philosophy may be one means of moving toward such identification, as might science of one kind or another, or poetry, or drawing. In the end, though, it is praise that marks the growth of such singling out of things, through their naming. If our movement toward such naming is blocked, overlooked, lost, or forgotten, then always there must be those who are caught in the woods alone, for a period, in a certain solitude, where they begin to hear the clamor of the world, otherwise lost in the trudging, or sometimes frantic reactivity of survival. The work of the single person is to give names to creatures that God has made. Jesus walks alone, in order to know the name of every sheep that is his (Matt 18:12; John 10:3).

## The Integrative Vocation of Work

Naming, in Genesis, is locating something within the generative genealogy of probative existence: the landscape of traversal, pilgrimage, skins. Hence, names are not only about sensibility about discrete objects; they are about place and ordered movement. Leviticus' concern with the clean and the unclean, this or that animal and plant, with the way in which sexual life is approached, and how the space of the home is arranged in this light, or the fields laid out and families allotted ground, the year measured in worship, and the vessels used within it—all this provides a framework for God's artifacts. It is a framework in which the particularities that mark God's created artifacts can actually either find their place in apprehended integrity or make their way in unapprehended integration, each to its temporal end, yet each providing some means of letting life *continue* to be suffered—that is, enjoyed within the limits of mortality. If the work of single persons aims at articulating these artifacts, displaying them somehow, this work is also a part of the larger work of ordering particularity for mortal existence in this way. Work that cannot do so, and thus turns back against the clarity of created form, is deadly.

One way of raising this question in general is to consider the way that work itself has tended, especially in the forms of modern developed economies, to flatten out differences. Work also tends, thereby, to reflect and increasingly encourage social values of interchangeability, not only among humans, but among their artifacts. "Jobs" are tasks that people are plugged into; and although individuals seek these tasks as "their own," in fact their presence in doing them is always dispensable. There is always someone else to take their place, and the job market, with its institutions and protocols, is organized in just this fashion, via formal and transferrable certifications and applications. What results is a kind of creaturely uniformity that is antithetical to the truth of difference and inequality. The Great Transition is only indirectly, and often only coincidentally, connected to industrialization; but within the last sixty years especially, forgetfulness of creaturely reality in terms of our biological character and in terms of the way production of artifacts is pursued have coalesced, with the result that "work" itself no longer serves createdness or expresses it as a form of praise. To the degree that eschatologically oriented visions of creaturehood, so common in both conservative and radical theological visions today, also express disinterest in intrinsic distinction, they too are reflections of this modern forgetfulness.

Whatever the merits of Ivan Illich's particular arguments in his controversial book *Gender*, the basic insight he laid out there is sound and properly challenging.[9] There are such things, and always have been such things until recently, as realms of life that clustered around the stages of the life span's arc and its communal ordering. Illich focused on these realms of activity and linked them to what he called the "vernacular," or universally localized, ordering of human life. Illich was especially concerned with those realms we now called "gendered," the spheres of life and work peculiar to women and men respectively. For most of human history, Illich argued that these gendered realms had boundaries that were clear and within which, he believed, creativity and individuality could flourish. By contrast, the modern interchangeable and atomistic worker, genderless and ageless, has destroyed these realms and with them a central character of human life. Critics rightly pointed out both historical errors in Illich's argument, as well as its tone deafness to actual experience within enforced gendered spheres. Spheres can, and have, become prisons. My own mother's personal struggles were partly tied up with the straitened demands of a certain kind of employment for women—in the 1940s and 1950s—that still lagged behind the hopes and self-understandings that women had come to share. But Illich's underlying point is nonetheless correct: when persons become inter-changeable, the specificity of created distinction within whole networks of human experience dissolves.

The realms of life in the past were all artifactually distinguished: the tools, space, and location of this or that person were peculiar to their task, their age, their vocation. One need not accept particular notions of socially prescribed roles in order to appreciate the fact that work becomes the place of genealogical integrity only to the degree that it can preserve and further the distinctiveness of created forms. No doubt, social roles and spheres should be variable, and thus flexible, and that includes those outlined here and there in the Bible. But *that* there should be differences is also obvious, and these will take malleable form precisely through the pressures of individuation, which can only happen as individual and sphere interact.[10] Gender and the ages of life all trace differences that, even if they cannot be organized and imposed according to a fixed tem-plate, must be ordered by real distinctions such as to permit the "things" of creation to be seen. It is through human work especially that this can happen. Exodus 35:35 provides a classic figure of this: the characteristic work of craftsmen laboring upon the tabernacle's forms bound up with a dual movement: genealogical life within the people of Israel, and the praise of God. Indeed, "wisdom," we are told, is located within this dual movement in a special way.

The creaturely meaning of single parenthood can be better seen in this context. The destructive pressures of single parenthood lie just in the direction of interchangeability, of one parent taking the place of two, as if this were possible given the particularities of a mother or a father, and of just *this* mother and just *this* father, and the complex and textured relationships each orders with and around a child. Single parents most often are forced to assume the "distracted" role of the married life, yet without the differentiations of persons that leaven the work of individu-ation. From Epictetus' perspective, it is the worst of both conditions. Within the order of skinful life, however—that is, within the order of life as given within the mortal limits of genealogical struggle—these

pressures can be and, as we know, often are transcended. A major part
in such potential transcendence is done by the adjustments and engagements of the larger community of extended family, friends, and churches
in relation to the lives of one-parent households. But it is necessarily a
struggle, one thrown at people from the outside usually. In this sense,
single parenthood's challenges are aspects of mortality's uncomprehending grasp of the whole of life, imposed by the difficulties of survival.
Single parenthood is thus an aspect of creaturehood's intrinsic limits, as
much as anything. When faithfully embraced, therefore, single parenthood can also be a path of wisdom. As with Job, however, it is perverse
to think of it as a path that can ever properly be chosen in freedom. Just
such choices that, in our era, are culturally enabled move against the
very particularity of human life that our struggles are called to engage.
A grasp of creaturely passability—that who we are, at root, is shaped by
our place and relations, not chosen or invented—is an essential way of
maintaining the integrity of particular creation.

Already in the nineteenth century we see efforts and movements of
reaction against the dissolving pressures of human interchangeability.
Communitarian experiments, often with explicit religious (though not
necessarily Christian) orientations, proliferated. Some of these efforts,
like William Morris' craft communalism, strike us today as the products of both privilege and romanticism. In our own era, however, the
ordering of communities, industry, food production, and retail practices
around spatial values of local "sphere" life—associated with concepts
like "the new urbanism" and earlier writers like Lewis Mumford and
Jane Jacobs—represents a more self-aware and experienced response.[11]
The French tradition of the "terroir,"[12] which has never disappeared,
constitutes a continued alternative for the literal cultivation of created
distinctiveness integrated within the genealogical context. Rooted in
the wine culture of France, and now applied to many other areas of
agriculture (e.g., tea, fruit, livestock production), the "terroir" refers to
the confluence of geography, geology, and climate that gives something
grown in a particular place its specific taste. Terroir also embraces the
full culture of those who grow and produce: their generational history,
their families, their homes and tools, their lifestyles and common commitments. As the philosopher Stiegler has argued, tools and technical
objects have their own "genealogy," of history, culture, place, and time.
More precisely, tools are distinctly interwoven into the genealogies of
persons. Thus, a major aspect of human "memory" is bound up with the

"life" of these objects themselves. They are intimate and distinct parts of human life, whose creaturely texture increasingly thins out as this memory itself is weakened or rejected outright.

If this general and even normative way of talking about work and its objects sounds much like the perspective of a pre-Transition world, that is probably the case. This is because the reality of creatureliness, exposed in the Scripture's figures, demands *at least* the maintenance of such relationships between people and things in the context of work, even if embodied in new ways. The monastic community and its map best typify this, in the way this form of life sketches out how individuals and groups live in their dependence upon each other. Monastic dependence is not only for biological survival but exists for the sake of the salvation of the individual soul that is the aim of common life (as St. Benedict writes in the prologue of his *Rule*). Monasticism, however, is but a type and need not stand as some kind of epitome to be grasped, so much as a witness for a more normal reality, made up of the family map and its community. Here toil becomes the ground where singularity and genealogy grow together, and the artifacts of the world are both displayed and deployed in thanks. An important claim emerges from this logic: singleness and married life are joined in work, not in analogues of sex.

## Work

Work itself is not some kind of threshold of distinction from "nature," as if the artifacts of technical tool making were opposed to the artifacts of created existence more broadly. Some sociologists have argued for such an opposition (e.g., the late Serge Moscovici), planting an evolutionary and conceptual line between nature and human labor.[13] It is a common philosophical claim, in fact; but it is also wrongheaded. One thing Marxian theory got right was that a human person's relation to his or her labor is primary to his or her human "being," not secondary: we are what and how we work. (Questions of how a society or political economy takes account of this rightly are also therefore central.) Work is the foundation of our created and generative existence, and hence "natural," according to Scripture: Adam and Eve are created for one another and for the construction of life together within the created sphere of God's gifts. Montaigne's dictum that our lives are our work derives from the fact that the act of living itself is bound up with the forms of our work. "We say: 'I have done nothing to-day.' What? have you not lived? that is not only the fundamental, but the most illustrious of all your occupations."[14]

We are never told in the Bible what the fundamental form of labor might look like concretely. Even before their disobedience, Adam and Eve are seen as "workers" or "tillers" of the garden (Gen 2:15); and it is the same work they will do in their exile (e.g., Gen 3:23; 4:12; etc.), now to the point that the word "work" itself becomes a synonym for "servitude." So, however we construe "work" in the garden, the disobedience of man and woman (the "fall") reorients the shape of their lives and leads to a transformation of work into a new direction of experience: toil. The Hebrew word (*itsabown*) is translated by the Authorized Version as such in Genesis 5:29: "And [Lamech] called his [son's] name Noah, saying, This same shall comfort us concerning our work and toil of our hands, because of the ground which the Lord hath cursed." In Genesis 3:17, the word is translated as "sorrow": "cursed is the ground for thy sake; in sorrow shalt thou eat of it all the days of thy life." "Toil" is itself from the old French and originally meant a violent struggle, and, later, in English, it referred specifically to the struggle of a certain kind of labor. ("Work," more generally, perhaps derives from the same root as the Greek *ergon*, an "act" or deed of some kind.) Ecclesiastes will fixate on this this kind of referent (*amal*) in its repeated discussion of the vanity of "labor," itself viewed as a kind of wearisome sorrow.

Hence, work is described first as a "curse." Work is hard; it is often miserable even; it is bound up with death in a way that seems to go beyond the more basic limits of created life. Yet it also becomes pervasive to human life, the "ground" of our living in a literal and scriptural way. Even if work itself did not arise from the fall, the relationship of survival between human beings and the blessings of the rest of creation was altered: the dust itself was no longer intrinsically fruitful for the needs of human beings, and survival became the result only of a long and laborious struggle. The "curse," however, is actually shown here to be a gift: it is given by God, in the shadow of failure, as a *means* for life. Life is now struggled after; yet still, it is life that is given. Thus, like the skins with which he clothes the first man and woman as they leave the garden, God provides toil, not for death, but for life in the face of death. Despite Ecclesiastes' claim that toil is without "profit" or value (cf. Eccl 1:3), there is an element in this judgment that reflects what we have done with it, not simply its intrinsic meaning.

We will not reflect directly on human sin until the conclusion, delaying our discussion in an effort at rebalancing certain tendencies in the Christian church and countertendencies within secular responses.

For to be a creature is not, in itself, to be sinful; it is to be mortal, and mortality itself is not sinful. But the character of our suffering in this world is bound up with more than our mortality. It is tied rather to the fact, embodied in Adam and Eve's disobedience, that we cannot *trust* in God's grace within our mortal existences. The fact that our lives are "all grace" in their givenness by God is what sin, at its center, rebels against. Our grabbing, manipulating, and fighting derive from this rebellion. Learning, in its widest sense of learning for the sake of wisdom, is the process of growing *back*, of being shaped back into a place of complete and perfect trust in God's grace. This is why humility has been properly seen, within the Christian tradition, as the pinnacle of wisdom. The curse of toil is a part of this learning backward; it "fits" into this movement of relearning grace, of being "humiliated" in the sense of being pressed back to the earth from which we came. The curse is a means of grace in the face of our sinfulness. That is a fundamental Christian conviction, although often misunderstood.

If one of Martin Luther's great theological contributions to the Christian church was a renewed understanding, from a particular perspective, of God's grace, just as important was his radical press for reconceiving the reality of "vocation." (This reading of Luther was common among many early twentieth-century readers of Luther, although it is less stressed by today's scholars.) Luther was really the first person to engage this reality of work in the world, which he linked to the Christian concept of "vocation," or of being "called" by God. Our labor, he argued, must be seen as a "calling."[15] It is important to get the order right: we do not work only where we are called; rather, it is in working that our calling is given shape. One text—although there were many—that Luther turned to was 1 Corinthians 7:20, where Paul writes, "Let every man abide in the same calling wherein he was called." Luther rejected what had become the common Christian limitation of "calling" to the vowed life of the monk or nun, in which one followed the "counsels of perfection" of poverty, chastity, and obedience. Rather, he insisted, God calls us to serve him and others through our worldly location and within it. This work is our vocation. Hence, study, labor, marriage, parenting, caring, tending—these are all locations of calling, wherein the fullness of our Christian lives, given in love of God and neighbor, can be pursued.

Toil is thus a vocational landscape, bound to our life as creatures but, more importantly, to the way that life is ordered to our purpose. Toil, in fact, is bound to our learning wisdom in terms of knowing God's grace as "all in all." As Luther writes, in his *Small Catechism* (discussing the Apostles' Creed):

> I believe that God . . . has given me my body and soul, eyes, ears and all my limbs, my reason and all my senses, and still preserves them; in addition thereto, clothing and shoes, meat and drink, house and homestead, wife and children, fields, cattle, and all my goods; that He provides me richly and daily with all that I need to support this body and life, protects me from all danger, and guards me and preserves me from all evil; and all this out of pure, fatherly, divine goodness and mercy, without any merit or worthiness in me; for all which I owe it to Him to thank, praise, serve, and obey Him. This is most certainly true.[16]

God bestows his earthly gifts by means of the vocations we *share*, and we follow God's calling for the sake of others and all of us together. Throughout his long series of lectures on Genesis, Luther returns to this theme: the seemingly lowly acts of both men and women—raising cattle, milking cows, ordering homes, plowing fields (when done in a spirit of thanksgiving, worship, and service)—embody the fullness of the Christian life and hope.[17] Thus, when we pray, "give us this day our daily bread" (again from the *Small Catechism*), we are really both asking and thanking God for a whole intricate web of human vocations, from farmers to friends:

> Everything that belongs to the support and wants of the body, such as meat, drink, clothing, shoes, house, homestead, field, cattle, money, goods, a pious spouse, pious children, pious servants, pious and faithful magistrates, good government, good weather, peace, health, discipline, honor, good friends, faithful neighbors, and the like.

The scheme is as large as it can be, yet as intimate as its force rightly presses into experiencing. If there was something problematic in Luther's recasting of vocation, it was in not being broad enough, and broad in the sense of gathering the particularities of lives in a more variegated temporal and social fashion. There is a sense in which the category of vocation, just because it was expanded on the model of the vowed religious life that Luther himself had followed, maintained the constraints of the monastic model: one had a "station" in life that was fixed, and movement and interaction among stations, by one individual, was difficult to imagine. Magistrates stayed in their roles, and were so defined; soldiers too; wives and milkmaids. Luther's world remained numbingly stable as well as suffocating for many. Much of this is a factor of era, and our own—with its mobility of place, education, and relationship—demands that our work also be as malleable as such movement allows and requires. Hence, it is right in our day to reconsider the household as a place of male and female work, just as we might see the professional workplace as both role-variant and shifting for any given individual. In some ways, then, we are better able today to see work as something beyond just our "job." Work properly encompasses the breadth of our daily life in many ways.

This is one reason why politics, at its root, is a form of labor rather than a category of life separate from toil. Various cultures have had political structures that that limited daily toil in politics only to certain persons. Most modern societies have made politics a part of common labor (just as it has made washing and transport, accounting and writing). I can only make the suggestion here: politics, and particularly its theological understanding, should properly be studied as a form of toil. If it were, many of the overtly ideological issues that preempt our proper reflections on political choices might at least recede somewhat. Politics is about survival and is bound up with feeding and security. Individuals engage political decision making not as a momentary product of discernment and assent but as a constant effort to *live*, and to do so in a way that offers wisdom. There are skills to be learned, and those to be passed on; there are ages of life in which this form of political life is pursued, and others where it is not; and much of the political "process" is simply difficult, a hard dragging against the edges of the world's jagged landscape. This does indeed make politics and moral life, sexuality and remunerative labor coexpressions of skindom. They all fall into the same boat—no more and no less.

Our vocations in every form of labor, then, reflect the very tenor of our creaturely life in its gracious being, in that they are always followed "in relation" to others. Our work never can be primarily about ourselves but must always find its substance in connection with others and with our common support of one another. Few are the hermits, let alone the single person more normally, who simply grow their own food for themselves, apart from the world. Even the solitary contemplative, it turns out, relies on others—if not people, then animals, as so many stories, like that of Herman of Alaska, point out. Herman stands as a type: living alone in the wilderness of the Aleutian Islands as an early Russian missionary, he describes his own survival as given through fish, vegetables, and the help of a few local native families. His disciple, Ignaty, speaks of the beasts—birds, ermine, and even bears—as his companions.[18]

It is impossible to overemphasize the fact that toil is always toil *for another*. Hence, its articulation within the curse of Genesis is within the dual life of Adam and Eve *together*. Though bound to the curse, work demonstrates how grace can turn curse into the redeeming work of love. Learning, as we have seen, is founded absolutely upon our basic engagement and relations with parents, adults, peers, and others. There is no learning in pure solitude (and even books, read in a prison cell, are about bringing others into our minds, as Stiegler insists). The Ages of Life are always being shared with others, which is what defines their character. When we speak of coming into the world "naked," and leaving it "naked" (Job 1:21), this does not refer to the ultimate "solitude" of human life, proverbialized in the phrase "every man dies alone" (*on mourra seul*, in Pascal's version).[19] The proverb is only partially true. It is not true, in that our vocation is to live for and with others, and we die to God, who has brought us into life with others. If we fail to realize this somehow, then the proverb fulfills itself in the way we are left to face the horror of some final aloneness. In any case, as long as we are alive, we are in the midst of a clamoring crowd, and that is our calling to grow through.

Work is an essential part of life at least in the following way: it is the ongoing and necessary means by which we are held within and integrated into the framework of our life as creatures, by which we grow in wisdom, and thus into our receipt of God's gifts.

## The Character of Work

### Survival

Everyone senses that our survival depends upon our labor. Even today's poor, who live within the welfare system of this or that state, actually need to work quite hard to engage these services. In Genesis, work-as-survival is given in terms of leaving the garden and its readily available fruit (however we take the tilling of Eden, alluded to in 2:15). Somehow, food in Eden was near at hand at every turn, immediately offered by God. Outside the garden, however, human beings need not only to till the soil but to do so within a context of physical resistance. They must rely on rain and deal with droughts, hail, storms, floods, and insects. Harvests are struggles; the grinding of flour is a matter of "sweat." Human beings raise animals, protect them, slaughter them, prepare them. There is the challenge of dwellings, of clothing and weaving, of trade finally and its mechanisms and justice. Much of the Law in the Old Testament is bound to these realities: how to organize fields and allow the poor to scrape out a living; what to do with property; ordering the use and distribution of livestock; clothing, tilling, distinguishing clean and unclean animals for eating, as we have seen, which amounts to understanding some kind of interplay of realms of responsibility and discretion among humans and the rest of creation. The very word "culture" comes from this larger realm of human work to survive: how one organizes food through agriculture or viniculture. Our societies are built around the toil of survival, and not, in the first instance, around enjoyment or leisure.

Of course, our sin takes place within our work for survival as well, as the first murder of Abel by his brother Cain describes. The primordial murder arises out of the distinctive character of each brother's toil— farming versus the raising of livestock, and how each saw the other's work in relation to God. This linking of survival and divine sacrifice is telling: our work is for life. Our work is God's own provision of life. As Luther writes, God could simply create new people from the earth; but instead God gives us the means to "survive" and pass on that survival to others through generation of children and the raising of families.[20] Work is about life, not about deadness. People who feel their work is "dead" may well need to take stock of what they are doing, and perhaps do something else. But the issue in such feelings is not the work itself but our ability to see its purpose and its central meaning. If we can grasp this purpose, there is no reason to work in any other way. Work is life. It is bound to "blood" and hence to the very character of our mortal vocations: sustenance in breath.

### Providing for Others

Toil, then, is itself the form of "life," the means of sustaining our createdness with God. But work is also more particularly the means of extending that life, of engaging in life giving. We work *for* others, always. This is more obvious when it comes to our spouses, our children, and our families. But in very particular ways, this reality touches the larger sphere of our neighbors. Again, Luther stresses this so well: our vocations and work are the places we serve others and exercise the fruit of our faith, which are the works of love. Without question, the contemporary Western notion of work as a personal fulfillment of identity and self-making undercuts this insight. To be sure, the notion itself is only imperfectly

held by many, and, even for those who seemingly have many opportunities, the reality of caring for a family, on the one hand, and contributing
to the health of other persons bound up with a system of work, on the
other, is usually inescapable, if rarely taught clearly.

Moments like local or national economic recession can at least bring
this home, as the demands for cost cutting, workforce shrinkage, and
layoffs quite concretely bring into view the symbiotic character of work.
In our era, we can even see, sometimes quite immediately, the way our
work is bound up with workers in other countries and parts of the world.
Universities involve far more than teachers and students; churches, far
more than pastors and organists; mission fields, far more than evangelists and listeners. The simple economics of these small-scale communities of labor makes this clear. More deeply, all communities involve the
shared character of work in which stability and consistency provide for
the life of others working within the network. Hence, the work of single
persons is just as much a part of this network of provision as is that of
married persons. One moral consequence of this laboring network is that
the way one works and the vision, character, and prayers that are a part
of one's work are all immediately obvious and pertinent with respect to
neighbors.

### Work Is Always Shared

Work is a central aspect of learning wisdom. Not only is work something done *for* the life of others; it is something done *with* others, in
the sense of engagement and relationship in an immediate and ongoing
way. After our infancy and childhood, and beyond our immediate family (although in the past, work was usually done *as* a family), our work is
the place we learn.

In every workplace—and that includes the "work" being done by
children in their schooling—there are the realities and challenges of simple human encounter, which can involve both tedium and emergencies
but mostly the vast realm that lies in between these extremes. We meet
new people; learn about the characters, foibles, and lives of others over
time; and engage in problem solving or in conflict and its resolution.
Dinner conversations often revolve around such work, especially among
families and friends.[21] In some contexts, such conversation is actually
limited for reasons of a certain discretion, since the topics are understood to be too profound for open discussion. As one of the main places
where we learn about truth and limits, love and forgiveness, evil and

resistance, the learning that takes place in work can be as demanding and revealing as intimate relationships are seen as being. The colleague with cancer; the student with a family struggle; the family with twins and all it means; the husband who was laid off; the loss of a bursary; the car accident; this failure or that; our feelings of anger or joy, satisfaction, or anxiety: the communities of work constitute disciplined schools for wisdom as much as do families.

One can rightly wonder about what this wisdom-provoking community of labor says regarding the way work is often organized in our society. The default habits of modern work tend both to contain existentially challenging encounters and to limit conscious avenues for their healthy engagement. Nonetheless, if it is the nature of work to be such a school for wisdom, then, whatever we do, specific aspects of work's blessing must begin to emerge.

### Work Is Receptive

Luther insisted that work is a form of *relatio*—that is, a way of relating for what we begin to learn in our labor; something that goes to our growth in wisdom is receptivity itself. In working, we receive from those with whom we work and for whom we work. As we grow in our laboring, we come to see our work not only as our responsibility for others but also as our own *dependence* upon them within the landscape of shared creatureliness under the providence of God.

Here, the moral character of our work comes into play. Until, in our work, we begin to see this dependence on others for our "daily bread"—surviving, breathing, being shaped, learning—and until we actually rely on our coworkers in this way for our deepest sustenance as human beings, then the "curse" aspect of work as mere toil continues to exert its force.

Just here the integration of married and single lives in the truthful exercise of creatureliness begins to bear fruit. We learn from others only to the degree that such otherness is actually assimilated as such and has traction upon our perceptions and responses. The character of dependence is partly the form of such perceptive response, and thus it is built up out of this engagement of persons within spheres of demanded cooperation. The service of singleness in its individuality is performed most regularly within the symbiotic sphere of work, where, in most cases, adult friendships find their initial roots.

It is not unusual for Christians to pray for coworkers. But the reality of learning from them and with them, of which such intercessory prayer is a feature, should rightly move in a further direction. For it is proof of our growth in wisdom within our work that we can also give *thanks* for those with whom we live, concretely and continually. This, after all, constitutes at least an initial form of love itself, which is bound up with the mature acknowledgment of grace that flows from the renewal of our understanding of life as the fundamental divine gift.

## Work Is Reflection

Contemporary Western culture has deeply failed us by making work a matter of individual or self-discernment for the sake of individual or self-fulfillment. This follows along with the shift of the meaning of "vocation" from God-given toil in all of its fullness to "vocation" as a personal quest for self-expression, that which is "right" for me (e.g., finding the "right" job that fulfills "my deepest desires").

We should not dismiss this impulse; it is both a necessary part of the movement of creaturely specificity we have called "individuation" and something inevitable in a world of almost countless choices about "careers" and "gifts" and so on. Our young people, though, while they have more possibilities for kinds of work than ever before in human history, have also been thrust into a world where "work" is not the issue any longer, but rather the self. At the same time, however, the actual dignity of work has been lost in the public mind, and we have come to scorn more and more the simple demands for stable employment that every human being both needs and was created and is a creature for.

But none of us can avoid the question our culture forces us to confront: "What is the 'right' work for me, as *this* person?" All of us have real desires as well as passions about the employment of our imaginations and energies, and if we dismiss them they will wreak a secret vengeance upon us. All the same, this question is not properly posed and pursued until we have grown in our sense of work itself. Although young people and their mentors must consider the question in order to organize their schooling, we will never get a good answer until we have grown in our sense of work as vocation in the way we have just described it. The proper place to pose the question of vocation fruitfully is always from within the context of responsibility, learning, and receiving in work with others. Only there can we begin to hear, to have the ears of our spirits opened, not simply to what we want, but to the ways that our gifts used in toil might more fruitfully serve a common purpose and hope. It is not the case that work is somehow sanctified in its wholeness simply by being pursued, such that out of it only good can come. One does not need to rely on the works of social deconstructionists to recognize that work is often ambivalent in its meaning, imposed out of base motives and taken up out of tactical response.[22] Nonetheless, work marks the quotidian tenor of the mortal life in such a way that its inevitability also becomes the source of its fruitfulness simply as a grace given within our traversal of life.

Within the arc of the life span, labor should be assumed at an earlier age than is now common, as a discipline and responsibility. At the same time, the kinds of choices that fix our singularity as creatures are probably better seen less as specific demands on the front end of our existences than as emerging clarities from the ongoing framing of our lives. A human person, simply because we are creatures whose lives are given in extenso through time and time's formation, can probably happily marry most anybody; hence, arranged marriages have had a long and consistent track record in human history that is more stable and positive than many people in today's societies of personal choice can imagine. Likewise, a person can live anywhere and flourish, because the issue is not who I am related to but how my relations are shaping me, opening me and teaching me. A Christian pastor, as the tradition has generally rightly insisted, can and should be able to work with faithfulness in any setting and context—rural, urban, big, small, with older people, with families, with the more and the less educated or wealthy. Homophily, and its individualistic analogues, is neither a specifically Christian nor a more broadly creaturely virtue.

We also remain peculiar individuals. Therefore, given the choices we are made to discern within a culture of multiplied possibility, we can also use our gifts for others in profoundly fruitful ways that are peculiar as well. To see this and be led by this fact in a way that is faithful as a creature of God is to find the space for listening. In such a space, our fruitfulness in labor can be spoken to us, usually by others, and not simply take form before our eyes out of personal desire. Our working neighbors mirror back to us the way our own work is a blessing, and we are responsible for receiving this reflection. The shape of such reception stands as an ongoing process. While work should be stable, it is never static precisely because we are living, relating, and learning. We are also, of course, limited, such that our choices are inevitably incomplete, cut off, and always uncertain. The test of our labor is its probative thrust: whether I am growing in a wisdom that properly reflects my life as God's creature, such that, whatever my choices, I am receiving and being received back again from God, within the web of other creatures, in the movement that is my life's essential grace.

Toil is vanity, Ecclesiastes asserts. But it is vanity to the extent that it is taken "all on its own," as a simple reality decoupled from everything else. "All is vanity," in fact, if all things, whatever their beauty, are taken only on their own. Work is actually the container God gives us, as creatures, for our learning of wisdom: surviving; providing; loving; receiving; learning; listening. Toil, it turns out, is a gift of a profound kind. People of the past have known this in ways we have forgotten, for it was through their work that the fullness of human relating took its form.

### Toil and Food

The toil that is our work is taken up for our survival. It is also the formative context of our generative existence, of our sociality in time. The common meal, therefore, becomes its active figure, as a matter of experiential logic: as we eat together, all the bits of our tunics of skin are held together.

Anthropologists and sociologists insist on this fact. They began studying the unique and powerful role of eating together systematically over a century ago, tellingly with discussions first of the Old Testament. In doing this, they were of course only articulating in an empirical and theoretical manner what human beings have long known and articulated in other ways. Meals are a fundamental, even essential, aspect of creaturely assertion—in families, first, and then in terms of the wider community.[23] Anthropologists like to speak about the "symbolic communication" among persons and within societies that meals represent. They look at issues of what and how things are eaten, where people sit, who shares what with whom, when do they do it, what happens before and after this or that meal. The inner goals and energies of an entire culture can be read out through the way people eat together, or alone. All of the meaning of how people understand themselves within a group is funneled into the common meal and its occasion. This is wonderfully interesting and almost overwhelming in its possible lines of exploration. There is, among many avenues of study on this topic, a Society for the Anthropology of Food and Nutrition (SAFN), with its own journal, *FoodAnthropology*, and simply dipping into this material opens up a breathtaking world of self-understanding and even mystery. Sociologists have been more interested in the formalized structure of a meal as a means of social/community identity formation. This obviously takes in aspects of politics itself. We can see some of this dynamic hovering over even the "oneness of the body" aspect that is central to the Eucharist in particular.

Important as these elements may be, there is more to a meal from a theological point of view. Meals are the actual embodiment of our lives as given and thus of our given genealogical identity as well. In this sense, meals are not a "symbol" of anything; they are the reality itself. It was an anthropologist, Gillian Feeley-Harnik, who made this point regarding the Eucharist in the early church, speaking of the immediate relationship of survival between people and land in the harsher and more contrastive geology and climate of Palestine. One eats in order to survive; one eats together for the same reason and out of the same dynamic. The food one takes into oneself, with whatever care and cherished wonder, is tied primarily to this fact. From an anthropological perspective, cultures often link food and sex, the one a symbol for the other, and frequently bind them (as in Christian tradition) to "passions" of the "flesh" and to parallel prohibitions. Some researchers have, in fact, suggested that there is a neurological link between the sensing arousals connected with each. The link, however, is even deeper and more concretized than this: food, as in the personal case of Jesus, *is* our life in a material fashion. It is the participation of life within its material givenness, as created by God. Hence, food marks the first and basic level at which societies engage in self-repair, and it is just where churches have most frequently expressed their ministries: soup kitchens, basement meals, celebrations, and, of course, peculiar liturgical actions.

For all these reasons and more, food has become the most broad and inclusive arena, in our contemporary Western societies, for the subconscious creaturely assertions of our existences, which have been displaced by the lost recognition of our larger creaturely traversal. Arguably, food is a more comprehensive arena for these assertions than even sex. As the Great Transition has increasingly occluded within our culture the central aspects of creaturely existence associated with mortality, eating is one of the few places where we still find our inescapable natures capable of some kind of expression, albeit one that is frequently deformed, in overwhelmingly powerful ways.[24] This compensatory dynamic, in the face of mortality's obscuring, explains why, in societies of plenty, food is even more important than ever before. "Food culture" (and with it, food politics) dominates Western culture in an astonishing way. Even Christians have been swept into this compensatory dynamic: first there were tentative explorations of culinary theology (e.g., by Robert Capon); then came a spate of books on biblical cooking, meals for saints' days; and finally there appeared the expanding moral concerns over production and distribution, nutrition and ethics, that have tracked with larger social anxieties. Part of this contemporary food focus is the result of successful marketing that expresses the internal dynamics of a consumerist economy. But the search for food meaning, possession and consumption, display and delight, is driven more deeply, and unfortunately.[25]

These matters have become the subject of several publishing fields in their own right and cannot be explored here. There is, however, an obvious element that can be drawn from all these studies: our food disorders are part of a larger shift in our sense of who we are, one that has little to do with the objects of ingestion in a simple way but that pertains instead to the limited way we now understand ourselves as creatures. From the perspective of the Christian tradition, by contrast, the meal emerges from the work of the creature, and that work is given in the genealogical movement of human creaturehood. This creaturely context is the only real place to understand what is at stake in, and the lens through which to grasp, the nature of our eating at its root. We skin animals and fruit both, before they are set upon the table. That is our work to live.

### The Ingesting God

Given this creaturely context, we can understand why the Eucharist lies at the center and even summit of our common life. The reason lies less in a complex theological train of deductions than in the straightforward meaning of our eating itself: we eat because we are alive; and since we are alive, then what follows must come down to generation, genealogy, toil, individuation, and probation. Hence, the Eucharist comprehends just these elements of creaturely existence as much as anything else— probably mostly these elements. We can see some of this expressed in Paul's discussion of the Corinthians' meal gatherings in 1 Corinthians 11:17-34. What he articulates in the specific terms of the Last Supper is informed (in this case negatively) by the realities within his congregation of "hunger" and "drunkenness," abundance and scarcity, hurry and isolation, division and disdain, and, finally, illness and death itself (v. 30). The meal is nothing but the prism of creaturely traversal in its difficult distinctions. This traversal, to be sure, is bound up with the New Man as much as with the Old; but it is traversal that defines the Eucharist.

Food itself is the bond between life as divine gift and the shape of such a life as distinct, as placed within the world of divine artifacts, as one among many. Hence, food is itself a form of created being, ingested by created being. If there is such a thing as the great "chain of being," as medieval and early modern theologians insisted, that chain is given in created ingestion itself, what contemporary biologists have popularized as "the food chain." The traditional English phrase that links "bread," and later any staple food, with the "staff" or support of life actually comes directly from the Hebrew. It translates Leviticus 26:26 and other similar texts: food is bound up directly with all that lives; and all that lives *leans* upon it, to move forward. If one takes food away, life collapses. As Donne insists, the "daily bread" of the Lord's Prayer is always a *memento mori*, which presents us with a sign of the *mors quotidiana* ("daily death") even as it gives us that life that is only God's to give and take.[26] Food is at the center of the garden's life, in Genesis, not merely as the "tree of life," but as an essential part of the initial relationship of creatures to God and to one another. Human beings are created to eat as food all seed-bearing—that is, generative—plants, just as are other animals (Gen 1:29-30). The fateful tree, furthermore, is known by the eating of its fruit (Gen 3:6)—such that the "shame" now tied to the self-consciously "genesic" sense (in Brillat-Savarin's nomenclature) is properly tied to the sense of "taste." In the same way, the "tree of life" in Revelation 22:3 bears "fruit" whose implied eating will, along with its leaves, bring renewed wholeness to all the "nations" and thereby the fulfillment of their generational order.

This kind of creaturely network of shared life, given through the creature-as-food, is bound up with work from the start: Adam is "put" into the "garden of Eden to dress it and to keep it" (Gen 2:15). What is altered in the act of disobedience, through the "curse," is that this labor should now become a struggle, toil. God curses the ground, so that "in sorrow shalt thou eat of it all the days of thy life; Thorns also and thistles, shall it bring forth to thee; and thou shalt eat of the herb of the field; In the sweat of thy face shalt thou eat bread, till thou return to the ground" (Gen 3:17-19). What the AV translates as "bread" does in fact refer to the product of grain, while the earlier word "meat," used in Genesis 1:29-30, translates a more general (and relatively rare) word for "food," which can be either plant or animal flesh. Food is thus brought into the realm of the great traversal that the man and the woman will enter upon as they venture out into the world of wilderness.

Whether the eating of animal meat—unmentioned in Genesis 1–3 —is itself now a sign of or adjustment to this fallen state (cf. Gen 9:3 on the Noachic "permission" to eat meat) has been much debated[27]—just as whether the skins with which God clothes Adam and Eve come from beasts that have died "naturally" or were killed for the purpose, much as Cain will later raise cattle for a host of uses. Christian vegetarianism has, in fact, been based in part on particular resolutions to these questions.

But the relationship of food and work, bound to the character of survival and the maintenance of life, remains steady, and not simply one of agonized demand. Food is often viewed in the Scriptures as a good to be delighted in: it "strengthens the heart" (Gen 18:5; Ps 104:15), and, in some of its forms, like wine, it even makes the heart "rejoice" (Ps 104:15), in the sense of giving thanks to God for blessings received. Indeed, such rejoicing is often bound up specifically with meals shared before God (cf. Deut 12:7 etc.). And the opening up of the gospel message to the nations as a whole is linked with a wide embrace of gastronomic abundance, in terms not of culinary aestheticism but of multitudinous creaturely provision:

> On the morrow, as they went on their journey, and drew nigh unto the city, Peter went up upon the housetop to pray about the sixth hour: And he became very hungry, and would have eaten: but while they made ready, he fell into a trance, And saw heaven opened, and a certain vessel descending unto him, as it had been a great sheet knit at the four corners, and let down to the earth: Wherein were all manner of fourfooted beasts of the earth, and wild beasts, and creeping things, and fowls of the air. And there came a voice to him, Rise, Peter; kill, and eat. But Peter said, Not so, Lord; for I have never eaten any thing that is common or unclean. And the voice [spake] unto him again the second time, What God hath cleansed, [that] call not thou common. (Acts 10:9-15)

This vision of Peter depicts the realm of Eden's fullness, restored in the realm of the meal. All of creation opens up insofar as it is received as food. Food, that is, remains a blessing in the same way that creaturely existence and its order, for all of its sorrow, is an incomprehensible gift "from heaven." Eating finds its place at the center of this donative framework, pulling together persons, their generative relations, their duties, their burdens, and their particular distinctions. Paul will tie eating and work together in a moral fashion—to eat, one must work. This is more reminiscent of the meal's pilgrimage character (cf. 1 Thess 4:11; 2 Thess 3:10-14; 1 Cor 9:6-9). At the same time, he will insist that "eating and drinking" be done "to the glory of God" (1 Cor 10:31), just as he sees the Lord's Supper as the epitome of such glorification. What Jesus does with his disciples, even and especially in the form of his resurrected life, is "eat and drink" with them (cf. Acts 10:41). But for all that, the Eucharist is a "work," an act of labor, not only for the Christians who participate in it, but, of course, for God's own self-giving in Christ Jesus. Food turns labor into praise and redeems the curse of toil.

The well-known Jewish "blessings" over God's gifts, especially food, known as the *Birkot-ha-mazon* are in line with this vision: "Blessed are you, Lord God, King of the Universe, who creates various kinds of sustenance . . . who brings forth bread from the earth . . . who creates the fruit of the ground . . . who creates various kinds of herbs."[28] These Talmudic prayers, still regularly said, have their origins in early rabbinic life, perhaps at the time of Jesus himself, as third-century fragments from the remarkable site of Dura-Europos demonstrate. These parchment snippets, found in the ancient rubble, include blessings offered to God for giving food for eating, preparing sustenance, and creating human beings to take nourishment from them. Eating, within this context, is the direct ingestion of God's creation, in a way that elicits praise. This was the early Jewish philosopher Philo's point as he explained the meaning of eating *un*leavened bread at certain times: the lack of yeast underscores how food, at its root, is "simply" given by God for life. It retains, even in the wilderness, the grace of Eden.[29] Whether or not these *birkot*, in some form, were part of the early Christian eucharistic practice, there are clear parallels. The second-century Christian text known as the *Didache*, or "Teaching of the twelve apostles," includes a short discussion of the Eucharist that provides prayers to be said over the wine and bread (chapters 9–10). These are explicitly oriented toward scriptural and christological figures; but they close with a familiar creaturely analogy:

> You, almighty Lord, created all things for the sake of your name, and you gave food and drink to human beings for enjoyment, so that they would thank you; But you graced us with spiritual food and drink and eternal life through Jesus your servant. (10:3)[30]

Thus, to this day, one of the most commonly used prayers from the current Roman Mass, the "Preparation and Presentation of the Gifts," follows this format, now expressly underlining the continuity of food as the fruit of human labor and the divine gift of Christ:

> PRIEST: Blessed are you, Lord God of all creation, for through your goodness we have received the bread we offer you: fruit of the earth and work of human hands, it will become for us the bread of life.

> ALL: Blessed be God for ever.

> PRIEST: Blessed are you, Lord God of all creation, for through your goodness we have received the wine we offer you: fruit of the vine and work of human hands it will become our spiritual drink.

> ALL: Blessed be God for ever.

Benedict XVI explained this "humble and simple gesture" in redemptive terms: "In the bread and wine that we bring to the altar, all creation is taken up by Christ the Redeemer to be transformed and presented to the Father."[31] Creation is "taken up" first by human hands, by work, by the deliberate set of processes, cultural and otherwise, by which food is taken from the soil and fashioned into edible form and shared. "Universally, eating and drinking are processes of bringing the natural world into the human domain," writes Amy Trubek. If so, then the Eucharist is the ingestion of "the natural world"[32]—that is, creation itself—into and through Jesus, such that the processes of toil become his own as they are "taken up" by God.

If the Eucharist involves "ingesting the natural world in Christ," there are implications that go beyond liturgical theology. For this "taking up of creation" by God in Christ is, to some extent, true of every other meal Jesus ate. The fact that God incarnate placed in his mouth, chewed, tasted, savored, swallowed, delighted in, and was nourished by the very creatures he had, in his wisdom, made from nothing stands, in relation to human understanding, in the same incomprehensible place as does the creation itself. It is also, just there, one of the overwhelming mysteries of our existence.[33] We are led to wonder if Jesus himself ate of the bread he broke and the wine he shared at the Last Supper—that is, of his *own* body and blood. (The indications in Luke 22:15-20 and Mark 10:22-25 seem to point in this direction.) Nothing could be more astonishing. In any case, in the Eucharist, the Christian ingests not just "Jesus as God" in some general fashion; rather, she or he is taking in the very fulfillment of God's specific *creation* through God's own creative and particular act in Christ. In the Eucharist, the Christian ingests not God, uncharacterized, but in particular the ingesting God himself.

To speak of "the ingesting God" is to trespass, whether we like it or not, into deep Trinitarian challenges. The way in which we are to understand the impassible God as "eating" within the economy of the incarnate life of the Son requires more than special care.[34] But we must nonetheless affirm this basic claim in a robust fashion. The New Testament—in John 6 and 1 Corinthians 11, for example—stresses the "body" of Jesus that is "eaten." In so doing, we are driven to understand this "body" in very particular creaturely terms. This is the "body" that has itself made the great traversal. This is the body that has been born, has grown, and has, in its "hidden years" in Nazareth, engaged familial challenge and perhaps travail, toil, and struggle. It is a body that has walked and slept, dreamed and hoped, wept, laughed, and pressed forward. The fact that "God eats" is the one marvelous authorization of our lives as creatures, and just so, in their creaturely form. In this sense, we can speak of a Great Transfiguration that emerges within and around the Great Traversal, and that must render relative, one way or the other, all the confusions of the Great Transition. This Transfiguration occurs in the so-called "words of institution" that mark the Last Supper's shape: this is a "body given" and "blood shed," in the very matter of the bread and wine of a common meal. Survival, work, and food are now taken and become the gift of life as a "new covenant" in forgiveness. God eats, insofar now as God "works."

### The Work of God

God eats, and thereby creaturely work itself is renewed. The "works" of God in creating are now given over to the works of humanity in creaturely life. The two are coordinated as terms (Gen 2:2; Exod 20:9-10). This is embraced anew by God in the "work still being done" (cf. John 5:17-20) that marks the traversal, tabernacling in the flesh of Jesus, to the cross. Toil finds its home in the "bosom" of the life of God (John 1:14, 18).

Here we come to a strange aspect, which turns food back toward the character of created life, in a way that must somehow include the Eucharist (or vice versa) rather than distinguish the two. The Scriptures amaze us as they demonstrate this, with their intertwining verses, words, and figures; dogmatic theology has sometimes done a disservice to the wonderful mystery embodied by this reality. Although a discussion of sin has been limited in the present volume, it has inevitably come up as the question, especially, of the fall is raised. While distinctions between sin and redemption, as they pertain to creaturely existence, must obviously be made, the two cannot be easily segregated. Furthermore, as David Kelsey has argued in discussing the basic biblical framework for talking about creation, it is deforming to press the element of fallenness too exclusively.[35] Scripture presents God's relation to human beings in various ways, from creating in blessing, to correcting in judgment, to perfecting in history. Creaturely existence is, in this light, that very place where fallenness and redemption, goodness and evil, divine creation and human rebellion, immaturity and perfection are mingled, precisely within the work of God. Both the challenge and wonder of life, as well as its moral demand, is to enter into this mingling rather than simply to classify the elements themselves as separate aspects for analysis.

The problem of creation and redemption's experiential contrast has never really been resolved theologically, in any case. Understandings of the Eucharist have simply followed aspects of this irresolution. There are those who would separate the sphere of redemption from that of lost creation. What follows practically from this is a claim to separate the saved from the lost themselves, as persons. While this makes the Eucharist a meal for the blessed and the pure, it leads to obvious historical contradictions, in that we know that such blessedness and purity have rarely been seen among the eucharistic faithful. In too many fundamental ways, the saved seem indistinguishable from the lost. The converse to this strictly segregated vision, what has been called a "realized eschatology," is no less hard to accept, and for just the same reasons: historical experience tells us otherwise. Everything is redeemed "already," we might insist; we just do not know it. According to this view regarding the hidden reality of the kingdom of God, in the Eucharist the veil is lifted and the curtains opened upon "what is really the case." But the case, as we see around us and within us, is one of living and expiring within the realm of skindom. A third alternative, then, often expressed in terms of the "already/ not yet" dynamic associated with Paul's "eschatological" perspective, has been articulated. (It was popularized by, among others, the French Protestant Oscar Cullmann.) This alternative is not really a resolution so much as an embrace of *ir*resolution. And since irresolution is intrinsically unstable, the approach generally settles into and becomes a stand-in for moral exhortation. Hence, it is popular with politically motivated

Christians: we must change this or that, *do* this or that, "because" it is
"already" true, even if it is "not yet" embodied.[36]

Sin, struggle, and the reality of our mortal limitations and suffer-
ings are all inescapable, for every person, Christian and non-Christian,
believer and unbeliever. This needs to be admitted within all theological
frameworks. It matters little what we wish to say about the fall, when
it comes to the *shape* of our created existence; one has altered nothing
by positing this or that "real" truth outside and alongside our creaturely time. We must all still live the strange challenges of Job and walk
through the same landscape as Cain, clothed in the same skins as John.

If, then, the Eucharist is the meal of the God who eats, then the
Eucharist is "just what is." What is, however, is God's. In the Eucharist,
God's complete life is given in the product of toil and ingestion. It is the
meal of God's human survival with us. When we say, in the light of the
Eucharist, that "what is, is God's," we are speaking of creation and the
redemption of creation both. It is not so much a matter of seeing "the
same thing" from two aspects as it is of seeing and participating in God
"working." God does many "works," some more peculiar than others,
at least in terms of human apprehension. But the eucharistic work of
God, who is ingesting in a creaturely way the divine creation, is God
working within our work, and thus it is a complete divine work insofar
as it includes our own. The Eucharist, as the meal it is, is *how* God "is,"
how God acts, and how God works. We can say that the Eucharist actually shows us why it is a terrible mistake to ignore, escape, or deny our
creatureliness as it is given in all of its straitened forms. In the Eucharist,
God works in the very fact that each of us is born as a woman or man,
from a father and mother, with siblings and family, lifted up through
the generations, with illness and struggle, with learning and work, with
friendships and their sharing, with perhaps the joining of flesh and the
conception and rearing of new life, with turning backward toward the
young, with weakening, and with death.

In the same way, "I have called you friends," says Jesus to the disciples
at the Last Supper (John 15:15). The language of friendship here is aimed
at just this creaturely gathering at the meal. Among the most potent
terms of friendship are those related to sharing bread, as in Psalm 43:9,
quoted by Jesus in John 13:18: love "betrayed" most deeply is the love
of one with whom bread has been broken. It is what in English we call
a "companion," or, literally, "one with whom we share bread." Companions are common bread eaters. Hence the eucharistic meal moves from

the disciples back to the common table, to a community, to married life, to family; it stretches back to genealogy, to generation, to survival. And all of these are gathered into the probative reach of friendship in Christ. This is our creaturehood as it is given, fallen and otherwise. This life we live as just these creatures is how God does what God does and is God. For "this is my body, given for you. . . ." We gather and eat the flesh and blood of God. The traversal is transfigured by being traversed with God.

Creation merges into its redemption because of this divine work. Temporality—with its progressions and dissolutions, its "before" and "after," its "already" and "not yet" aspects—is not so much ordered as made the very work of God. The resurrection, to be sure, can rightly be dated in terms of its apprehension by human creatures. In that sense, we can speak of a "before" and "after" with respect to a given act of God in Christ. But the resurrection itself cannot be located in terms of its being according to the clock, at a given minute and second. It is probably that there were no minutes at all attached to the resurrection, just as there were none attached to creation itself. Yet Jesus returned to eat (Luke 24:30, 42; John 21:12-13), over and over. The giver became the gift, repeatedly. How that happened is as much a mystery as how we ourselves came to be—even more so. As a "new creation," the resurrection stands beyond our historical grasping. No more than our own births and deaths, we cannot stand "outside" the reality of our redemption to gaze upon it or to measure its form, except as it is in fact given to us, in the figure Scripture describes: a transfigured traversal.

It is not true that every meal is sacramental, or eucharistic, except in the most basic sense that every meal is given in this passage with God. This is important enough a thing to say. Historically and figurally both, "every meal" is only a meal such as it is, *because* the Eucharist is given and shared. God is always first, and God's work is "before" any work we might do, hence before our toil and our eating. This means that the table joins with the workplace in a special form, an opening out to the transfigured sensibilities of divine love. Although we eat to live, in Christ we live to eat as well. With that eating, we do not erase our creaturely existence but rather move backward from the meal into all the stages of our lives, from birth to death, and discover there the work of God. God is named in his works, and in the Eucharist we are given the fullness of linguistic expression, so as to proclaim, "You, Lord, have made me."

*The Creature's Sabbath Meal*

As the work of the ingesting God, the meal finds itself at the end of the long arc of time, even as it was tasted along the way. It is consummating, just in its divine expression as creative. At the last meal, we shall discover God, as just the God who has come to us. Here, many traditional understandings of the Eucharist itself come into play: the heavenly banquet, the gathering of all peoples at a place of joyful eating and drinking. In a celebrated text, Isaiah writes: "And in this mountain shall the LORD of hosts make unto all people a feast of fat things, a feast of wines on the lees, of fat things full of marrow, of wines on the lees well refined" (Isa 25:6). Isaiah goes on to explain how, on this mountain, the Lord will take away the "veil" spread over the nations and "swallow up death in victory" (vv. 7-8), such that eating is bound up with a new knowledge and vision as well as with a new kind of relationship with mortality. Isaiah speaks of a culminating time but also a time richly filled with the actual stuff of created being. Jeremiah, also describing such a time, stresses the young age of the animals, their recent birth and vigor, as well as the fertility of the soil and its growth. "Therefore they shall come and sing in the height of Zion, and shall flow together to the goodness of the LORD, for wheat, and for wine, and for oil, and for the young of the flock and of the herd: and their soul shall be as a watered garden; and they shall not sorrow any more at all" (Jer 13:12).

In our earlier discussion of the "ages of life," we pointed to Augustine's notion of the Seventh Age, that of "eternity" itself. Within the enumerated schema he used, bound up with biblical figures, Augustine called this final age history's "Sabbath"; it marked as well the individual Christian's entry after death into God's kingdom. Sabbatical time is understood as a kind of contrast to temporality. Thus, the historical location of the Eucharist can be seen as itself a grasp of the "end time" or "eschaton," as "timeless," or even "outside time," as popular Orthodox, Catholic, and related liturgical traditions will often say. "Sabbath time," in this vision, is not time at all but something nontemporal. The early church fathers as a whole tended to speak of the Sabbath also as a state of being for the Christian, enveloping all days, rather than falling on a specific day of the week (as the Decalogue certainly seems to indicate). Christ's fulfillment of the Law made his own person a perpetual Sabbath, as it were, available to all believers at all times.

While the notion of "fulfillment in Christ" cannot be avoided for the Christian, such language is probably not the best way to frame the reality of creaturely eating that is at issue here. The reason the Eucharist is a meal is because it is a creaturely act, although now one that God "does." The Eucharist is indeed a "work," not a moment of "rest." But it is also the work of *God*, who actively created for six days and then rested. Divine rest is included within the being of a God who creates, and vice versa. To "keep the seventh day" is a weekly duty, itself ordered by the clock, and rigorously so. All the same, it is a duty that touches upon God—in prayer and adoration, in the thanksgiving even for eating, though an eating whose "work" precedes it. Better to go hungry on the day before Sabbath, writes the Mishnah, so as to approach the meals of the Sabbath with a more fervent joy. The Sabbath is about creation, but creation as utterly God's, not our own (Exod 16:26; 20:10-11; Isa 58:13-14). Because it is God's, it is filled with moral imperative (Isa 1:13). Thus, however impregnated with eternity, the Eucharist is utterly timely, though it is a time where creature and Creator have come to the same table—we from our path, God from God's. "In a mysterious way, God makes the profane sacred without changing its character. We finally see God in the profane—reversing all our expectations, crushing our delusions, and freeing us from the material constraints of the mind."[37] Both popular Jewish writers (e.g., Abraham Heschel) and Christian writers (e.g., Josef Pieper) have written in challenging ways about how a "sabbatical" understanding of the world must transform not only our vision but also our schedules and tasks.[38]

Christians have had difficulty holding to the notion of a "day of rest," coming and going over the centuries, with laws and reactions to them, finally now wholly confused as to the meaning of such marking of time altogether. That work ceases on a given day and for a given period is rational simply from the perspective of health, even in times of critical survival. But the claim that on a given day, just as in a given meal, this life is denuded of its human pretensions and allowed somehow to be the life we are given—this is difficult for us to grasp, only because such a claim is particularly difficult to face in this era. Because of our contemporary confusion in the face of mortality, timelessness is often seen as the simple contrast to temporal existence. It is not.

To eat together takes time, and, sabbatical or not, the heavenly banquet is a timely feast. To it stream the nations, from east and west (Matt 8:11), of every form, especially the lowly (Luke 13:29-30). There are "feasts" aimed simply at eating together, as in Isaiah 25. When we hear of one, it is usually for life and joy (e.g., Gen 21:8, where Abraham celebrates Isaac's survival and growth as a child). There are also the many sacrificial meals, associated with festivals and specific moments of ritual prayer. These are commonly described in the Old Testament (cf. early in Exod 5:1). Their pagan counterparts are alluded to as well in the New Testament in connection with meat sold from the remains of sacrificial worship (Rom 14). The heavenly banquet, whatever it is exactly, is a gathering of particulars, human creatures and nonhuman; it is marked by ingestive joy; it is filled with "noise." Although God participates in this kind of meal (cf. Exod 24:11), just because of all this and of the God who in fact is there, creaturely reality is not shed at such a banquet; it is most deeply shared.

This sharing challenges our generally dichotomous way of thinking about time and eternity, in that it leaves room for all the ruptures we wish to escape and insist have no place with God: our losses and our deaths, and thus everything that gave them their space and shape, the traversal itself. One may still die on the Sabbath day, as during the Eucharist. It has happened to many persons. Somehow, all this too is gathered at the table. When Jesus invites to his meal, he calls "the poor, the maimed, the lame, the blind" (Luke 14:13). This gathering is not symbolic of some *other* work, a work no longer done in a timely way, something different from the encounter of just these persons. The timely meal of eternity is always about just these limbs, just these sores, and just these rags.

The heavenly banquet does not eliminate creatureliness; it founds it. Those who see God face to face are those whom God has created and to whom God has in this meal. In the resurrection, Augustine thought, our bodies would be formed as mature and vigorous adults, thirty years of age perhaps, the blemishes gone, the scars removed except for the martyrs, whose wounds resemble Christ's.[39] Both the claim Augustine makes and the exception he provides are telling. Bodies are our identities, Augustine insisted, so that even in cases of cannibalism, the parts eaten by another person would, at the resurrection, necessarily return to their "rightful owner." But death must first intervene. Those who gather at the table, whatever their form, will just as surely be those who have died as any other. Even among those few mysteriously "caught up" at the Son's coming (cf. 1 Thess 4:7), memory will not have shriveled and been cast off—those "caught up" will have been formed as much by all the turns and crevices of their path as any other. It is important that the "not yet" of those who have "wandered about in sheepskins and goatskins" (Heb 11:37), "of whom the world was not worthy" (v. 38), is not severed from the "already" of the "us" (v. 40), for whom "perfection" is given. That perfection, finally, is given in running "with patience the race that is set before us" (Heb 12:1), following Christ Jesus. That "race," literally the *agon* of the traversal, is the place where "wandering" is made, in Christ, the "way."

> O LORD, raise up (we pray thee) thy power, and come among us, and with great might succour us; that whereas, through our sins and wickedness, we are sore let and hindered in running the race that is set before us, thy bountiful grace and mercy may speedily help and deliver us; through the satisfaction of thy Son our Lord, to whom with thee and the Holy Ghost be honour and glory, world without end. *Amen.* (Collect for Advent 4, 1662 Book of Common Prayer)

This way of talking about even the heavenly banquet may tend too closely towards a view of human life that reduces it to "brute existence" rather than expanding it towards a conception of the human soul. This is Rémi Brague's worry regarding our culture's general dismissal of more metaphysical ways of construing the human person, in favor of just these features of temporal contingency. The return of the "soul" as a modern interest, however, has actually accompanied the rise of materialist world views. Descartes being generally disdained as the purveyor of a nefarious dualism of body and spirit, rescuers of the spirit initially tried to do this on a materialist basis (e.g., the seventeenth-century Anglican philosopher Henry More). But others moved in a direction that more fully emphasized the immaterial aspect (cf. the Quakers in the seventeenth century, and Emmanuel Swedenborg and his followers in the eighteenth and nineteenth centuries). These ideas, however, merged with other philosophical movements, like Hegelian idealism, and biological evolutionism and the press for the human "spirit" moved into models that managed to turn materialism on its head, with claims regarding "emergent" consciousness and the spirit or soul. It is hard to tell whether some of these new notions, now caught up with contemporary systems and cognitive theory, are materialist or etherealist. But it is clear that talking about the human "soul" has become a difficult means of disciplining thought along traditional Christian lines, one way or the other.

While reflection on the human soul is a necessary Christian theological enterprise, it cannot be used to pry apart creaturehood's character as an integration of temporal traversal and intrinsic dignity. No human being lives outside of the created world, however much we wish to speak of our "belonging to" or being "citizens" of another. Souls, in any case, are as much created entities as are bodies, shaped by the same constraints of creaturely being. There is no Christian orthodoxy on the matter of "what happens to us when we die" with respect to souls and bodies, understood as distinct categories. But the tradition has been generally united against Origen's idea that souls preexist the creation of bodies, as a kind of original stable of divine creaturely being, to be fitted with material existence only later and for a brief time. Instead, alternative theories maintained a common commitment: for example, the ideas of a Tertullian, that the human soul was passed along, as it were, through the act of generation, from parents to children; or the idea (e.g., of Ambrose) that God creates a soul immediately upon the generation of each individual person. Both these views are rooted in and express the constraints of human generation and mortality in temporal terms, but clearly as aspects of the very blessing that is human creation itself.[40] Brague's rejected category of "brute existence," in this context, is not so much mortal existence-as-temporal passage; it is rather a view of that existence, minus creaturehood as its definition and reality.

The human creature is bound to this "way of Christ," our God who has taken creation and ingested it as a creature himself. All of creation, as it is, will be brought together, driven by the lines of each's probative aim from their long or shortened pilgrimage; and whatever judgment is, the sheep and the goats, known by their names, will go their way just as they are, but now on a "way" that takes the final steps of God's own movement through the world: descending and ascending (Eph 4:8-10), though in a manner whose future passage for our own lives we cannot now fathom. We shall be like him; for we shall see him "as he is" (1 John 3:2). It is as the famous Collect for the First Sunday of Advent in the 1662 Book of Common Prayer has put it:

> Almighty God, give us grace that we may cast away the works of darkness, and put upon us the armor of light, now in the time of this mortal life in which thy Son Jesus Christ came to visit us in great humility; that on the last day when he shall come again in his glorious majesty to judge both the quick and dead, we may rise to the life immortal; through him who liveth and reigneth with thee and the Holy Ghost, one God, now and for ever. Amen.

For those who sit at the table before that "glorious majesty," the food and drink, the noise and smells, the voices and rousing touch will all contain the time that is our time now. "Teach us to number our days," therefore, in the time of this mortal life, "that we may apply our hearts unto wisdom" (Ps 90:12). Teach us as you have taught all things, through your word come among and with us. Teach us as you also grew in wisdom and grace (Luke 2:52). Teach us to number ours, just as you numbered your own. Teach us to take stock of our birth, our feeding, our growing, our parents, our families, our learning; our movement, from generation to generation; our coupling and progeny; our toil and provision; our weakness and deaths. On each day of our labor, as we move from day to day, let us number each and mark the beauty and singularity of each marvelous element—and so discover, through our mortal frames, your making of us, O Lord God, King of the Universe. Blessed be your Name.

# Conclusion
## *The Church's Vocation to Number Our Days*

The argument of this book has been that thinking about who we are as created human beings comes down to numbering our days. To "number our days" is not really a theological "locus," in the technical sense. It is not a specific category meant to fit into the network of topics that together build a theological "system," or dogmatics. Day-numbering is not "soteriology," the study of our redemption, at least not in any direct way. It does not leap into the realm of Trinitarian thinking. Nor is it really ethics or applied theology. To be sure, numbering our days is not without implication for these and other traditional theological subjects. But it stands more fundamentally toward these subjects as their necessary ground, something that has been ruinously forgotten within the church's habits of formation. To be sure, there has been a great interest, especially more recently, in taking up issues of created being in central ways that can relate "embodiedness" to God's own being and purpose. Enormous energies have been focused on discussing the *imago Dei*, the "image of God" embedded within human creation (Gen 1:27), and explicating its corporeal character in ways linked to Trinitarian elements, like relationality, divine personal diversity, and mutual engagement. Gender—or the sexed character of human bodies—has likewise found a place within these theological areas of study. On the basis of these kinds of orientations, day-numbering must seem theologically deficient, and profoundly so: there is God, of course, in such numbering; and a good deal of Jesus

229

Christ, but only in an assumed form; and nothing much about the Spirit; finally, the mutual relations of Father, Son, and Spirit have no obvious place at all. Scripture, instead, looms large as an unquestioned matrix for day-numbering, but in an almost unorganized way: like a catalogue, the Bible tells us about this and that, and it holds these together in the course of a set of human lives.

Although day-numbering is not a topic of systematic theology, it is nonetheless the matter of theology, the "stuff" we must deal with and out of which we do this dealing, when we talk about God truthfully. Day-numbering constitutes the form in which we reflect upon created being. Such being is not a *natura pura*, or "pure nature," a category that Thomists and others fought over in the early twentieth century, and Karl Barth engaged as well. There is no metaphysical entity we can work with that is "simply" the "being" of a created human person. For being cannot be "simply" what it is, by definition, since it is from God and is perceived as such only from within the contours of creaturely existence itself. All talk about God—theology—is bound to the matter of created apprehension. That apprehension is not just limited as a result. Our talk of God is given through the matter of created apprehension in the sense that what we have as we turn to God are the things God has given us out of our nothingness. That, of course, must include himself in some fashion, but still in the fashion of our created reception. So, for instance, if we wish to engage the *imago Dei* theologically, we can only begin with the fact that it is a gift, not something we can define. (Attempts to define the *imago* have led only to a kind of Promethean attempt to create it for ourselves.) What we *do* know, from the Scriptures, is that Christ ultimately is the image of God and that he is thus the image of the self-giver, the God in whom our skins are taken up. In a sense, this leaves us where we truly are: mortal creatures. Our iconic representation of God can involve no more than what we have been given, as it constitutes that which generates our lives themselves from nothing.

Day-numbering, as reflecting on the created being in this sense, marks a certain subjective turn, although not one in any decidedly modern form. It is closer to the kind of natural theology practiced by premodern and early modern Christians, who had no choice but to receive from God all of their lives within the context of the created landscape in which God had placed them. This was a terrain in which one could speak of God only for a few years, with a few breaths, and within the concentrated display of created purpose such little time actually afforded. These words, then, were vocalized far differently than today and therefore stand as a different kind of theology than what is normally practiced today. Even Eastern theology, with its notions of *theosis* as human "divinization" or participation in God (2 Pet 1:4), was not nearly so otherworldly as modern Christians sometimes imagine. For such divine participation was seen as founded on rigorous ascetic practice that involved the control and finally shedding of human bodily passions. Apart from these practices, which take created being as their "matter," even the Trinitarian reflections of, for instance, the Cappadocian fathers, so attractive in our day, are nonsensical. God can be received only from the perspective of the creature God has made us.

David Kelsey's wide-ranging work on Christian anthropology, *Eccentric Existence*, is one of the few systematic theological anthropologies to have been written in the last few decades. One of Kelsey's key decisions was to take as a central scriptural context for his discussion the so-called Wisdom books of the Bible: for example, Proverbs and Ecclesiastes. Some have criticized Kelsey for this specific scriptural focus: by choosing to mine books like Proverbs for his theological anthropology, Kelsey decided implicitly to imbue the "everydayness" of these limited texts with universal application. Surely everybody is not really like the generationally defined actors—drawing lessons from patriarchal families, agriculture, and local markets and meals—who inhabit the ancient Middle Eastern text that constitutes Proverbs. To assume this, some have argued, is to leave things in human life "the way they are," when in fact, for all kinds of important reasons, things are not only diverse; they are diversely deformed and must be changed. For this reason, getting back to the "real" essence of the creature, intellectually distilled in some fashion or another apart from the historical contingencies of mortal life, is a necessary imperative for Christian reflection upon the human person. On this score, Kelsey's scriptural choices have been challenged by liberationist and political approaches to human life, approaches that demand the eschatological as their motive force, or perhaps some metaphysical notion of "nature," and that the everyday interest of the Wisdom books cannot seem to supply.

The practice of day-numbering responds to these kinds of questions by insisting that even liberationism cannot do away with the "matter" of theology, which is our creatureliness, a reality (not simply a concept) for which God is the necessary condition. Liberationist or political theologies of one kind or another (to the Left or Right) often have left this matter behind, and, when they have, they have ruined lives, as much of their Western appropriation has done within our churches in just those areas where the skinful character of human life has been denied. By contrast, when the matter of theology—what I will call "material theology"—is maintained, then there is quite precisely and materially the ground of accountability for the political: food, shelter, family, generation, genealogy, probation—in short, the skins. The occlusion of this "matter" within much modern Christian theology has in fact been deeply problematic. Observers, like the anthropologist Graham Harvey, looking in on what theologians and churches say about their faith today can therefore claim that Christianity is not even a "religion" at all in the normal sense but rather a gnostic set of intellectual claims, untethered to the world of created existence.[1] (Oddly, Kelsey himself has said that, despite his interest in the material aspects of human life, he quite deliberately believes these specifically filiative elements—gender, sexuality, etc.—are *not* a part of human persons' "basic personal identities." They are, instead, more variable "quotidian identities" that are secondary matters to Christian anthropology, important though they may be.)

Material theology—the theological concern with the "matter" that other more proper theological disciplines need to work with—may not have its own technical "locus." "Theological anthropology" is probably already oriented in wider conceptual concerns. Still, material theology has its own genre. It is committed to describing, naming, and ordering the artifacts of our existence for the purpose of engaging the fuller breadth of God's creation.[2] Since this descriptive naming and ordering is ultimately fulfilled within the Scriptures, the genre both is scriptural and presumes to be engaged with matters of truth. It answers questions that are both urgent and gnawing, even in their marginal evocations: What does a human person grasp about his or her being alive? How do we perceive the death of one of our children? What does our work amount to? Who are we related to, and so what? What does it mean to have a mother and a father, or not? When we speak, where do our words go? Why do mushrooms taste so good, yet sometimes kill us? How then shall we cook them and share them?

Day-numbering *is* material theology in its practice. It is something we must all do, and theologians as much as anybody. All theologians die. This is not a minor point made simply to relativize inflated academic claims written down in books by finite human beings. We must, even in our furthest and most sophisticated and yearning reach toward God, return to the dust of our coming. That is not the end of the matter. But it is the end of *this* matter, the specific toil of this specific person born to this place and filiative set. Our yearnings themselves come to an end, insofar as they are ours, and this must shape the nature of our speaking, not in its systematic form but in "what" we are talking with, as we talk.

In a wonderful meditation on just what this kind of talking consists in, the philosopher Harald Weinrich gathered up a host of literary reflections on the nature of our existence that he entitled *On Borrowed Time*.[3] Much of what he gathers together is colored by the central observation that "life is short" and therefore that the "time we have" is always pressing its limitations upon our existence. Our life always feels—and should feel—"borrowed." Weinrich ends his survey with his own definition of time. It is, he argues, a kind of human "sense." Time is not so much a cognitive sense, as Kant argued it was, forming a certain prism of perception. It is a sense in a very physiological way, Weinrich says, based in the felt rhythm of the circulatory pulse within our bodies. In earlier eras, this was often checked and hence located within the temples on each side of the head, whose throbbing marked the flow of blood through the body. The temples actually make a "sound" to our touch: "tum te tum te tum." Hence, Weinrich speculates, we can understand the overlapping semantics and etymologies even of "time" in various languages (i.e., Latin and French) where *tempus* and *templum* coincide. When we are awake, we can "sense" time pressing us, from within our flesh itself; and when we sleep (another word overlapping with time-related semantics), we feel ourselves to be "timeless," simply because this sense is stilled from our consciousness. And like our blood, and its imperious constraints upon our lives, all of us live with a time we know to be "in limited supply." The hourglass is like a body, sand like the dripping fluids of our flesh. While Aristotle defined time spatially—the measuring of the movement from "before" to "after"—Weinrich instead sides with Hippocrates' notion of time as a bound to physical life. "Someone who has not internalized what makes time short does not yet know what time is."[4]

Maybe this makes no difference. Weinrich goes on to ask if it is only the old and ill who need to think about such things. The sense of time, after all, is often unnoticed for most people even when waking:

> Someone who is young and healthy does not need—whether questioned or not—to know or even to sense what time is and how short the limits set on existence are. Under such conditions, even the pulse beat can be disregarded and for the time being counted among the

things taken for granted in life. Only when—usually at an "untimely" moment—the pulse (or some other sign of corporeality) announces that the pleasant carelessness of youth and good health has become fragile, does the "true time in which we live and which is our inner measure" (Carlo Levi) make an uncalled for appearance and disturb our previously so robust idea—which was in fact a lack of awareness—of time.[5]

Whether this sense of time is universal or morally demanded, Weinrich has no interest here in Christian theology. So he draws no strong religious conclusions from his survey. Still, it is interesting that he ends his book with an excerpt from Hugo von Hofmannsthal's libretto for Richard Strauss' opera *Der Rosenkavalier* (1911). Time is a problem, of course, for more than the old. It comes up in relationships of love or the chasms of generational and physical separation. "Nevertheless, one must not fear it. / It is also a creation of the Father / Who has created us all" (*Auch sie ist ein Geschöpf des Vaters, der uns alle erschaffen hat*).[6] Time, just in its sensing as being borrowed, is indeed a part of the giftedness that constitutes our lives.

This, at any rate, is a precious and essential Christian claim. The issue of life's brevity, its "borrowed" character, outstrips the concern of just a few philosophers, as Weinrich shows. The most famous and influential treatment of the theme is the Roman philosopher Seneca's, in his much-read moral essay *"De brevitate vitae"* (On the Shortness of Life). The essay became a popular Christian model for centuries. But it lacks precisely the essential Christian claim of time's donative character. Seneca, picking up Hippocrates' maxim that "life is short, art is long," goes on to point out that the problem human beings have in this regard is not really life's brevity. Rather, it is the fact that we waste so much of it (ending life just as we begin to live it, as he famously says). The essay is really nothing more than a long description of the ways people throw their lives away. We allow others to "trespass" on our life, gobbling it up with their demands. We get caught up in the endless exercise of professional ambition and greed, luxury and self-indulgence. We fritter away our time, "precious" like money, on the merely "distracting." What should we be doing instead? Reading philosophy! Thereby, Seneca says, we come to understand, in good Stoic fashion, how we are "our own masters" in what we feel and suffer. One reason we read these philosophical authors whom Seneca recommends is because they are "past," exist beyond the fleeting moment of today, and thus can be our "chosen parents," free from the actual people Fortune throws at us.[7]

The last observation is telling: for Seneca, the "matter" of life (e.g., our actual parents) should not be the matter of our living. Day-numbering, however, forcefully argues against this view. In fact, although Seneca became a kind of model for Christian thinkers, it was only in the most superficial of ways. For substantive discussions, Christian preachers and essayists on life's brevity turned rather to the Scriptures, like Psalm 90:12. Here, the notion of day-numbering came to form its own genre, within the larger category of material theology itself. "Consideration of the shortness of life" was a constant theme in preaching, taking its title from Seneca, yet filling up the text with something very different. To take one late and utterly unoriginal example, we can examine the standard remarks of the eighteenth-century archbishop of Canterbury, Thomas Secker (1693–1768). In two coordinated sermons on "a just estimate of the shortness of human life," Secker tells his listeners that the topic is perhaps the most useful of all for preaching.[8] Instead of dealing with theological "speculations," it zeroes in on "truths" that lead most concretely to the "mending of hearts." Because death is inevitable, we are "naturally" forced to this place of consideration. Secker here hints at the proper character of natural theology.

Taking as his text Psalm 90:12, he goes on to explain what this might mean with respect both to our lives "in this world" and to our life in eternity. Numbering our days as mortal creatures has a specific set of meanings for Secker. In the first place, he says, it simply indicates that our days are not many. Yet nor are they "too short" given our condition as creatures of God and given the work God has called us to during this time. All life and work is proportional to our place and our gifts; that is, our life is given to us by God, and its faithful living, within its mortal limits, is exactly what our lives are meant to be in their blessing. Secker goes on: To number our days also serves, just because of this creaturely condition, to encourage prudence and temperance in life, which in fact is healthy and extends life usually. To number our days means, as well, to live with good people, "reciprocally," so that we share with each other the support and encouragement that social relations provide. In this, we are better able to grasp the blessings of life and so to "live more"—that is, more fully. To number our days means also to pursue the fulfillment of our duties, learned from God and others. It means to avoid greed and ambition (useless things, evidently, and here Secker follows Seneca). It means that, seeing what everything in fact amounts to in this short life, we are "calmed" by this vision of proportional significance. Finally,

Secker concludes, to number our days is to realize that there is another world, and we should aim our purposes and hopes in that direction. This other world is one that is given in God and through the gospel of Son Jesus Christ.

Secker then moves, in the accompanying sermon, to speak of day-numbering in terms of eternity, of this "other" world. Secker begins with one of the great ancient texts describing a nihilistic worldview—that is, the reflections of the "ungodly" in Wisdom 2:1-12: "For the ungodly said, reasoning with themselves, but not aright, Our life is short and tedious, and in the death of a man there is no remedy: neither was there any man known to have returned from the grave" (2:1). With nothing but a swift death in store, the ungodly urge self-indulgence and violence. "Let our strength be the law of justice: for that which is feeble is found to be nothing worth" (2:11). "Voluptuousness and injustice" is their creed. But we are actually persons of "dignity" before God, Secker counters, whose lives are "honored" by our meekness before him (Sir 10:28). From this point to the end of the sermon, Secker picks up the "probative" nature of our short life on earth now and pursues it vigorously, under three headings. First, as we number our days with an eye to eternity, we do so with the "conviction of the necessity of applying diligently to know and do our duty" (this turns us back, paradoxically, to an interest in *this* world of created work). Second, we are encouraged "to persist in it to the end against temptation." And finally, we are given "support under the afflictions to which we are exposed in the mean while."[9] All this drives us to the Scriptures, where we can dwell with the form of Christ, searching after "the kingdom of God" in all we do, according to his words and figure.

At this point, Secker has moved from texts associated with scriptural and apocryphal Wisdom books and has fastened firmly onto the New Testament. He ends with a vision of the Great Traversal, beginning with Jacob's words of blessing to Pharaoh, and ending with Hebrews' image of the city of God:

> And Jacob said unto Pharaoh, The days of the years of my pilgrimage [are] an hundred and thirty years: few and evil have the days of the years of my life been, and have not attained unto the days of the years of the life of my fathers in the days of their pilgrimage. (Gen 47:9)
>
> For he looked for a city which hath foundations, whose builder and maker [is] God. (Heb 11:10)

We can easily see how this "numbering of our days" as Secker presents it goes well beyond the Senecan paradigm. It moves through the troubled engagement of the Wisdom literature with time, struggles through to the creaturely character of life's givenness, wonders over the implications of its divine shape, and discerns, through scriptural searching and habitation, the figure of Christ with and within the passage of our lives. As a result, life on this earth is reordered according to a sense of thanksgiving for the "duties" of common and ordinary filiative existence.

An earlier Christian exemplar of the genre, the Baptist minister Thomas Hardcastle, described this as a way we approach created matter itself, the stuff of our lives. He titled his reflection on "numbering our days" a *Christian geography and arithmetick; or, A true survey of the world: together with the right art of numbring our dayes therein.*[10] The discussion is much like Secker's later. But Hardcastle framed it quite explicitly in terms of a certain kind of "thinking," a divine "arithmetic" and ordering of spaces within our lives. This permits us to lay out the "distinctions" of the world as we encounter them. As with Secker, our "work" is central to this and is a large part of simply "living" through and with these encounters. But as we work, so we can see, just as Secker insists, the blessings of these encounters in full relief. They are the form of that aspect of our createdness that frames all things as we meet them.

Secker believed that there was an intimate relation between this kind of "matter" that we number and the deeper "truths" of Christ he saw as central and final, yet in a sense as only coming into view within the press of a more material engagement. Christ mingled with the food of the wilderness does indeed become, for our vision, the ascending King of Glory. But there are no shortcuts available to us in grasping this relationship. The very temptation of a shortcut, encouraged by our own forgetfulness of mortal time and its generative form, has afflicted our theological stamina. The twentieth-century Catholic theologian Josef Pieper has much to teach us here, particularly about grasping the proportional shape of a faithful human life. That shape not only involves understanding the proper relationship of various tasks and activities but ordering their temporal engagement in terms of "useful" work, festival, worship, leisure, and contemplation. Pieper deeply opposed the modern tendency to turn all of life into a utilitarian project. He called this project "total work." The grand utilitarian scheme of modernity is a voracious dynamic that has engulfed scholarship, art, even theology. And although he viewed work as something necessary and inescapable, he saw "contemplation," a form of truthful and receptive vision, both as more fundamental and as the final aim of human life.

Pieper has been criticized, perhaps rightly, for this segregating of spheres of life. But he was correct in arguing that a central feature of our lives as creatures is "to see the world aright."[11] It is, after all, work that gives rise to festival—not purely as its reason, but as its road to reason. And it is thanksgiving that gives rise to worship, joined to that holy fear that stands in the face of the Creator. Both of these—work and thanksgiving—are founded in the actualities of the world as it is *given*. Thus, to see this world as such is what will give the proper order to our timekeeping. How this timekeeping takes form is another matter, involving complex cultural issues that probably emerge from, rather than themselves order, the character of life.

Seeing the world as it is is critical. The fact that there are no shortcuts in this seeing is the important link to the specifically Christian truths that a purely material theology may seem to miss. We see as we move, with eyes open, and in this we are led, we persist, we learn. Moving in this way involves just those Christian "virtues" that the tradition has rightly both placed at the center of the Christian life and also seen as given through the living presence of the Triune God: faith, hope, and love. As we are led through our life, it is our faith that is nurtured and exercised: we receive from others; we encounter with openness; we marvel at the shapes we touch or rub against, questioning yet taking hold or being taken hold of. Augustine, typically, linked "faith" to the apprehension of "truths" about God, such as those given in the creed. These are crystallizations of what God gives us of himself, but the actual movement of faith is a temporal one, moving through the arc of our lives according to and apprehending different ways appropriate to the times. It is the true revelation of God that is taking place in all this, the coming close of our Maker, but more and more in the forms that are shared through divine self-offering in Scripture and church. The creed rightly gives names to this, which are true and indicate a path.

As a pathway, we follow it and are led along it, wondering who it is who leads us and who it is who lets us suffer our time with new energies or simply with solemn implacability. Such strength as we have on this passage is our hope, and that hope is given in the person of God's own self, in the Christ who has offered and led and now stands beside and beneath even as he awaits. The Great Traversal is accomplished, finally, only in such a hope. It is never accomplished, however, apart from the gifts we receive, the constant showering of forms and shapes upon our bodies and thoughts, in work and rest. That there is time that is still ours is something that we can take hold of only in hope. The alternative is to drift, to forget, to slip. This is all part of what day-numbering implies and what supports it. The divine arithmetic of life can be achieved in no other way except in faith and hope. And if it can be achieved in this way, that is only because it is carried out in the presence of the self-revealing God.

God is seen—seen from below, through the sense of grace that creaturely existence is all about, but also seen, as it were, "from above," from the very motion of God's self-offering that permits this grace of our being to be such at all. Thus seeing, through a divine motion, we love. To learn is to love, because only in coming-to-see, which is learning itself, is our joy, thanks, pleasure, and affection in response to what we are given provided its fullest form. To be sure, this is not made in a moment alone, as a threshold crossed. But like our lives themselves, our love is given over time, and grows, through both spurts and fallow seasons, or by the simple increments of instants. Wisdom joins with love in this movement: love "beareth all things, believeth all things, hopeth all things, endureth all things" (1 Cor 13:7), not because it is perfect in itself, or even a thing in itself, but because we have lived. Love is a created life lived "fully," in Secker's phrase.

It is easy to schematize the "theological virtues" of faith, hope, and love, and doing so has been a temptation in the tradition. But wise Christians have always understood how faith, hope, and love cannot be pulled apart, any more than can Father, Son, and Holy Spirit, who are given to our faith, relied upon in our hope, and rejoiced in through our love. Etymologically, in English, "love" is related to the word "belief" (as in, "by your leave/lief"): it is a kind of pleasure and attraction, and finally trust. But "love" is also related to words meaning "hope" itself. The theological virtues all emerge in overlapping ways, from the single traversal of the human creature, and are in fact most firmly expressive of a material theology, which orients us toward and opens us up to the love of our Maker—that is, of "being made" in every breath by just this God, who is Father, Son, and Spirit.

To number our days, then, is indeed a specifically Christian practice, although we apprehend it as such only as we pursue it as just these creatures that we are. This is finally why it is such a terrible thing when a Christian, or the Christian church, lets go of its place within the Great

Traversal. For outside of this place, known, understood, and seen, the Gospel is heard in vain:

> For the scripture saith, Whosoever believeth on him shall not be ashamed. [*But to believe is to be led through this landscape.*] For there is no difference between the Jew and the Greek: for the same Lord over all is rich unto all that call upon him. [*To call upon the Lord is to face the needs of just this journey—Gen 4:26.*] For whosoever shall call upon the name of the Lord shall be saved. How then shall they call on him in whom they have not believed? and how shall they believe in him of whom they have not heard? and how shall they hear without a preacher? [*To learn to call is to be among those who know how to call and who teach according to their lives.*] And how shall they preach, except they be sent? as it is written, How beautiful are the feet of them that preach the gospel of peace, and bring glad tidings of good things! (Rom 10:11-15) [*To be sent with this message is to love the One who has loved us as such, just here and in just this way.*]

I have argued that the Great Health Transition has obscured much of the Great Traversal, of Adam to Adam. This is not meant to be a reductive sociological explanation for the Christian church's muteness. That the enormous creaturely blessings associated with the novel extension of life in the last century have led to forgetfulness rather than to thanksgiving is no fault of the blessing itself. Indeed, the scriptural story of the traversal actually begins with the same blessing yet more fully extended, even after the expulsion from Eden: Adam lives to 930 years of age; Seth, 812 years. Through Noah, these life spans, we are told, were common. Noah himself lived 950 years, longer even than Adam (though, as many know, Methuselah himself takes the honors for Scripture's longest human life, at 969 years). Yet in the midst of all these long-lived progenitors there is murder and violence, profligacy and dishonor, by those most blessed of all. While, it seems, the bulk of humanity lived no more than 120 years (Gen 6:3), this span, a marvel to our own age still, was itself a standard for human debasement. So comes the flood, brought on by "the wickedness of man [that] was great in the earth" and by the "imagination" of "his heart" that "was only evil continually" (Gen 6:5). Long life has a history of being squandered in the most terrible of ways.

That the Great Transition is a divine blessing, partially achieved through sacrificial labor and love of human beings, cannot be overstated. We should have no nostalgia for a time when mothers and children died at the rate of one in three, and when disease or hunger could be expected to limit one's sight of God's creation to but a few, and often pain-filled, years. The Great Transition is a divine blessing. But this character of blessing has been rejected. Whatever our life span, we are creatures who exist solely by God's blessing, and because of this we actually embody blessing in our mortal forms. People, and thus the church, should care about how we are conceived; how we are born; how we are raised and raise others; how we grow; how we work; how we have sex; how we eat; how we age; how we share our ages; how we die. We should care about all this, however, in a way that takes seriously the shape of these elements within their created order in the life span, whether stretched or compressed. From Methuselah to the Palestine of Jesus, and even to the most recent present of our globe, the elements of this ordering proved stable, however much their form varied or their embrace was deliberately rejected. Longer lives do not mean lives without their skins.[12] The skins themselves, stretched over our mortal frames, still determine the movement of generation, genealogy, and probation that constitute the material form of our life's meaning. In Christ, that form is transfigured, but it is not cast aside.

Whatever the church's full vocation may be at this time of unprecedented global transformation, it must include as a central element the ministry of day-numbering. The controversies over sexual life that have so riven both our churches and our civil cultures are to be expected in this context; nor can we run from them. Weariness over the seemingly intractable divisions on these matters have led many to give up, or to reevaluate the significance of the debates, or to simply change the subject. These are understandable reactions but ultimately improper ones. One should certainly question the way these debates have been pursued, subverting, as they have, the very virtues of Christian witness that the topic's significance ought to engage: trust, hope, charity. The debates themselves have devolved into argumentative jargon, proof-texting (from whatever authoritative text one claims), and abstracted slices of experience. These have been starkly divorced from the rich texture of that life that is given as a creaturely traversal of the world, into death and the grace that God's promises hold in that place of ending. So, the church must not shy away from the struggle to understand the blessings of life given in mortal flesh, including sexuality; but she must engage them in ways that are much fuller, broader, and truer to the constraints of our own existence as we have been given them.

Perhaps that is part of the problem: Christians, too, do not wish to face the limits of their lives as given utterly by God. We are tempted, like all human creatures, to forget our deaths, to dispense with the responsibilities of our generation, to reject the demands of our social existence as "children of men, turned to destruction" (Ps 90:3), yet for whom obedience provides the genealogy of righteousness through time. "For the moth shall eat [the unrighteous] up like a garment, and the worm shall eat them like wool: but my righteousness shall be for ever, and my salvation from generation to generation" (Isa 51:8). The blessing of life, which is always shaped in the manner of this traversal, is easily forgotten. So Christians are called to number their days, and the days of their church as it is made up of such children, in the fashion of all the children of men. Numbering our days is a practice, a discipline, a habit, and finally a joy.

On the cusp of modernity, we can observe a flourishing of celebratory numbering, as if people of the era sensed the coming dawn of new means of health. The poetry, for instance, of Guillaume de Salluste du Bartas constitutes one of the most popular and influential products of the Christian culture of the time. It was edited and republished at an astonishing rate, translated into many European tongues, and directly touched the compositions, in English alone, of writers from Shakespeare to Milton, including even Anne Bradstreet in New England. Du Bartas was a Protestant soldier, son of a rich merchant, whose relation to the court of Henri de Navarre was intimate. In 1578 his *Sepmaine, ou creation du monde* ("The week, or the creation of the world") was published in Paris; two later volumes extended the work through the history of Israel's captivity.[13] This book, almost completely forgotten today, utterly entranced du Bartas' era and a century afterward. The numbering of creation according to the seven days of Genesis was presented according to each long day's details, which du Bartas described in terms of the range and particularity of divine artifacts, from each animal and plant to medicines, astronomy and color, to sound and vision. On the sixth day, with Adam and Eve's creation, du Bartas ranges from human life as a piece to its smaller elements—disease, clothing, food; work and handicrafts, virtues and vices; families and their rearing; children and their deaths. The poem was meant to be an encyclopedia of creation, arranged and ordered by the Creator's time itself.

Just these temporally numbered details accounted for the astonishing attraction of this work, which gave rise to many other compositions. The "history" of Adam, which du Bartas would carry on in later volumes, still using the seven-day enumeration, was tightly and complexly tied to the character of material life and its distinctions and limits. This made every sense in the world to readers of the age, lifted up by du Bartas' laudatory language of thanksgiving and praise to God. In Pieper's terms, the poetry let "the world be seen" for what it is, and we within it, at a time when such a seeing in Europe demanded all the Christian virtues a person might summon. Creation and creature were the realm of God's revealing. The two brief excerpts below cast a flickering light on this now lost enthusiasm. In the first, du Bartas quickly moves through several smaller creatures, having spent lengthy pages on many others. (The sixteenth-century translation is by the Puritan Joshua Sylvester, whose sumptuous version became yet more famous than du Bartas himself within Great Britain.)[14]

> There skips the *Squirrell*, seeming Weather-wise,
> Without beholding of Heav'ns twinkling eyes:
> For, knowing well which way the winde will change,
> Hee shifts the portall of his little Grange.
> Ther's th' wanton *Weazell*, and the wily *Fox*,
> The witty *Monkey*, that mans action mocks:
> The sweat-sweet *Ciuet*, deerly fetcht from far
> For Courtiers nice, past *Indian Tarnassar.*
> There, the wise *Beuer*, who, pursu'd by foes,
> Tears-off his codlings and among them throwes;
> Knowing that Hunters on the *Pontik* Heath
> Doo more desire that ransom, then his death.
> There, the rough *Hedge-hog*; who, to shun his thrall,
> Shrinks up himself as round as any Ball;
> And fastning his slowe feet under his chin,
> On's thistly bristles rowles him quickly in.
> But th' Ey of Heav'n beholdeth nought more strange
> Then the *Chameleon*, who with various change
> Receiues the colour that each obiect giues,
> And (food-les else) of th' Aire alonely liues.[15]

On the creation of Eve, several hundred pages into the long discussion of creation, du Bartas provides an account that by now has accumulated the details of such a variegated world from God's hand. That store of divine artifact means that the glorious discovery by Adam of a new person to be loved and cherished is neither dogmatic nor pedantic but rises out of the natural features of the world, as it tumbles into a Christian purpose of its own right that, again, naturally embraces the generative, genealogical, and probative movement of creation as a whole:

> You that haue seen within this ample Table,
> Among so many Modules admirable,
> Th' admired beauties of the King of Creatures,
> Com, com and see the Womans rapting features:
> Without whom (heer) Man were but half a man,
> But a wilde Wolf, but a Barbarian,
> Brute, ragefull, fierce, moody, melancholike,
> Hating the Light; whom nought but naught could like:
> Born solely for himself, bereft of sense,
> Of heart, of loue, of life, of excellence.
> God therefore, not to seme less liberal
> To Man, then else to euery animal;
> For perfect patern of a holy Loue,
> To *Adams* half another half he gaue,
> Ta'en from his side, to binde (through euery Age)
> With kinder bonds the sacred Mariage. . . .
> He took a rib, which rarely he refin'd,
> And thereof made the Mother of Mankinde:
> Grauing so liuely on the liuing Bone
> All *Adams* beauties; that, but hardly, one
> Could haue the Louer from his Loue descry'd,
> Or know'n the Bridegroom from his gentle Bride:
> Sauing that she had a more smiling Ey,
> A smoother Chin, a Cheek of purer Dy,
> A fainter voice, a more inticing Face,
> A Deeper Tress, a more delighting Grace,
> And in her bosom (more then Lillie-white)
> Two swelling Mounts of Ivory, panting light.
>
> Now, after this profound and pleasing Traunce,
> No sooner *Adams* rauisht eyes did glaunce
> On the rare beauties of his new-com Half,
> But in his heart he gan to leap and laugh,
> Kissing her kindely, calling her his Life,
> His Loue, his Stay, his Rest, his Weal, his Wife,
> His other-Self, his Help (him to refresh)
> Bone of his Bone, Flesh of his very Flesh.
>
> Source of all ioyes? sweet *Hee-Shee*-Coupled-One,
> Thy sacred Birth I neuer think upon,
> But (rauisht) I admire how God did then
> Make Two of One, and One of Two again.

O blessed Bond! O happy Mariage!
Which doost the match 'twixt Christ and vs presage!
O chastest friendship, whose pure flames impart
Two Soules in one, two Hearts into one Hart!
O holy knot, in *Eden* instituted
(Not in this Earth with bloud and wrongs polluted,
Profan'd with mischiefs, the Pre-Scaene of Hell
To cursed Creatures that' gainst Heav'n rebell)
O sacred Cov'nant, which the sin-less Son
Of a pure Virgin (when he first begun
To publish proofs of his drad Powr *Diuine*,
By turning Water into perfect Wine,
At lesser *Cana*) in a wondrous manner
Did with his presence sanctifie and honour!

By thy deer Fauour, after our Decease,
We leaue behinde our liuing Images,
Change War to Peace, in kindred multiply,
And in our Children liue eternally.
By thee, we quench the wilde and wanton Fires,
That in our Soule the *Paphian* shot inspires:
And taught (by thee) a loue more firm and fitter,
We finde the Mel more sweet, the Gall less bitter,

Which heer (by turns) heap vp our human Life
Eu'n now with ioyes, anon with iars and strife.[16]

Du Bartas' work spurred both copiers, summarizers, and novel depar-
tures.[17] There was, for instance, Edward Brown (mentioned above in
chapter 4), whose take on the genre emphasized a kind of moral ency-
clopedism, where each day, or the labor of toil and eating, are laid out,
in order to contrast them with the heavenly goods of faith and devotion. While these kinds of moves somewhat subvert the open embrace
of engraced mortal existence that du Bartas praised, they nonetheless
keep strongly intact the connection between that existence and its Giver,
albeit now driven by a moral and often ascetic fire more closely associated with the early church.

But whatever transformations his work was subjected to, by the
eighteenth century, du Bartas—who had been compared to Homer and
Vergil—had begun to slip from the reading public's attention. "Joys, jars,
and strife" were drifting into some other realm of meaning. It was at the
same period wherein Yonnet has traced the beginnings of a significant

shift in France's own relationship with life span and generation. It is an era in which we can observe, more broadly, the gradual but decisive closing of the "two books," of Nature and of Scripture, as texts to be read side by side. With du Bartas, still, everything is given a paired and intertwining reading. But by the end of the eighteenth century, it was one book or the other that was scrutinized, often one against the other.[18] Much misunderstanding regarding the relationship of the "two books" still exists in Christian circles, where many think they have a moral duty to valorize the authority of one over the other.

Yet Scripture speaks within the context of nature, just as each of the two books speaks within the context of the scriptural canon itself taken more broadly. Nature and Scripture are not so much equivalent as they are mutually demanding—because creatively coherent—frames of reference. This means that there is no material theology apart from Christ; though it also means that Christ's teaching is apprehended according to the forms of our created being. What some have called "natural theology"—what we learn of God from the created matter of the world—is, after all, a theology of the Eucharist at its base, for anything we know about God in relation to the created world is finally given through the divine ingestion. But such natural theology is therefore also a theology of the traversed landscape of the world that is given in the one, singular, and particular body of Jesus. The "coherence" of the two books is essential to grasp for Christians. The great twentieth-century theologian Karl Barth is still remembered for his resounding "No!" (*Nein!*) to any claim that God's truth is to be constrained by our experiences within the world.[19] He aimed this savage stricture against what he called "natural theology," which he linked to a kind of experiential culturalism that he associated with, among other things, the rise of National Socialism in Germany. But whatever Barth really thought, the popularized notion of his *Nein!* has proven unhelpful to the maintenance of a serious consideration, among Protestants especially, of the divine gift that creatureliness constitutes. This popular *Nein!* has thus undermined the ability, again of Protestant churches especially, to engage our creaturehood as itself a revelation of God indirectly, as Giver of all that we are, in terms of utter receipt. Neither Luther nor Calvin would have followed in this modern Protestant trajectory, and early Reformed documents, like the Belgic Confession (article 2), expressly uphold the idea of the "two books":

> We know God by two means: First, by the creation, preservation, and
> government of the universe, since that universe is before our eyes like a

beautiful book in which all creatures, great and small, are as letters to make us ponder the invisible things of God: . . . Second, God makes himself known to us more clearly by his holy and divine Word, as much as we need in this life, for God's glory and for our salvation.[20]

None of this is particularly relevant to the so-called "argument between science and religion," reembraced in a stunted form within the creationist-evolutionist debates of the past few decades. Pitting science and religion against each other actually derives from a *rejection* of the whole two books outlook. For all traditional discussants of the Two Books image, Scripture was viewed as somehow the more fundamental articulator of the matter of nature. Hence, it was never the case that the Bible was a "book of science," to be read in the same fashion as natural history. Rather, the notion was that the stuff of nature, understood according to our best reasoning abilities, cohered with the deeper truths of Scripture and could be grasped only in its meaning within the forms of scriptural truth[21]—all the more reason, then, that the clearly demarcated forms of human mortality in its temporal movement should find their true significance within the figures of Scripture's own discussion, not so as to disappear within that discussion, but in order to be illuminated in their clearest outlines. Only thus could they be seen finally in their transfigured forms.

It is therefore metaphysically illogical that so many Christians do not seem to grasp the deep connection between, on the one hand, the sorrowful brokenness of the earth's landscape, brought on by human greed and the fury of desire and now disclosed in the yet unnumbered burdens of climate change, and, on the other, the forgotten realities of mortal existence. Both are twin failures to understand and embrace the ordering of giftedness. The church has little to offer the world as gospel if the elements of nature's integrity and the integrity of human mortality are separated. The political entailments of our reflections are, in fact, concrete just in this nexus of this connection, though they cut in directions that will clearly discomfort many. One great irony of the Great Transition is manifested at the moment before it gathered steam, in the seventeenth century. This moment constituted the nadir of the human life span, buffeted by famine, plague, and, in the Americas, the dissolution of entire peoples. Yet this was also the moment that was expressed, by du Bartas and his company, in one of the most remarkable human displays of divine abundance within the arts and theological discourse of the day. This was an era when, for the first time, it seems, the clean and unclean both were given voice to praise their Maker. Yet in our day, spoken out of a context of untold prosperity, all is colored with the pale and fading tint of scarcity: at every turn, we are met by the messages of dwindling supplies and possibilities, even as more and more is being gathered into the barn. All the shades and tinctures of abundance are being covered over.

Today, therefore, the church is called to praise God in a time of perceived drought. It is wrongly perceived yet horribly experienced. The church is faced with a vocational decision. In humanity's perverted experience of drought, the Christian church can be like Jonah, sitting testily in the heat and awaiting doom. She can instead be like Joseph, numbering the years and harvests, counting out the gifts of this day and the next; touching the faces of his brethren long unseen; gathering and then receiving a father and his family who had been lost, "his sons, and his sons' sons with him, his daughters and his sons' daughters, and all his seed" now "brought with him into Egypt" (Gen 46:7).

This scriptural figure, one of many like it, is normative for the human creature and describes what just such a creature is. Our urgent responsibility is to rediscover the "just suchness" that constitutes human creaturehood. While the culture wars rage, as they really do, fueled by the dried timber of human creaturely self-knowledge cast aside, the church is called to gather her children, born as such, with their families given as such; she is called to tend their survival as such, to frame their growth as such, to nurture their friendships as such, to order their learning as such. She is called to carry them into death as just such creatures, now formed by a faith, hope, and love that is recognized as Jesus Christ himself, standing with and in the church in all of this, their Lord and their God, who has, even before the foundation of the world, made it his own.

So the church prays the prayer of all numbering, that the prayer offered to the one who gives gifts before they are even known, and hence can only now be described because they were given before they were sought (Matt 6:8):

> *Our Father, who art in Heaven*
> There is only one God, there is only God before and after even our thoughts, and we are his creatures, made by his hand, for no reason other than his love. We are made, not from God in heaven, but from the very incomprehensible thing that is not God, the dust of the earth, that he has made before us. We cannot know God as he is, but only as a Father who gives. And we know ourselves only as a gift from this Giver.

Our knowing is all gift, and thus our knowing is all Christ Jesus who has made the Father known. For our Father is in Heaven, and we are of the earth. Help us to number our days.

*Hallowed be thy Name.*

There is nothing to claim from this fact. It is all God. We do not constitute our own lives, even if we are but ourselves here upon the earth. The dignity of our being is given in that this being is not ours at all, but given us. We look, then, to Him, and only Him. We have, as our first word, God's name, and call upon it because it is the source of our being, our turning, our speaking. Speak to me, we ask; and He speaks. Let me speak of You; and You speak. Who am I? You shall tell all to me, just as You have told me into being. For me to speak, then, is only to listen as You speak first.

*Thy Kingdom come!*

Let me then hear! Let me live in such a way that every sound is also the gift that envelops the gift of my life. Let me grow and learn, that Your voice becomes the words whispered in my ear in the night time, waking me at dawn, calling me through the daylight, and inviting me at dusk. For You have taken the same journey as have I, and come back to make it mine; that is, to rule all things, since they exist only at your calling and persist only in your coming.

*Thy will be done on earth as it is in heaven!*

So I am made. I am made as You would have me made. I shall live as You would have me live. This earth, thistled and barren, or moist and thick, is the place of my being made, and it is Yours. Just this life, is the life of my being made in just this place. Yet it is Your making, as it is Your earth, and thus all my days are Your days, the ones You have counted out in Your book, the ones You have numbered in Your own flesh, heaven to earth, and earth to heaven, Word descended, Word arisen and uttered to the ends of all ages.

*Give us this day*

There is no Name, no Kingdom, no Will accomplished but on this day. For I am myself given, and this day speaks to this gift, from sunrise to sunset. There is no other day that shall be but now. This day is the fullness of Your love for me. This day is the only manner of my being and standing towards You and all the world. That there is this day, is the fact of my life, its length of days being but the account of the wonder of one day or another. Let me have no other day but this one, since I am but a creature of a day.

### Our daily bread

Today, I shall find You in the crumbs under the table. I shall find you in the wine or water on my tongue. I shall find you in my hunger and my satisfaction on this day, walking from minute to minute, and being fed by the ravens of your mercy. I shall find You upon my mother's breast, nourished by my father's labor, within the cloak wrapped around me, by a stove or open window, by my sister, and her friends, in digging and reading, in speaking to a stranger whom I will learn to love, in building and being torn down. I eat and I live because You have made others to eat and live with me and me with them. For I have found You, my breath, my day, my bread within the realm of many. My bread is the bread that is ours together.

### And forgive us our trespasses

Because You feed us together, You have made me a creature who learns from others, and learning has become the mark of my dignity as your creature. My learning has opened my eyes to the fullness of Your making, a gift that is many gifts, creatures that are manifold. My world is a landscape, littered with things; and the air, filled with voices. They are all that I am given, in the form of our common life, on just this day. Let us hold to just these limits of our lives as marks of Your own generosity. Let us know that our births and deaths are Yours to order. Let us never close our eyes to You.

### As we forgive those who trespass against us

By knowing You, we shall know in each the frailty of our days as Your own gift. Learning to eat, we shall learn the tending of a vine that too must perish, and just in this, has fruit to bear on just this day. Hearing each voice, we shall also hear the silencing of each. We are turned to each other, we tend to each other, we watch each other come to our ends. Therefore, we can never turn aside from the path we were placed upon together. Young and old, born and yet-to-be-born; woman and man; married and single; toiling and resting; eating and waiting to eat; weakening and passing away: let us carry on with them, for all our sins are gathered in the confusions of these days, and all our hope in Your own illumination of their passage.

### Lead us not into temptation, but deliver us from evil

We are fearful, and fear is something good in such a place and passage as this. All that You give us is good, yet it is not ours. You take us away in an instant! Our loves are powerless, our angers consuming. We pray; we cry out; we call upon Your Name: have mercy on us, O Lord! We learn so slowly, distracted, seeing nothing ahead. We are tested and assaulted, as all the forms of the world overwhelm us, so that what is beautiful we come to hate, and what demands our attention we come to despise. Draw us out of these pits of our own making; sell us to traders if need be, to be taken to Egypt, and flourish; let us at least live long enough to see Your light. Have mercy on us Lord for our "days are consumed like smoke" and our "bones are burned as an hearth" (Ps 102:3), so that we "forget to eat our bread" (102:4). Let us never forget.

*For thine is the Kingdom, the power, and the glory, for ever and ever.*

"But now, Lord, what wait I for? my hope is in thee" (Ps 39:7). For "whom have I in heaven but thee? and there is none upon earth that I desire beside thee" (Ps 73:25). "I will praise thee; for I am fearfully and wonderfully made: marvellous are thy works; and that my soul knoweth right well" (Ps 139:14).

# Notes

*Preface*

1   Most of what I have written on this has been occasional and delivered within church settings or Internet discussions. A few essays are devoted to the topic in my *Hope among the Fragments: The Broken Church and Its Engagement of Scripture* (Grand Rapids: Brazos, 2004); or again, my essay "The Nuptial Mystery: The Historical Flesh of Procreation," in *The Nuptial Mystery*, ed. by Roy Jeal (Eugene, Ore.: Wipf & Stock, 2010), 85–115. Again, "Blessing: A Scriptural and Theological Reflection," *Pro Ecclesia* 19, no. 1 (2010): 7–27. As will become apparent, I was deeply challenged by my study of Leviticus; see *Leviticus* (Grand Rapids: Brazos, 2008). The fact is, as I will indicate in this book, that the topic itself is hard to treat systematically.

2   John Donne, sermon preached before the king, April 1, 1627. In John Donne, *The Sermons of John Donne*, ed. Evelyn Mary Spearing Simpson and George Reuben Potter (Berkeley: University of California Press, 1954), 7:400. I have made some attempt at outlining this in the opening chapters of *Time and the Word* (Grand Rapids: Eerdmans, forthcoming).

3   Perhaps one cannot make such sweeping statements. But despite the recent interest in "popular religion" or "religious cultures" in, e.g., medieval Europe, which tends to fragment thinking and experience, there *do* seem to be "general" attitudes at work. Cf. K. L. French, *The People of the Parish: Community Life in a Late Medieval English Diocese* (Philadelphia: University of Pennsylvania Press, 2001); or some of the essays in Norman Tanner, *The Ages of Faith: Popular Religion in Late Medieval England and Western Europe* (London: I. B. Taurus, 2009).

*Chapter I*

1  The most famous visitor in this respect was the seventeenth-century British scientist Robert Boyle, who was one of the first to compare the universe to a great clock, on the basis of the Strasbourg machine. See Edward L. Schoen, "Clocks, God, and Scientific Realism," *Zygon* 37, no. 3 (2002): 555–79.

2  For material on the Strasbourg clock in particular, see Alfred Ungerer, *L'horloge astronomique de la cathédrale de Strasbourg* (Strasbourg: Impr. Alsacienne, 1922); Henri Bach, Jean-Pierre Rieb, and Robert Wilhelm, *Les trois horloges astronomiques de la cathédrale de Strasbourg* (Strasbourg: Éditions Ronald Hirlé, 1992); F. C. Haber, "The Cathedral Clock and the Cosmological Metaphor," in *The Study of Time II: Proceedings of the Second Conference of the International Society for the Study of Time, Lake Yamanaka, Japan*, ed. J. T. Fraser and N. Lawrence (Berlin: Springer-Verlag, 1975), 399–416. For a somewhat more philosophical take on the clock, see Brian Hays, "Clock of Ages: When One Millennium's Bright Ideas Become Inscrutable Legacies for the Next," *Sciences* 39, no. 6 (1999): 9–13. More broadly on clocks, time, and the culture of time in the Middle Ages, see Nancy Mason Bradbury and Carolyn P. Collette, "Changing Times: The Mechanical Clock in Late Medieval Literature," *Chaucer Review* 43, no. 4 (2009): 351–75; John Scattergood, "Writing the Clock: The Reconstruction of Time in the Late Middle Ages," *European Review* 11, no. 4 (2003): 453–74.

3  John Donne, *The Variorum Edition of the Poetry of John Donne*, ed. Gary A. Stringer, vol. 6, *The Anniversaries and the Epicedes and Obsequies* (Bloomington: Indiana University Press), 180.

4  Karl Barth, *Church Dogmatics*, vol. III.2, *Man in His Time*, edited by G. W. Bromiley and T. F. Torrance (Edinburgh: T&T Clark, 1960), 417–651.

5  Jacques Ellul, *The Meaning of the City*, trans. Dennis Pardee (Grand Rapids: Eerdmans, 1970).

6  An English translation of the play can be found in *Antonin Artaud: Selected Writings*, ed. Susan Sontag (New York: Farrar Strauss & Giroux, 1976), 555–74. The quoted original can be found in Antonin Artaud, *Oeuvres completes* (Paris: Gallimard, 1956), 13:83.

7  Milton, *Paradise Lost* 10:211–23; this is conveniently available in Dartmouth College's online edition: https://www.dartmouth.edu/~milton/reading_room/pl/book_10/text.shtml.

8  Hugh Broughton, *A Comment upon Coheleth or Ecclesiastes: Framed for the Instruction of Prince Henri Our Hope* (London: W. White, 1605), 2.

9  We can see how the two "trees," of knowledge and life, fasten all that God has made into a fulfilled harmony (Gen 2:9,17; 3:22; Rev 22:2).

10 For references, see Gerhart B. Ladner, *The Idea of Reform: Its Impact on Christian Thought and Action in the Age of the Fathers* (Cambridge, Mass.: Harvard University Press, 1959), 176, on "skins" and fathers. See also Gary Anderson, *The Genesis of Perfection: Adam and Eve in Jewish and Christian Imagination*

(Louisville, Ky.: Westminster John Knox, 2001), esp. 117–34, which offers Jewish traditions on the matter. For more, see Panayiotis Nellas' *Deification in Christ: Orthodox Perspective on the Nature of the Human Person*, trans. Normal Russell (Crestwood, N.Y.: St. Vladimir's Seminary, 1987), 44–63; Alexandra Parvân, "Genesis 1–3: Augustine and Origen on the *Coats of Skins*," *Vigiliae Christianae* 66 (2012): 56–96.

11  On some of this, see Jonathan Z. Smith, "The Garments of Shame," *History of Religions* 5, no. 2 (1966): 217–38.

12  Warren S. Thompson, *Population Problems* (New York: McGraw-Hill, 1930); Adolphe Landry, *La revolution démographique: Études et essais sur les problems de la population* (Paris: Sirey, 1934); Frank W. Notestein et al., *The Future Population of Europe and the Soviet Union: Population Projections, 1940–1970* (Geneva: League of Nations, 1944).

13  Alfred Sauvy, *Les limites de la vie humaine* (Paris: Hachette, 1961). Sauvy himself was not worried about overpopulation, since falling birthrates would take care of that quite "naturally."

14  James C. Riley, *Rising Life Expectancy: A Global History* (Cambridge: Cambridge University Press, 2001), esp. 1–57. Emphasis added.

15  Rémi Brague, *Les ancres dane le ciel: L'infrastruture métaphysique* (Paris: Éditions de Seuil, 2011), 97–98.

16  See Robert Woods, *Children Remembered: Responses to Untimely Death in the Past* (Liverpool: Liverpool University Press, 2006), 33–60, with its rich references. For the demography of life expectancy at the beginning of the Reformation, see Deborah Youngs, *The Life Cycle in Western Europe, c. 1300–c. 1500* (Manchester: Manchester University Press, 2006), 11–38.

17  Ralph Houlbrooke, ed., *English Family Life, 1575–1716: An Anthology from Diaries* (Oxford: Blackwell, 1988), 109.

18  Riley, *Rising Life Expectancy*, esp. 1–57.

19  Arthur E. Imhof, "Is Japan Following Europe towards a Society of Singles? Possible Impacts of the Rapid Increase in Life Expectancy on Japanese Social Structure—as Seen by a European Historical-Demographer," *Keio Economic Studies* 23, no. 1 (1986): 21–47.

20  Philip A. Mellor and Chris Shilling, "Modernity, Self-Identity and the Sequestration of Death," *Sociology* 27, no. 3 (1993): 411–31; Zygmunt Bauman, *Mortality, Immortality, and Other Life Strategies* (Stanford: Stanford University Press, 1992). The notion that "denial of death" is a long-standing human characteristic, rather than a very recent phenomenon, is historically absurd. Ernest Becker's famous *The Denial of Death* (New York: Free Press, 1973) disseminated this idea, wrapped in a relatively powerful psychological framework. Nonetheless, Becker simply failed to take seriously a whole range of religious realities on their own terms rather than on the basis of a more generalized theory of "religion," which he understood to be based on a broad human search for immortality. Becker's own view of a "good" religion is in fact closer to pre-Transition

attitudes. Still, there are those who have taken Becker's mistaken historical perspective and turned it into a popular "science of mind": cf. Ajit Varki and Danny Brower, *Denial: Self-Deception, False Beliefs, and the Origins of the Human Mind* (New York: Twelve/Grand Central, 2013).

21   Francis C. Notzon et al., "Causes of Declining Life Expectancy in Russia," *Journal of the American Medical Association* 279, no. 10 (1998): 793–800.

22   Robert Putnam, *Bowling Alone: The Collapse and Revival of American Community* (New York: Simon & Schuster, 2001).

23   C. P. Snow, *The Two Cultures* (Rede Lecture, 1959) (Cambridge: Cambridge University Press, 1961), 28–29.

24   Condorcet (his full name was Marie Jean Antoine Nicolas de Caritat, marquis de Condorcet) was a mathematician, whose remarkable contributions to probability theory, statistics, and other areas of the discipline were driven by a keen belief in the immutability and discoverability of the "laws" by which the universe works. As he puts it in the final chapter of his famous *Esquisse d'un tableau historique des progrès de l'esprit human* (1795), as humankind understands more and more the nature of these laws, it can not only predict the future but order its life so as to adjust to reality so perfectly that its life will itself achieve its own natural "perfection." This will mark the path of inevitable social "progress." But just what are these "laws"? And how are they reflected in human life? Condorcet's rejection of Christianity was in part driven by his rejection of Christianity's insistence upon human finitude, in its cognitive realm, and human sin both. See the original translation, M. de Condorcet, *Outlines of an Historical View of the Progress of the Human Mind* (London: J. Johnson, 1795), 316–17. Condorcet, ironically, was the victim of the very revolution he encouraged, and the work was published posthumously. Christopher Lasch's *The True and Only Heaven: Progress and Its Critics* (New York: W. W. Norton, 1991) remains one of the great contemporary social discussions on this theme, within the American intellectual context. Lasch's posthumous collection of essays, *Women and the Common Life: Love, Marriage, and Feminism* (New York: W. W. Norton, 1997), deserves special notice. Its historical observations as well as critiques overlap with many elements in the present book.

25   See the section of Charles Taylor's book that he entitles "The Immanent Frame," in his outline of the "Conditions of Belief" in the modern world, in *A Secular Age* (Cambridge, Mass.: Harvard University Press, 2007), 539–93. For a description of how to speak of nonutilitarian transcendence within an immanent framework, see the wonderful essay "Monks and Morals" by the philosopher R. G. Collingwood (an excerpt of a longer work), in Collingwood, *Essays in Political Philosophy*, ed. David Boucher (Oxford: Oxford University Press, 1989), 144–49.

26   See the article by Rebecca Krawiec, "Garments of Salvation Representations of Monastic Clothing in Late Antiquity," *Journal of Early Christian Studies* 17, no. 1 (2009): 125–50.

*Chapter II*

1  Athanasius, *On the Incarnation*, trans. Archibald Robertson (London: David Nutt, 1891), 4.

2  The key text in Augustine is *The Literal Meaning of Genesis* I.204–5. See Augustine, *On Genesis: A Refutation of the Manichees. Unfinished Literal Commentary on Genesis. The Literal Meaning of Genesis*, trans. Edmund Hill (Hyde Park, N.Y.: New City, 2002).

3  For Augustine, see his *Literal Meaning of Genesis* I.204–5.

4  Cf. *A Select Library of Nicene and Post-Nicene Fathers, Second Series*, ed. Henry R. Percival (Grand Rapids: Eerdmans, 1955), 14:496.

5  This can be found easily in John Calvin, *Commentaries on the First Book of Moses, Called Genesis*, trans. John King (Edinburgh: Calvin Translation Society, 1847), 1:179–80.

6  The classic Seventh-Day Adventist work on this topic is the two-volume treatise by Le Roy Edwin Froom, *The Conditionalist Faith of Our Fathers: The Conflict of the Ages over the Nature and Destiny of Man* (Washington, D.C.: Review & Herald, 1966). It can be accessed online at http://docs.adventistarchives.org//doc_info .asp?DocID=52969 (accessed November 25, 2015).

7  Irenaeus, *Against the Heresies* (*Adversus haereses*) IV.39.2.

8  Edgar Morin, *L'homme et la mort* (Paris: Corrêa, 1951). The volume has gone through several revisions since. Raymond Kurzweil and Terry Grossman's book *Fantastic Voyage: Live Long Enough to Live Forever* (Emmaus, Pa.: Rodale, 2004) has generated enormous interest and follow-up. The linking of life extension and "life forever" with the development of artificial intelligence has been part of Kurzweil's own thinking. Other medically and genetically oriented pursuits of not only life extension but the possibility of overcoming the process of "aging" altogether are numerous. There is even a large and distinguished society, the American Academy of Anti-Aging Medicine, that organizes the dissemination of research and so on: http://www.a4m.com/. One promising line, for instance, involves the identification of a specific enzyme, telomerase, that may control the genetic reproductive circuits, by which genetic information for cell reproduction is either turned "on" or "off." Needless to say, this kind of research—originally linked to cancer-related interests—remains primitive in its knowledge base at best.

9  On suicide and sexuality, see Michel Henry, *Barbarism* (1987), trans. Scott Davidson (New York: Continuum, 2012), 82–87.

10 Sigmund Freud, "Reflections on War and Death," in *On Murder, Mourning, and Melancholia* (London: Penguin Books, 2005), 169–94.

11 Freud, "Reflections on War and Death," 175.

12 Cf. Amber Peterman, Tia Palermo, and Caryn Bredenkamp, "Estimates and Determinants of Sexual Violence against Women in the Democratic Republic of Congo," *American Journal of Public Health* 101, no. 6 (2011): 1060–67.

13  K. Johnston et al., "Association of Sexual Violence and Human Rights Vio-
    lations with Physical and Mental Health in Territories of the Eastern Demo-
    cratic Republic of Congo," *Journal of the American Medical Association* 304, no.
    5 (2010): 553–62. See, more widely, Lara Stemple, "Male Rape and Human
    Rights," *Hastings Law Journal* 60, no. 3 (2009): 605–46.

14  Daniel Bergner, *The Other Side of Desire: Four Journeys into the Far Realms of Lust
    and Longing* (New York: Ecco, 2009).

15  See *Culture, Medicine, Psychiatry* 36, no. 2 (2012): 183–419; this issue is devoted
    to the topic, covering a worldwide set of case studies, and filled with up-to-
    date references. See also relevant chapters in Rory C. O'Connor, Stephen Platt,
    and Jacky Gordon, eds., *International Handbook of Suicide Prevention Research,
    Policy and Practice* (Malden, Mass.: Wiley, 2011).

16  IV.29, in Joseph I. Gorfinkle, trans., *Sayings of the Jewish Fathers: Pirke Abot*
    (New York: Bloch, 1916), 73.

17  Thomas Aquinas, *Summa Theologiae* II.II.64.5. Translation from Thomas
    Aquinas, *Summa Theologica, Second Part of the Second Part . . .* , trans.
    Dominican Fathers of the English Province (New York: Benzinger Bros.,
    1947); easily accessible at http://www.ccel.org/a/aquinas/summa/SS/SS064
    .html#SSQ64A5THEP1.

18  See John Donne, *Biathanatos: A Modern-Spelling Edition*, intro. and commen-
    tary by Michael Rudick and M. Pabst Battin (New York: Garland, 1982).

19  One of the most daring interpretations of Donne's intention was Borges', who
    linked Donne's picture of Jesus as a "divine suicide" with elements of bizarre
    Gnosticism: God creates by killing himself. The interpretation, at least in terms
    of authorial intention, is absurd. See Jorge Luis Borges, "Biathanatos," in his
    *Selected Non-fictions*, ed. Eliot Weinberger (New York: Penguin Books, 1999),
    333–36.

20  Cf. James Kuzner, "Donne's *Biathanatos* and the Public Sphere's Vexing Free-
    dom," *ELH (English Literary History)* 81, no. 1 (2014): 61–81.

21  Jennifer Michael Hecht, *Stay: A History of Suicide and the Philosophies against It*
    (New Haven, Conn.: Yale University Press, 2013).

22  Hecht, *Stay*, 7.

23  A six-volume critical edition has appeared, as Robert Burton, *The Anatomy of
    Melancholy*, ed. Thomas C. Faulkner, Nicolas K. Kiessling, and Rhonda L. Blair,
    intro. by J. B. Bamborough (New York: Oxford University Press, 1989–2000).

24  World Health Organization 2014 statistics; accessed at http://www.who.int/mental
    _health/prevention/suicide/suicideprevent/en/ (accessed November 25, 2015).

25  Hecht, *Stay*, 136.

26  Hecht, *Stay*, 143.

27  Cf. the fascinating work being done in this area by the National Institutes of
    Health, at the Human Microbiome Project; http://www.hmpdacc.org/.

28  David Benatar, *Better Never to Have Been: The Harm of Coming into Existence*
    (New York: Oxford University Press, 2006). Benatar stands in the line of the

more popular ethicist Peter Singer but takes Singer's utilitarian logic to its extreme. See Singer, *Rethinking Life and Death: The Collapse of Traditional Ethics* (New York: St. Martin's, 1994).

29   Two helpful openings to phenomenology—one more historical and textual, the other more thematic—are respectively Dermot Moran, *Introduction to Phenomenology* (London: Routledge, 2000); and Robert Sokolowski, *Introduction to Phenomenology* (Cambridge: Cambridge University Press, 2000). Neither, however, speaks to Michel Henry or Jean-Luc Marion. A good introduction on that score is Christina M. Gschwandtner's *Postmodern Apologetics? Arguments for God in Contemporary Philosophy* (New York: Fordham University Press, 2013).

30   Four volumes of Michel Henry's collected material, under the title of *Phénoménologie de la vie*, have appeared (Paris: Presses Universitaires de France, 2003–2004), which cover a full range of topics. Henry's foundational 1963 work was translated into English as *The Essence of Manifestation*, trans. Girard Etzkorn (The Hague: Nijhoff, 1973). His later works dealing with Christianity, however, are somewhat more user friendly (though still difficult) and make use of many of his more abstract categories from his philosophical work: *I Am the Truth: Toward a Philosophy of Christianity* (1996), trans. Susan Emanuel (Stanford: Stanford University Press, 2003); *Words of Christ* (2002), trans. Christina M. Gschwandtner (Grand Rapids: Eerdmans, 2012). *Barbarism* (1987), trans. Scott Davidson (New York: Continuum, 2012), remains perhaps his most accessible book. A good introduction to his religious outlook is Michelle Rebidoux, *The Philosophy of Michel Henry (1922–2002)* (Lewiston, N.Y.: Edwin Mellen, 2012).

31   Cf. Denis Edwards, *The Breath of Life: A Theology of the Creator Spirit* (Maryknoll, N.Y.: Orbis, 2004). Also Amos Yong, *The Spirit of Creation: Modern Science and Divine Action in the Pentecostal-Charismatic Imagination* (Grand Rapids: Eerdmans, 2011).

32   Like Henry, Marion has already written a vast amount. For an introduction to Marion's work in English, see Jean-Luc Marion, *The Essential Writings*, ed. Kevin Hart (New York: Fordham University Press, 2013). One of his major works is translated as *Being Given: Toward a Phenomenology of Givenness*, trans. Jeffrey L. Kosky (Stanford: Stanford University Press, 2002). More manageable is his *The Reason of the Gift*, trans. Stephen E. Lewis (Charlottesville: University of Virginia Press, 2011).

33   See Marion's "Sketch of a Phenomenological Concept of Sacrifice," in *Reason of the Gift*, 69–90.

34   John Adams, *An essay concerning self-murther wherein is endeavour'd to prove that it is unlawful according to natural principles: With some considerations upon what is pretended from the said principles, by the author of a treatise intituled, Biathanatos, and others* (London: Th. Bennet, 1700), 65–66.

35 William Denny, *Pelecanicidium; or, The Christian adviser against self-murder together with a guide and the pilgrims passe to the land of the living: in three books* (London, 1653).

36 Petrarch's *De remediis utriusque fortunae* does not exist in a modern English translation. The original Latin version can be found in reproduced forms as printed in Cremona, by Bernardinus de Misintis and Caesar Parmensis, 1492. Thomas Twyn published a translation in 1579, entitled *Phisicke against fortune, as well prosperous, as adverse, conteyned in two books . . .* (London: R. Watkyns, 1579). A rather unhelpful English translation, still used, is that of Susannah Dobson, published as *Petrarch's View of Human Life* (London: John Stockdale, 1791).

37 Dobson, *Petrarch's View*, 307; quote from "De Rota," in *Remediis utriusque fortunae*, dialogue 118. See Twyn's sixteenth-century translation of this popular work: "furie agaynst a mans owne selfe, and the forgetfulnesse of his owne estate" (*Phisicke against fortune*, 328). The original Latin is rather more complex.

*Chapter III*

1 Guy Krivopissko and François Marcot, eds., *La vie à en mourir: Lettres de fusillés* (Paris: Talleandier/Seuil, 2003), 247; translated by the present author.

2 A readable and illuminating, if one-sided, account of some of this, set within the context of marriage debates, is given in George Chauncey, *Why Marriage: The History Shaping Today's Debate over Gay Equality* (New York: Basic Books, 2009). Chauncey's discussion of AIDS is framed by an interest in legal protections over decision making and property among gay couples.

3 Again, a one-sided but for all that helpful account is given in Caroline J. Addington Hall, *A Thorn in the Flesh: How Gay Sexuality Is Changing the Episcopal Church* (Lanham, Md.: Rowman & Littlefield, 2013).

4 See some of the narrative material in Robert R. Reilly, *Making Gay Okay: How Rationalizing Homosexual Behavior Is Changing Everything* (San Francisco: Ignatius, 2014). Reilly's highly polemical book has some very useful discussions of the political dynamics involved in legal decision making, research, and teaching.

5 These figures are from amfAR, the Foundation for AIDS Research; http://www.amfar.org/.

6 From the World Health Organization; http://www.who.int/hiv/en/ (accessed November 25, 2015).

7 See the work of Edward C. Green—e.g., *Rethinking AIDS Prevention: How the Experts Went Wrong* (Westport, Conn.: Praeger, 2003); *Broken Promises: How the AIDS Establishment Has Betrayed the Developing World* (Sausalito, Calif.: PoliPoint, 2011). Green, a respected and mainstream researcher, has borne the brunt of critique from colleagues for following the "evidence" as he sees it, in ways that have put him at odds with "establishment" thinking. If nothing else (although I believe there is much more), he is useful for articulating views held by many leaders, religious and otherwise, in places like East Africa.

8   See the overview, especially the epilogue, in Heather Murray, *Not in This Family: Gays and the Meaning of Kinship in Postwar North America* (Philadelphia: University of Pennsylvania Press, 2012).

9   Benatar, *Better Never to Have Been.*

10  Philip Jenkins has been a major writer on these topics. See his *The New Faces of Christianity: Believing the Bible in the Global South* (New York: Oxford University Press, 2006); Jenkins, *The Next Christendom: The Coming of Global Christianity*, 3rd ed. (New York: Oxford University Press, 2011). For Anglicanism in particular, if already somewhat out of date, see Miranda K. Hassett, *Anglican Communion in Crisis: How Episcopal Dissidents and Their African Allies Are Reshaping Anglicanism* (Princeton, N.J.: Princeton University Press, 2007). Some of the larger dynamics of internationalizing sexual conflict, as it were, are explored, albeit rather tendentiously (but in a helpfully provocative way too) by Dennis Altman, *Global Sex* (Chicago: University of Chicago Press, 2001).

11  P. D. James, *Children of Men* (London: Faber & Faber, 1992).

12  David Trobisch, *War Paulus verheiratet? Und andere offene Fragen der Paulusexegese* (Munich: Gütersloher Verlagshaus, 2011).

13  Key history and documentary references can be found in David G. Hunter, *Marriage, Celibacy, and Heresy in Ancient Christianity: The Jovinianist Controversy* (Oxford: Oxford University Press, 2007).

14  Cf. *Confessions* IX.6.14.

15  ICUR stands for Inscriptiones Christianae Urbis Romae, the official gathering of inscriptions from the city of Rome relating to Christianity. The nineteenth-century edition, from which these have come, is by G. B. de Rossi, ed., *Inscriptiones Christianae urbis Romae septimo saeculo antiquiores*, 2 vols. (Rome, 1857–1888), although a new series was begun in 1922. An important discussion is given in Jos Janssens, *Vita e morte del Cristiano negli epitaffi di Roma anteriori al sec. VII* (Rome: Università Gregoriana Editrice, 1981). Likewise, Carlo Carletti, *Iscrizioni cristiane de Roma: Testimonianze di vita Cristiana (secoli III–VII)* (Firenze: Nardini, 1986). The particular inscriptions and translations here are taken from Antonio Baruffa, *The Catacombs of St. Callixtus: History, Archaelogy, Faith*, trans. William Purdy (Vatican City: L.E.V., 1993), 125–31.

16  Cf. Steven E. Ozment, *When Fathers Ruled: Family Life in Reformation Europe* (Cambridge, Mass.: Harvard University Press 1983), among several of his studies of this theme.

17  Tertullian, *De carne Christi* 4.1; quoted in M. A. Williams, *Rethinking Gnosticism* (Princeton, N.J.: Princeton University Press, 1999), 26.

18  See Paul Beauchamp, *Création et separation: Étude exégétique du chapitre premier de la Genèse* (Paris: Aubier-Montaigne, 1969).

19  See also Janet Martin Soskice, "*Imago Dei* and Sexual Difference: Toward an Eschatological Anthropology," in *Rethinking Human Nature: A Multidisciplinary Approach*, ed. Malcolm Jeeves (Grand Rapids: Eerdmans, 2010), 295–306. The notion of an original and/or eschatological human "androgyn," or

simply original male, on the analogy with unsexed angelic nature, goes back to patristic sources, not to mention pagan ones (cf. Gregory of Nyssa); some later Jewish mystical traditional picked it up as well. But such ideas have generally been marginal or outright rejected in the Christian tradition. For some references here, see various chapters in Kari Elisabeth Børresen, ed., *The Image of God: Gender Models in Judaeo-Christian Tradition* (Minneapolis: Fortress, 1995).

20  Georges Vigarello, *Le proper et le sale: L'hygiène du corps depuis le Moyen Âge* (Paris: Seuil, 1985); Emily Cockayne, *Hubbub: Filth, Noise, and Stench in England, 1600–1770* (New Haven, Conn.: Yale University Press, 2007). On bodily fluids in general, including relationship to the skin, see some of the essays in Manfred Horstmanshoff, Helen King, and Claus Zittel, eds., *Blood, Sweat, and Tears: The Changing Concepts of Physiology from Antiquity into Early Modern Europe* (Boston: Brill, 2012).

21  The Roman Catholic judgment, in its *Catechism* (2357–58), that homosexuality is an "intrinsically disordered inclination" is related to this line of thought and certainly does not deserve the ignorant opprobrium launched against it by many.

22  The most notorious case of this fallacy, according to which what we see determines what is "natural," is that of John Money, the radical sexologist whose determination that a boy without a penis should become a girl led to a sex-reassignment therapy that ended in tragedy. See John Colapinto, *As Nature Made Him: The Boy Who Was Raised as a Girl* (Toronto: HarperPerennial Canada, 2000). The story itself is not very illuminating of the question at issue, but it does demonstrate how confused the prejudices can be, from any direction, as to what counts as "natural physical determination."

23  Sermon preached at White-hall, February 29, 1627. See John Donne, *The Oxford Edition of the Sermons of John Donne,* vol. 3, *Sermons Preached at the Court of Charles I,* ed. David Colclough (Oxford: Oxford University Press, 2013), 91–104; quote on 93.

24  Anne-Marie Kilday, *A History of Infanticide in Britain, c. 1600 to the Present* (New York: Palgrave Macmillan, 2013), 215. See also Geoffrey Nathan, *The Family in Late Antiquity: The Rise of Christianity and the Endurance of Tradition* (New York: Routledge, 2000); Odd Magne Bakke, "Upbringing of Children in the Early Church," *Studia Theologica* 60 (2006): 145–63; Reidar Aasgaard, "Paul as a Child: Children and Childhood in the Letters of the Apostle," *Journal of Biblical Literature* 126, no. 1 (2007): 129–59.

25  Jean-Luc Marion, *La rigueur des choses: Entretiens avec Dan Arbib* (Paris: Flammarion, 2012), 199.

26  Jean-Claude Guillebaud, *La Tyrannie du Plaisir* (Paris: Editions du Seuil, 1998).

27  Cf. David Novak, "Response to Martha Nussbaum's 'A Right to Marry?'" *California Law Review* 98, no. 3 (2010): 709–20.

28 Danilo Kiš, "The Encyclopedia of the Dead (The Whole Story)," in *The Encyclopedia of the Dead* (Evanston, Ill.: Northwestern University Press, 1997), 37–65.

29 Paul Yonnet, *Famille I: Le recul de la mort; L'avènement de l'individu contemporain* (Paris: Gallimard, 2006).

30 Charles Péguy, *The Mystery of the Holy Innocents and Other Poems*, trans. Pansy Pakenham (London: Harvill, 1956), 155; *Oeuvres Complètes de Charles Péguy, 1873–1914* (Paris: Nouvelle Revue Française, 1919), 6:214–15.

*Chapter IV*

1 Péguy, *Mystery of the Holy Innocents*, trans. Pakenham, 160–62; *Oeuvres Complètes*, 6:226–28. Pakenham translation.

2 Gilbert Highet, *Talents and Geniuses* (New York: Oxford University Press, 1937/1957), 44.

3 Quoted in Harald Weinrich, *On Borrowed Time: The Art and Economy of Living with Deadlines*, trans. Steven Rendall (Chicago: University of Chicago Press, 2008), 2.

4 Joseph Butler, *The Analogy of Religion, Natural and Revealed, to the Constitution and Course of Nature* (1736); cf. *Analogy of Religion*, intro. by Ernest C. Mossner (New York: F. Ungar, 1961).

5 Venantius Fortunatus' sixth-century poem "Pange lingua," has become a famous hymn ("Sing my tongue the glorious battle . . ."). For some explorations of the theme, tracing some of the legends of the origin of the "tree" (in paradise, with Moses, etc.), see Arthur Sampson Napier, *History of the Holy Rood-Tree: A Twelfth Century Version of the Cross-Legend* (London: Early English Text Society, Kegan Paul, original series, no. 103, 1894).

6 Georges Bernanos, *The Diary of a Country Priest*, trans. Pamela Morris, intro. by Rémy Rougeau (New York: Carroll & Graf, 2002).

7 Alison Gopnik and Andrew N. Meltzoff, *Words, Thoughts, and Theories* (Cambridge, Mass.: MIT Press, 1997).

8 Lev Vygotsky, *The Vygotsky Reader*, ed. René van der Veer and Jaan Valsiner (Oxford: Blackwell, 1994); Jerome Bruner, with Rita Watson, *Child's Talk: Learning to Use Language* (New York: W. W. Norton, 1983); Bruner, *Acts of Meaning* (Cambridge, Mass.: Harvard University Press, 1990).

9 Cf. Michael Newton, *Savage Girls and Wild Boys: A History of Feral Children* (London: Faber & Faber, 2002).

10 Aelred of Rievaulx, *On Jesus at Twelve Years Old* (*De Jesu pueor duodenni*), trans. Geoffrey Webb (London: Mowbray, 1956)

11 Cf. Gillian Cohen and Stephanie Taylor, "Reminiscence and Ageing," *Ageing and Society* 18, no. 5 (1998): 601–10; Mark Byrd, "Elderly Individuals' Reminiscences about the Life Span Development of Their Family," *International Journal of Aging and Human Development* 52, no. 3 (2001): 253–63.

12 Iris Murdoch, *The Sovereignty of Good* (London: Routledge, 2014), 91.

13 Two works where Iris Murdoch deals creatively with the issue of tragedy and the narrative of our lives are *Metaphysics as a Guide to Morals* (London: Penguin,

1993); and *Existentialists and Mystics: Writings on Philosophy and Literature*, ed. Peter Conradi (New York: Penguin, 1999). On her marriage and Alzheimer's, see her husband's volume: John Bayley, *Elegy For Iris* (London: St. Martin's, 1999).

14  Cf. Peter Brooks, *Realist Vision* (New Haven, Conn.: Yale University Press, 2005).

15  For this, see the wonderful discussion in Francesca Murphy, *God Is Not a Story: Realism Revisited* (New York: Oxford University Press, 2007): 201–36.

16  R. Larry Overstreet, "The Greek Concept of the 'Seven Stages of Life' and Its New Testament Significance," *Bulletin for Biblical Research* 19, no. 4 (2009): 537–63; see 549.

17  A wonderful book on a key period of elaboration on this theme is Elizabeth Sears' *The Ages of Man: Medieval Interpretations of the Life Cycle* (Princeton, N.J.: Princeton University Press, 1986).

18  Cf. Andrew Hofer, O.P., "The Old Man as Christ in Justin's *Dialogue with Trypho*," *Vigiliae Christianae* 57, no. 1 (2003): 1–21.

19  Martha Nussbaum, *Upheavals of Thought: The Intelligence of Emotions* (Cambridge: Cambridge University Press, 2003).

20  Bernard Lynch, *A Guide to Health through the Various Stages of Life* (London, 1744).

21  Edward Browne, *A description of an annual world; or, Briefe meditations upon all the holy-daies in the yeere, with certain briefe poeticall meditations of the day in general and all the daies in the weeke* (London, 1641), 22–24.

22  Act 2, scene 7, lines 139–66, in William Shakespeare, *As You Like It*, ed. Cynthia Marshall (New York: Cambridge University Press, 2004), 165–67.

23  References for Augustine and his context can be found in Paul Archambault, "The Ages of Man and the Ages of the World: A Study in Two Traditions," *Revue des études augustiniennes* 12 (1966): 193–228. Augustine posits six ages of man and the world in *De Genesi adversus Manichaeos* 1.23.35–1.25.43; and *De vera religione* 26.49–27.50 (a seventh, after death or apocalypse, is generally presumed). Sermon 259 gives eight ages to history, while *De diversis quaestionibus* 66 speaks of four ages to individual lives and *The Enchiridion* 118 speaks of four ages to history. Augustine does not settle upon one shared structure exclusively; that there is a parallel between individual human life and history exists seems to be the crucial point.

24  Cf. Janette B. Benson and Marshall M. Haith, eds., *Social and Emotional Development in Infancy and Early Childhood* (London: Academic/Elsevier, 2009); which is a collection of the relevant articles from the much larger three-volume *Encyclopedia of Infant and Early Childhood Development* (Boston: Elsevier/Academic, 2008).

25  Philippe Ariès' *Centuries of Childhood* (London: Penguin, 1962) was by far the most influential proponent of the childhood-as-modern-construction claim. Among critics of Ariès, one of the best was Linda Pollock, *Forgotten Children:*

*Parent-Child Relations from 1500 to 1900* (Cambridge: Cambridge University Press, 1983). More recently, Peter N. Stearns, in *Childhood in World History* (New York: Routledge, 2008), while maintaining the value of Ariès' work, presents a tableau that depicts the widespread and long-standing recognition of childhood's special status. Ivan Illich did much to popularize Ariès' views, as extended to the area of institutional education, in his *Deschooling Society* (New York: Harper & Row, 1971).

26  For a standard and "official" view about these matters, see Barbara L. Frankowski, "Sexual Orientation and Adolescents," *Pediatrics* 113, no. 6 (2004): 1827–31.

27  Lene Arnett Jensen, ed., *The Oxford Handbook of Human Development and Culture: An Interdisciplinary Perspective* (New York: Oxford University Press, 2015); David F. Greenberg, *The Construction of Homosexuality* (Chicago: University of Chicago Press, 1988); Jenell Williams Paris, *The End of Sexual Identity: Why Sex Is Too Important to Define Who We Are* (Downers Grove, Ill.: InterVarsity, 2011).

28  Arnold Van Gennep, *The Rites of Passage* (London: Routledge, 2004).

29  Henrik Urdal, "A Clash of Generations? Youth Bulges and Political Violence," *International Studies Quarterly* 50, no. 3 (2006): 607–29.

30  In Francis Bacon, *Bacon's Essays, with Annotations by Richard Whately* (London: John W. Parker, 1856); see "Of Youth and Age," 386–88.

31  Cf. Cohen and Taylor, "Reminiscence and Ageing." The ordering aspect of such reminiscence is stressed in most studies.

32  David Baily Harned, *Patience: How We Wait upon the World* (Cambridge, Mass.: Cowley, 1997).

33  Karl Rahner, *On the Theology of Death* (1961), trans. Charles H. Henkey (New York: Herder & Herder, 1972).

34  Thérèse of Lisieux, *The Story of a Soul (L'Histoire d'une Âme): The Autobiography of St. Thérèse of Lisieux; With Additional Writings and Sayings of St. Thérèse*, trans. Thomas Taylor (London: Burns, Oages & Washbourne, 1912), 16.

*Chapter V*

1  For an overview, see Hubert Cancik, "The Awareness of Cultural Diversity in Ancient Greece and Rome," in *Exploring Humanity: Intercultural Perspectives on Humanism*, ed. Mihai Spariosu and Jörn Rüsen (Taipei: National Taiwan University Press, 2012): 123–44. Robert E. Belknap, *The List: The Uses and Pleasures of Cataloguing* (New Haven, Conn.: Yale University Press, 2008).

2  Bart Moore-Gilbert, " 'New Worlds, New Selves': Montaigne, 'the Atlantic,' and the Emergence of Modern Autobiography," *Atlantic Studies* 2, no. 1 (2005): 1–14; Ann Hartle, *Michel Montaigne: Accidental Philosopher* (Cambridge: Cambridge University Press, 2003); Albrecht Classen, ed., *East Meets West in the Middle Ages and Early Modern Times: Transcultural Experiences in the Premodern World* (Boston: De Gruyter, 2013); Anthony Padgen, *European Encounters with the New World: From Renaissance to Romanticism* (New Haven, Conn.: Yale University Press, 1993); David Abulafia, *The Discovery of Mankind: Atlantic Encounters in the Age of Columbus* (New Haven, Conn.: Yale University Press,

2008); Fernando Operé, *Indian Captivity in Spanish America: Frontier Narratives* (2001), trans. Gustavo Pellón (Charlottesville: University of Virginia Press, 2008); Lynn Hunt, *Inventing Human Rights: A History* (New York: W. W. Norton, 2007); Lynn Hunt, Margaret C. Jacob, and Wijnand Mijnhardt, *The Book That Changed Europe: Picart and Bernard's "Religious Ceremonies of the World"* (Cambridge, Mass.: Harvard University Press, 2010). For a nicely concise summary of some of the questions of diversity as they were pondered, see Voltaire's dialogue between a "savage" and a "bachelor of arts," originally in *Mélanges de littérature et d'histoire de philosophie* ("Entretiens d'un sauvage et un bachelier"), 1761; see *Oeuvres complètes de Voltaire* (Paris: Hachette, 1860), 18:444–48. See also, more broadly, and in what follows, Timothy J. Reiss, *Mirages of the Selfe: Patterns of Personhood in Ancient and Early Modern Europe* (Stanford: Stanford University Press, 2003), and his notion of "passability" as the general self-understanding of premodern Europeans.

3  J. S. Davies, "The Social Exclusion Debate: Strategies, Controversies and Dilemmas," *Policy Studies* 26 (2005): 3–27; H. Silver and S. M. Miller, "Social Exclusion: The European Approach to Social Disadvantage," *Indicators* 2 (2003): 1–17; Thomas K. Holcomb, *Introduction to American Deaf Culture* (New York: Oxford University Press, 2013).

4  For a range of perspectives related to this, see the extensive anthology, edited by Christopher McCrudden, *Understanding Human Dignity* (Oxford: Oxford University Press for the British Academy, 2013).

5  Mary Douglas, *Purity and Danger: An Analysis of Concepts of Pollution and Taboo* (London: Routledge & Kegan Paul, 1966).

6  Mary Douglas, *Leviticus as Literature* (New York: Oxford University Press, 1999).

7  Michel Serres, *Genesis* (1982), trans. Geneviève James and James Nielson (Ann Arbor: University of Michigan Press, 1995), 123–39.

8  Cf. George Sikes, *The Book of Nature: Translated and Epitomiz'd by George Sikes* (London, 1667), 105.

9  Most well known, Charles Taylor, *Sources of the Self: The Making of the Modern Identity* (Cambridge, Mass.: Harvard University Press, 1989); but also Paul Yonnet, *Famille. I. Le recul de la mort: L'avènement de l'individu contemporain* (Paris: Gallimard, 2006).

10 Cf. the questions raised (and some of the resources offered) in Kathryn Lilla Cox, "Toward a Theology of Infertility and the Role of *Donum Vitae*," *Horizons* 40, no. 1 (2013): 28–52. Not all potential analogies between singleness and childless marriages are valid. Singleness can be (it is not always) a "chosen" form of life, intentional, as it were. But childless marriages, if intentional (e.g., out of opposition or indifference to procreation), are not faithful vocations. Childlessness within marriage can constitute the fullness of marriage when it is itself "given" by God. It is thus a part of the encounter of experience that marks any marriage as itself a form of growth in wisdom. Catholic theology has long worked with this set of questions, whatever success it has had, in a way

that Protestants have failed to do. In any case, a childless marriage partakes of a certain kind of friendship that, in the present discussion, is analogous to that of single persons.

11 Julia Duin, *Quitting Church: Why the Faithful Are Fleeing and What to Do About It* (Grand Rapids: Baker, 2009); Julia Ludy, *Sacred Singleness: The Set-Apart Girl's Guide to Purpose and Fulfillment* (Eugene, Ore.: Harvest House, 2009). These represent popular laments over the challenges of single people without Christian churches.

12 Eric Klinenberg, *Going Solo: The Extraordinary Rise and Surprising Appeal of Living Alone* (London: Penguin Books, 2012), 5, 1–3.

13 Cf. See David E. Garland, *1 Corinthians* (Grand Rapids: Baker Academic, 2003), 332–34.

14 Epictetus' *Discourses* III.22, in *The Discourses of Epictetus*, trans. George Long (London: George Bell, 1890), 259–60.

15 Judith L. Kovacs, ed. and trans., *1 Corinthians: Interpreted By Early Christian Commentators* (Grand Rapids: Eerdmans, 2005), 124–27.

16 Augustine, *De bono viduitatis* ("On the excellence of widowhood") 19.23. Translation in Augustine, *Treatises on Various Subjects*, trans. Sarah Muldowney et al. (New York: Fathers of the Church, 1952). Related works can be found in Augustine, *Treatises on Marriage and Other Subjects* (New York: Fathers of the Church, 1955).

17 Lucius Annaeus Seneca, "On the Shortness of Life," in Seneca, *Moral Essays*, trans. John W. Basore, Loeb Classical Library (London: William Heinemann, 1932), 2:286–355.

18 Bernard Stiegler, *Acting Out*, trans. David Barison, Daniel Ross, and Patrick Crogan (Stanford: Stanford University Press, 2009). Stiegler's views are hardly novel, and the literature on "individuation" is extensive. But his own personal experience of and interest in the way individuation ought to be ordered to an educational engagement with "past" traditions is uniquely intriguing.

19 St. Methodius, *The Symposium: A Treatise on Chastity*, trans. Herbert Musurillo (Westminster, Md.: Newman, 1958); Ephraim Radner, *Hope among the Fragments: The Broken Church and Its Engagement with Scripture* (Grand Rapids: Brazos, 2004), 121–38.

20 Elizabeth Chen's "Caught in a Bad Bromance" (*Texas Journal of Women and the Law* 21, no. 2 [2012]: 241–66) covers a good deal of this ground, but from the misguided perspective that friendships are best encouraged among men by completely dismantling sexual difference altogether.

21 Alan Bray's *The Friend* (Chicago: University of Chicago Press, 2003) garnered much publicity for its documentation of relatively numerous medieval (and later) funerary arrangements for same-sex pairs of friends, in Britain especially. What was missing from Bray's provocative research, however, was any means by which to engage just what was involved in the "friendships" marked by common burial. His own not-so-cautious speculation involved homoerotic

friendship, and this unsubstantiated conclusion was eagerly embraced by participants in the sexuality debates of the decade. In fact, though, the character of same-sex friendship during the epochs Bray examines was informed by cultures of celibate relationships for which there are today few parallels. In this case, we barely understand the past, so deep is the chasm that separates our experiential outlooks.

22  Neera Kapur Badhwar, ed., *Friendship: A Philosophical Reader* (Ithaca, N.Y.: Cornell University Press, 1993); Albrecht Classen and Marilyn Sandidge, eds., *Friendship in the Middle Ages and Early Modern Age: Explorations of a Fundamental Ethical Discourse* (Berlin: De Gruyter, 2010); Barbara Caine, ed., *Friendship: A History* (London: Equinox, 2009); Graham Allan, *Friendship: Developing a Sociological Perspective* (Boulder, Colo.: Westview, 1989); M. Mcpherson, L. Smith-Lovin, and M. M. Cook, "Birds of a Feather: Homophily in Social Networks," *Annual Review of Sociology* 27 (2001): 415–44; William K. Rawlins, *The Compass of Friendship: Narratives, Identities, and Dialogues* (Los Angeles: Sage, 2009); Gilbert Meilaender, *Friendship: A Study in Theological Ethics* (Notre Dame, Ind.: University of Notre Dame Press, 1981).

23  Montaigne, *Essays* I.27 ("On Friendship"). The English translation is from the classic version by John Florio, in *The Essays of Montaigne: Done into English by John Florio anno 1603*, ed. George Saintsbury (London: David Nutt, 1892), 1:202; the French original, from the 1595 edition, can be found in Michel de Montaigne, *Essais* (Bordeaux: P. Villey et Saulnier, 1595), 1:73.

24  C. S. Lewis, *The Four Loves* (New York: Harcourt, Brace, 1960).

25  On Irenaeus, see his *Against Heresies* (*Adversus Haereses*) IV.13.4 and IV.16.3–4. On marriage and friendship, see Stephanie Coontz, *Marriage, a History: How Love Conquered Marriage* (New York: Penguin, 2006); John Witte Jr., *From Sacrament to Contract: Marriage, Religion, and Law in the Western Tradition*, 2nd ed. (Louisville, Ky.: Westminster John Knox, 2012); Leon Battista Alberti, *The Family in Renaissance Florence: Books One–Four of I libri della famiglia* (1969), trans. Renée Neu Watkins (Long Grove, Ill.: Waveland, 2004); Amyrose J. McCue Gill, "Rereading *I libri della famiglia*: Leon Battista Alberti on Marriage, *Amicizia* and Conjugal Friendship," *California Italian Studies* 2, no. 2 (2011), https://escholarship.org/uc/ismrg_cisj?volume=2;issue=2.

26  Stanley Hauerwas, *The Hauerwas Reader*, ed. John Berkman and Michael Cartwright (Durham, N.C.: Duke University Press, 2001), 513; but see also Gilbert Meilaender, "Time for Love: The Place of Marriage and Children in the Thought of Stanley Hauerwas," *Journal of Religious Ethics* 40, no. 2 (2012): 250–61.

*Chapter VI*

1  Vernon Lee, *Hortus Vitae: Essays on the Gardening of Life* (London: J. Lane, 1904).

2  Bruno Latour, *We Have Never Been Modern* (1991), trans. Catherine Porter (Cambridge, Mass.: Harvard University Press, 1993).

3  The myth of Christian responsibility for ecological destruction is usually sourced to the historian Lynn White Jr. and his seminal essay "The Historical Roots of Our Ecologic Crisis," *Science* 155 (1967): 1203–7. White argued that a culture of anthropocentric instrumentalism lay behind the devastation of the nonhuman world and that Christianity (and Judaism behind it) constituted "the most anthropocentric religion the world has seen" (1205). White's own views were more nuanced than critics often claimed (and he was himself a believing Christian), but his article was picked up and made to justify a much larger revolt against the culture of Judeo-Christianity in the following decade.

4  Kristine Koozin, *The Vanitas Still Lifes of Harmen Steenwick: Metaphoric Realism* (Lewiston, N.Y.: E. Mellen, 1990); Liana De Girolami Cheney, ed., *The Symbolism of* Vanitas *in the Arts, Literature and Music: Comparative and Historical Studies* (Lewiston, N.Y.: E. Mellen, 1993); Raymond J. Kelly III, *To Be, or Not to Be: Four Hundred Years of* Vanitas *Painting* (Flint, Mich.: Flint Institute of Arts, 2006); Mina Gregor, *La Natura Morta Italiana: Da Caravaggio al Settecento* (Milan: Electa, 2003); Mina Gregori, Alberto Veca, and Lanfranco Ravelli, *Vanitas* (Bergamo: Fondazione Credito Bergamasco, 2007); Eric S. Christianson, *Ecclesiastes through the Centuries* (Malden, Mass.: Blackwell, 2007).

5  Élisabeth Barillé, *Petit éloge du sensible* (Paris: Gallimard, 2008), 48–49.

6  Jean Anthelme Brillat-Savarin, *The Physiology of Taste; or, Meditations on Transcendental Gastronomy* (1825), trans. M. F. K. Fisher (New York: Vintage, 2011); Suzanne Simha, *Du gout: De Montesquieu à Brillat-Savarin; De l'esthétique galante à l'esthétique gourmande* (Paris: Hermann, 2012).

7  Michel Serres, *Genesis* (1982), trans. Geneviève James and James Nielson (Ann Arbor: University of Michigan Press, 1995).

8  Isaiah Berlin, *Concepts and Categories: Philosophical Essays* (1978), ed. Henry Hardy (London: Pimlico/Random House, 1999).

9  Ivan Illich, *Gender* (New York: Pantheon, 1982).

10  Karl Barth is helpful in grounding the variation-in-stable-form aspect of sexual difference within a christological frame: Christ is the perfect "superordinary" and the perfect "subordinate" both; and the male-female ordering of first and second, in which modern concepts of male "headship" rest, is often turned upside down in this framework. See his *Church Dogmatics* III.2 (*The Doctrine of Creation*), trans. G. W. Bromiley and T. F. Torrance (Edinburgh: T&T Clark, 2004), 315.

11  See, e.g., Congress for the New Urbanism, http://www.cnu.org/; Emily Talen, *New Urbanism and American Planning: The Conflict of Cultures* (New York: Routledge, 2005).

12  Amy B. Trubek, *The Taste of Place: A Cultural Journey into Terroir* (Berkeley: University of California Press, 2008).

13  Serge Moscovici, *Essai sur l'histoire humaine de la nature* (Paris: Flammarion, 1968); idem, *Society against Nature: The Emergence of Human Societies* (1974), trans. Sacha Rabinovitch (Hassocks, UK: Harvester, 1976).

14  Michel de Montaigne, *Essays*, book 3, "On Experience"; in *Les Essais de Michel de Montaigne*, ed. Fortunat Strowski and François Gebelin (Bordeaux: F. Pech, 1909), 3:419.

15  Gustav Wingren, *Luther on Vocation*, trans. Carl C. Rasmussen (Philadelphia: Muhlenberg, 1957).

16  *Triglot Concordia: The Symbolical Books of the Evangelical Lutheran Church; German-Latin-English; Published as a Memorial of the Quadricentenary Jubilee of the Reformation anno Domini 1917 by Resolution of the Evangelical Lutheran Synod of Missouri, Ohio, and Other States* (St. Louis: Concordia, 1921), 543.

17  See also Martin Luther, "Exposition of Psalm 147," in *Luther's Works*, ed. Jaroslav Pelikan and Daniel E. Poellot (Saint Louis: Concordia, 1958), 14:110–35.

18  Michael Oleska, ed., *Alaskan Missionary Spirituality* (New York: Paulist, 1987), 43.

19  Pascal, *Pensées*, trans. A. J. Krailsheimer (London: Penguin, 1966; rev. 1995), 51. Fragment 151, in the Lafuma enumeration.

20  Luther, "Exposition of Psalm 147," 14:114.

21  Shoshana Blum-Kulka, *Dinner Talk: Cultural Patterns of Sociability and Socialization in Family Discourse* (New York: Routledge, 2012).

22  Michel de Certeau's tendentious, jargon-filled, yet nevertheless wonderfully creative masterwork, *The Practice of Everyday Life*, thus comes into its own, not in the theory-laden first volume, which dissects the "imposition" side of things, but in the second volume, written with Pierre Mayol and Luce Giard, which engages in interviews with real workers. Here we see something more miraculous going on: actual persons emerge in their intrinsic interest, character, agency, and often beauty, for all their struggles. It is a reality that simply disappears amidst the previous theory. But even theory cannot obscure people at work. See Michel de Certeau, Luce Giard, and Pierre Mayol, *The Practice of Everyday Life*, vol. 2, *Living and Cooking*, trans. Timothy J. Tomasik (Minneapolis: University of Minnesota, 1998).

23  James L. Watson and Melissa L. Caldwell, eds., *The Cultural Politics of Food and Eating: A Reader* (Malden, Mass.: Wiley, 2004); Janet A. Flammang, *The Taste for Civilization: Food, Politics, and Civil Society* (Champagne: University of Illinois Press, 2009); Gillian Feeley-Harnik, *The Lord's Table: The Meaning of Food in Early Judaism and Christianity* (1981; repr., Washington, D.C.: Smithsonian Institution Press, 1994); Nathan MacDonald, *Not by Bread Alone: The Uses of Food in the Old Testament* (New York: Oxford University Press, 2008); Esther Koble, *Dining with John: Communal Meals and Identity Formation in the Fourth Gospel and Its Historical and Cultural Context* (Boston: Brill, 2011).

24  Carrie Arnold, *Decoding Anorexia: How Breakthroughs in Science Offer Hope for Eating Disorders* (New York: Routledge, 2012).

25  Patricia Caplan, *Feasts, Fasts, Famine: Food for Thought* (New York: Bloomsbury Academic, 1994); Robert F. Capon, *Supper of the Lamb: A Culinary Reflection* (Garden City, N.Y.: Macmillan, 1989).

26 Cf. the wonderful treatment by John Donne in one of his great sermons: "Sermon on Psalm 89:47/8," on Easter Day (March 28, 1619), in *The Sermons of John Donne*, ed. George R. Potter and Evelyn M. Simpson (Berkeley: University of California Press, 1955), 203.

27 Rachel Muers and David Grummet, eds., *Eating and Believing: Interdisciplinary Perspectives on Vegetarianism and Theology* (London: T&T Clark, 2008).

28 Lawrence H. Schiffman, ed., *Texts of Traditions: A Source Reader for the Study of the Second Temple and Rabbinic Judaism* (Hoboken, N.J.: KTAV, 1998), 693–98. Hube van de Sandt and David Flusser, *The Didache: Its Jewish Sources and Its Place in Early Judaism and Christianity* (Minneapolis: Fortress, 2002); Clemens Leonhard, "Ritual Practices on the Move between Jews and Christians: Theories and Case Studies in Late Antique Migration," in *Liturgy in Migration: From the Upper Room to Cyberspace*, ed. Teresa Berger (Collegeville, Minn.: Liturgical, 2012), 19–42; Bryan D. Spinks, *Do This in Remembrance of Me: The Eucharist from the Early Church to the Present Day* (London: SCM Press, 2013).

29 Philo, *On the Special Laws* 2:158–60. See *The Works of Philo Judaeus, the Contemporary of Josephus*, trans. C. D. Yonge (London: Henry G. Bohn, 1855), 3:285.

30 Aelred Cody, O.S.B., "The *Didache*: An English Translation," in *The "Didache" in Context: Essays on Its Text, History, & Transmission*, ed. Clayton N. Jefford (Leiden: Brill, 1995), 10.

31 Benedict XVI, *Sacramentum Caritatis* (2007), 47.

32 Trubek, *Taste of Place*, 6.

33 Paolos Mar Gregorios, "New Testament Foundations for Understanding the Creation," in *Tending the Garden: Essays on the Gospel and the Earth*, ed. Wesley Granberg-Michaelson (Grand Rapids: Eerdmans, 1987), 83–92.

34 See the provocative and helpful exchange by Bruce D. Marshall, "The Absolute and the Trinity," and Paul D. Molnar, "A Response: Beyond Hegel with Karl Barth and T. F. Torrance," in *Pro Ecclesia* 23, no. 2 (2014): 147–64 and 165–73, respectively.

35 David Kelsey, *Eccentric Existence: A Theological Anthropology*, 2 vols. (Louisville, Ky.: Westminster John Knox, 2009).

36 R. Barry Matlock, *Unveiling the Apocalyptic Paul: Paul's Interpreters and the Rhetoric of Criticism* (Sheffield: Sheffield Academic, 1996); Oscar Cullmann, *Christ and Time: The Primitive Christian Perspective of Time and History* (1946), trans. Floyd V. Filson (Philadelphia: Westminster, 1950); idem, *Salvation in History* (1965), trans. Sidney G. Sowers et al. (New York: Harper & Row, 1967); Beth Felker Jones, *Marks of His Wounds: Gender Politics and Bodily Resurrection* (New York: Oxford University Press, 2007).

37 Christopher D. Ringwald, *A Day Apart: How Jews, Christians, and Muslims Find Faith, Freedom, and Joy on the Sabbath* (New York: Oxford University Press, 2007), 204.

38   Abraham Heschel, *Sabbath: Its Meaning for Modern Man* (New York: Farrar, Straus & Giroux, 1951); Josef Pieper, *Leisure: The Basis of Life*, trans. Alexander Dru (London: Faber & Faber, 1952).

39   Cf. Augustine, *De civitate Dei* 22:15, 20.

40   Cf. Mark Graves, *Mind, Brain and the Elusive Soul: Human Systems of Cognitive Science and Religion* (Aldershot, UK: Ashgate, 2008).

*Conclusion*

1   Graham Harvey, *Food, Sex and Strangers: Understanding Religion as Everyday Life* (Durham, UK: Acumen, 2013).

2   Paul S. Fiddes, *Seeing the World and Knowing God: Hebrew Wisdom and Christian Doctrine in a Late-Modern Context* (Oxford: Oxford University Press, 2013).

3   Harald Weinrich, *On Borrowed Time: The Art and Economy of Living with Deadlines*, trans. Steven Rendall (Chicago: University of Chicago Press, 2008).

4   Harald Weinrich, *On Borrowed Time*, 207.

5   Harald Weinrich, *On Borrowed Time*, 207.

6   Harald Weinrich, *On Borrowed Time*, 208–9.

7   "On the Shortness of Life," in Seneca, *Moral Essays*, 2:286–355.

8   Thomas Secker, "A Just Estimate of the Shortness of Human Life and Our Proper Employment Here" (sermons 106 and 107), in *The Works of Thomas Secker* (Edinburgh: J. Dickson & W. Laing, 1792), 3:153–65.

9   Thomas Secker, "Just Estimate," 165.

10   Thomas Hardcastle, *Christian geography and arithmetick; or, A true survey of the world: together with the right art of numbring our dayes therein* (London, 1674).

11   Josef Pieper, *Leisure: The Basis of Life*, trans. Alexander Dru (London: Faber & Faber, 1952); idem, *In Tune with the World: A Theory of Festivity*, trans. Richard and Clara Wilson (Chicago: Franciscan Herald, 1973); John Hughes, *The End of Work: Theological Critiques of Capitalism* (Malden, Mass.: Blackwell, 2007), esp. chap. 6, "The End of Work: Rest, Beauty, Liturgy," 161–210.

12   The idea that improved longevity will somehow take us back to paradise is long standing. Even in the early modern era, someone like Thomas Burnet, in one of the great imaginative constructions of the era, would use his biblical tables of life span to show how the flood marked the beginning of true mortality, implying that Eden might be reduced to a health issue. Cf. Burnet, *The Sacred Theory of The Earth: Containing an Account of the Original of the Earth and of All the General Changes Which It Hath Already Undergone, or Is to Undergo, Till the Consummation of All Things: The Two First Books Concerning the Deluge and Concerning Paradise*, 2nd ed. (London: R. Norton, 1691), book 2, p. 162.

13   Guillaume de Salluste du Bartas, *Sepmaine, ou creation du monde* (Paris: Jean Feurier, 1578).

14   Joshua Sylvester, *Du Bartas, his deuine weekes and workes translated: and dedicated to the Kings most excellent Maiestie. Now thirdly corrected & augm.* (1611).

15   Joshua Sylvester, *Du Bartas, his deuine weekes and workes translated*, 148.

16   Joshua Sylvester, *Du Bartas, his deuine weekes and workes translated*, 171–73.

17   See Chloe Wheatey, *Epic, Epitome, and the Early Modern Historical Imagination* (Burlington, Vt.: Ashgate, 2011), esp. chap. 4, "Du Bartas in Epitome."

18   Augustine, *Enarrationes* on Psalm 45 (7, on v. 4): "Liber tibi sit pagina divina, ut haec audias: liber tibi sit orbis terrarum, ut haec videas," *Patrologia Latina* 36: 518D; see also Jitse M. van der Meer and Scott Mandelbrote, eds., *Nature and Scripture in the Abrahamic Religions: Up to 1700*, 2 vols. (Leiden: Brill, 2008), esp. in vol. 1.

19   Emil Brunner, *Natural Theology: Comprising "Nature and Grace" and the Reply "No" by Karl Barth*, trans. Peter Fraenkel (London: G. Bles, 1946).

20   Version of the Christian Reformed Church (Grand Rapids: Faith Alive Resources, 2011), at http://www.crcna.org/welcome/beliefs/confessions/belgic -confession (accessed on November 25, 2015).

21   N. Max Wildiers, *The Theologian and His Universe: Theology and Cosmology from the Middle Ages to the Present*, trans. Paul Dunphy (New York: Seabury, 1982).

# Scripture Index

# General Index

Abel, 15, 17, 96–97, 102, 117, 168, 206
Abraham, 15, 20, 35, 69–70, 94, 105, 121–22, 140–41, 181, 187, 223
Adam (old/first), 5, 8, 13–17, 20, 35, 37–41, 46, 72, 78, 87, 100, 105, 107, 115–17, 119, 130, 143, 151–52, 167–68, 177, 187, 200–202, 205, 214–15, 240, 242–44, 254n10
Adams, John, 70, 259n34
Aelred, of Rievaulx, 129, 180, 263n10
AIDS, 33, 76, 78, 78–86, 90, 104, 112, 260n2, 260n5, 260n7
Ambrose, 180, 226
amortality, 34, 41
Aquinas, Thomas, 53–55, 67, 258n17; *Summa Theologiae*, 53, 258n17
arc of life, **113–58**, 175, 186–88, 197, 210, 222, 238
Aristotle, 54, 160, 179–80, 184, 233
Augustine, 17, 20, 38, 54, 57, 64, 87–88, 138–41, 145, 150, 152–53, 174, 176, 222, 224, 238, 255n10, 257n2, 257n3, 264n23, 267n16, 272n39, 273n18; *City of God*, 54, 57; on the ages of the life of man and the world, 138–41, 145, 150, 152–53, 264n23

Babel (tower of), 44, 165–67
Bach, Johannes Sabastian, 118–19
Bacon, Francis, 146–47, 265n30
Barillé, Élisabeth, 194, 269n5; *Petit élogue du sensible*, 194
Barth, Karl, 11, 230, 246, 254n4, 269n10, 271n34, 273n19; *Church Dogmatics*, 254, 269n10
Belgic Confession, 246
Benatar, David, 62, 84, 258n28, 261n9; *Better Never to Have Been*, 62, 258n28, 261n9
Benedict XVI, 217, 271n31
Benedict, Saint, 200
Bergner, Daniel, 47–48, 258n14; *The Other Side of Desire*, 47, 258n14
Berlin, Isaiah, 196, 269n8